Edward Tuckerman Mason

Personal Traits of British Authors

Edward Tuckerman Mason

Personal Traits of British Authors

ISBN/EAN: 9783744678094

Printed in Europe, USA, Canada, Australia, Japan

Cover: Foto ©ninafisch / pixelio.de

More available books at **www.hansebooks.com**

WILLIAM WORDSWORTH.

PERSONAL TRAITS OF

BRITISH AUTHORS

WORDSWORTH—COLERIDGE—LAMB
HAZLITT—LEIGH HUNT—PROCTER

EDITED BY

EDWARD T. MASON

WITH PORTRAITS

NEW YORK
CHARLES SCRIBNER'S SONS
1885

CONTENTS.

PREFACE.

THIS volume presents a company of friends. These men were bound together by strong sympathies, yet differed enough in temperament and character to give zest and variety to their intimacy. That intimacy was unmarred by dissension or misunderstanding, and was only broken by death. There was one exception—Hazlitt quarrelled with Wordsworth and Coleridge on account of their conservatism. He had known them in youth as ardent enthusiasts, advocates of the French revolution, and could not forgive a change of political convictions which, to him, seemed mere apostacy. His fiery intolerance made him regard his old friends as time-servers and renegades. This, however, was the only break in the harmony of these comrades.

Suppose that some lucky man were enabled to wander back into the past, and to place himself at will in the scenes and among the companions of his choice. After due deliberation, he decides to spend

a day with this company of cronies, at Wordsworth's
house. The lucky man will not choose hastily ; he
hesitates ; he weighs the matter thoroughly; it is in
his power to drink a cup of sack with the poets at
the Mermaid Tavern ; to ramble through green
meadows with Isaac Walton ; to go with Sir Richard Steele to see Betterton play Hamlet ; or to
listen to the debates of that club over which Samuel
Johnson presides. But at length he makes his decision, and speedily arrives at Rydal Mount. As he
talks with Wordsworth he finds unwonted meaning
in the commonest things around him, and sees a
new beauty in the earth and sky. Should he grow
a little weary of his host's proprietorship of nature,
and the too frequent repetition of the favorite personal pronoun, he can stroll to the lake with Hunt,
whose good spirits and cheerful optimism make him
the benefactor of all who come under his sunny influence. Presently they return to the house, where
Hazlitt is telling of new treasures he has found ;
delighting his friends by his own delight in the
Elizabethan poets, and showing a keen insight
which discerns every phase of strength and beauty.
But, by some mischance, the talk turns to English
politics. All is changed. The calm reasoner and
clear-sighted critic becomes a furious partisan. His
voice is choked by rage, his face convulsed by passion. The startled visitor feels the air grow hot

and heavy ; his ears are stunned by passionate de-
nunciation and wild invective. At the first opportunity he leaves the furious radical, and finds a grateful relief in chatting with a more congenial companion ; for by yonder window, whither he has retreated
from the din, stands young Procter, in whose modesty and gentle quietness there is nothing dull or
insipid. Evening comes ; the candles are lighted ;
now the talk of Coleridge flows forth with majestic
sweep, musical, eloquent, unwearied—"a river deep
and wide." Some may find the voyage long ; some
may be left stranded upon shoals, while the mighty
stream moves onward ; but for them, here is Charles
Lamb, whose quaint thought and delicate fancy
stammer themselves forth in broken sentences, unstudied epigrams of mingled humor and wisdom.
He will joke with a Church dignitary as freely as
with a clerk in the India House. He walks undis-
mayed in a twilight of doubts and questionings ;
guessing at truth ; prizing an apt suggestion above
the most conclusive demonstration. He loves to
startle prosaic minds by the assertion of whimsical
paradoxes ; and his catholic sympathy confesses to
a certain tenderness for a sheep-stealer. Could one
wish himself in better company than this group of
friends ?

   These kindly and high-natured men were held up
to contempt and reproach as madmen and outlaws.

Some of them were assailed with a violence which could scarcely have been greater had they been strange monsters of crime, combining in their own persons the cruelty of Nero and the baseness of Judas, instead of being quiet, law-abiding citizens, and workmen whose labors were destined to shed the highest honor on their land, and to be a source of joy to all mankind.   Not even Lamb escaped the malevolent spirit of the time.   In England, sixty years ago, politics influenced all judgments of literature to an extent which now seems hardly credible. When the critic, in those days, sat down to deal with the writings of a political opponent, he lost sight of the common obligations of humanity.   No misrepresentation was too reckless, no personality too indecent, for his purpose.   He was not content with a wholesale condemnation of the author's work, but proceeded to impugn his motives and to besmirch his moral character.   It may be interesting to note one or two typical instances of this ruffianism.   In 1818, *Blackwood's Magazine* called Leigh Hunt " the meanest, the filthiest, and the most vulgar of Cockney Poetasters."   The good-mannered critic also spoke of " the leprous crust of self-conceit with which his whole moral being is indurated," and called attention to " that loathsome vulgarity which constantly clings round him like a venomed garment from St. Giles."   A few years later, in 1823, the same journal paid its respects to William Hazlitt, after this fashion :—"A mere ulcer, a sore from head to foot, a poor devil, so completely flayed that there is not a square half-inch of healthy flesh on his carcase." The *Quarterly Review* was but little behind *Blackwood* in the virulence of its attacks upon Hunt and Hazlitt ; but the extracts already given will suffice.

Happily, there were other and widely different observers, who have left us records exceptionally graphic and satisfactory. By their aid we may join Wordsworth and Coleridge as they stroll together upon "the ribbed sea-sand," talking of the " Ancient Mariner," unwritten as yet. We may visit the blithe prisoner, Leigh Hunt, in his gaily decorated rooms at the Horsemonger Lane Jail, and learn how to make the best of misfortune. Or, seated in some cosy London inn, we may hear the midnight chimes in company with Hazlitt. These pleasant chronicles tell us how Lamb went to spend a few days with Wordsworth at Grasmere, and found it necessary to stay his mind by recalling his wonted haunts in town, and consoled himself by the reflection that he should soon return to the "sweet security of streets." They lead us to the comfortable, low-ceiled chambers in Inner Temple Lane, where Charles and Mary Lamb welcome their guests. The punch is brewed, the pipes are lighted, the fire burns cheerily.

Leigh Hunt flits about from one to another ; whis-
pering good-natured gossip to Mary Lamb ; joking
with his host about those "immaterial legs," encased
in the rusty black small-clothes—a joke sure to be
repaid with interest. Now he delights Wordsworth
with the heartiest praise of his neglected verses ;
and now he mildly deprecates the wrath of Hazlitt,
who calls down the vengeance of Heaven upon the
Tory ministry. With graceful, unsuspected skill
he lulls the storm ; the angry man grows calm, and
suffers himself to be lured away from his passionate
resentments, and enticed into genial talk upon the
repose and beauty of Italian art. Coleridge, with
face aglow, discourses volubly to Barry Cornwall,
most patient and receptive of neophytes ; and as he
soars away into the cloudy region of metaphysics,
the reverent but tired listener, too courteous to free
himself, glances rather wistfully toward Lamb, the
centre of a laughing group by the fireside. Lamb
'sees and understands the glance. He quickly makes
his way to his "dear boy's" side, breaks in upon the
unconscious sage, and interrupts the stately monologue with—" D-dont mind C-coleridge—it's only
his f-f-fun !" Happy evenings ! Happy and fortunate friends ! Hunt and Procter lingered for many
years after all the others had gone ; and in their old
age the white-haired poets often sat together, recalling bygone years, smiling at pleasures past, talk-

ing with fond remembrance of "the old familiar faces."

Extracts have been made from the following American copyrighted books : Ralph Waldo Emerson's "English Traits" (Boston, 1856) ; James T. Fields's "Old Acquaintance" (J. R. Osgood, Boston, 1876) ; Nathaniel Hawthorne's "Our Old Home" (Ticknor & Fields, Boston, 1863) ; the "English Note-books" of the same author (Fields, Osgood, & Co., Boston, 1870) ; R. Shelton Mackenzie's "Life of Charles Dickens" (Philadelphia, 1870) ; N. P. Willis's "Famous Persons and Places" (Charles Scribner, New York, 1854) ; "Pencillings by the Way," by the same author (Charles Scribner, New York, 1853) ; Mary Balmano's "Pen and Pencil" (D. Appleton & Co., New York, 1858) ; *Scribner's Monthly* (Scribner & Co., New York) ; *The Atlantic Monthly* (Houghton, Mifflin & Co., Boston) ; George Ticknor's "Life, Letters, and Journals," 2 vols. (Houghton, Mifflin & Co., Boston, 1876) ; *Harper's Magazine* (Harper & Brothers, New York). Permission was kindly granted to make selections from these works, and the courtesy of their respective owners is thankfully acknowledged.

CHRONOLOGY.

Born.		Died.
1770.	WORDSWORTH.	1850.
1772.	COLERIDGE.	1834.
1775.	LAMB.	1834.
1778.	HAZLITT.	1830.
1784.	HUNT.	1859.
1787.	PROCTER.	1874.

WILLIAM WORDSWORTH.

1770–1850.

INTRODUCTORY NOTE.

WORDSWORTH lacked those qualities which inspire spontaneous enthusiasm, and endear a man to those around him. He had little of the personal charm which obtains instant and joyous recognition. His merits were not fitted to win popular admiration and applause, while his failings were peculiarly adapted to provoke strong dislike, harsh judgment, and hostile criticism. His biographers seem to have been painfully conscious of these facts, for they have evaded unpleasant truths. This is unfortunate ; because the facts in this instance are sure to be discovered. The sympathetic reader of the Rev. Christopher Wordsworth's memoir of his famous uncle, receives the impression of a beautiful and elevated character ; a nature far removed from the common weaknesses of humanity, dwelling serenely above the vulgar din of the world. A rude shock awaits him ; for upon turning to the pages of De Quincey, Harriet Martineau, Charles Cowden Clarke, and Julian Charles Young, he will find evidence, abundant and conclusive, that the demigod was the victim of some very earthly frailties. Indeed, the warmest admirer of this great man must admit that he was sadly lacking in a due regard for the feelings of others, that he practised an economy which trenched upon meanness, and displayed an egotism which assumed truly astonishing proportions.

His egotism was largely a result of his isolation. It was the natural outgrowth of a solitary life ; and his lack of any adequate perception of the ludicrous betrayed him into frequent and comical exhibitions of his profound self-satisfaction. Moreover, for many years his most zealous and enthusiastic partisan was William Wordsworth. Such partisanship cannot be beneficial to any man, least of all to one prone to introspection. Yet, when all injurious admissions have been fairly made, there remains enough of sterling worth to justify a sincere admiration for the man, no less than for the poet. We may not altogether like him—but we must respect him. Hearty and unreserved self-consecration to a lofty purpose must always command respect ; and Wordsworth's whole life was an illustration and example of such consecration. His mode of life, with its seclusion and manifold deprivations, was deliberately chosen by him as that which he deemed most favorable to his design of becoming a great poet. Who shall say that he was mistaken, and that he did not rightly understand the requirements of his own genius ? That which gives dignity to Wordsworth's life, and constitutes his highest claim to personal regard—and even to veneration—is his steadfast devotion to an intelligent sense of duty.

The following works may be consulted with advantage : Rev. Christopher Wordsworth's " Memoirs of William Wordsworth ;" F. W. H. Myers's

volume in the "English Men of Letters" series ;
Wordsworth's Poems, edited by William Knight,
now in course of publication in Edinburgh ; Thomas
Carlyle's "Reminiscences ;" Rev. R. P. Graves's
"Recollections of William Wordsworth ;" J. C.
Young's "Memoir of C. M. Young ;" Harriet Mar-
tineau's "Autobiography ;" Henry Crabb Robin-
son's "Diary ;" Thomas De Quincey's "Literary
Reminiscences ;" Caroline Fox's "Memories of Old
Friends ;" and an essay by R. W. Church, in the
fourth volume of T. H. Ward's "English Poets."
The most valuable and impartial estimate of Wordsworth, the most satisfactory view of his personal
character, as well as of his literary achievements, is
the essay by J. R. Lowell, in the second series of
"Among my Books."

LEADING EVENTS OF WORDSWORTH'S LIFE.

1770.   Born, April 7th, at Cockermouth, Cumberland.
1778.—(Aged 8.) His mother dies.
1783.—(Aged 13.) His father dies.
1787.—(Aged 17.) Enters Cambridge University.   Publishes a
                sonnet in the *European Magazine.*
1790.—(Aged 20.) Visits France during the summer vacation.
1791.—(Aged 20–21.) Graduates in January.   Goes to France in
                November.
1792.—(Aged 22.) Returns to London.
1793.—(Aged 23.) He publishes his first volumes of poetry,
                "An Evening Walk," and "Descriptive
                Sketches."
1795.—(Aged 25.) Hires a cottage at Racedown, in Dorsetshire,
                where he lives with his sister.
1798.—(Aged 28.) Publishes "Lyrical Ballads," the joint pro-
                duction of Coleridge and himself.   Goes
                to Germany with his sister and Coleridge.

1799.—(Aged 29.) Begins the composition of "The Prelude." Hires a cottage at Grasmere, where he lives with his sister.

1800.—(Aged 30.) Publishes the second edition of "Lyrical Ballads," in two volumes; the second volume being exclusively his own work.

1802.—(Aged 32.) Marries Miss Mary Hutchinson.

1805.—(Aged 35.) Finishes "The Prelude." ("The Prelude" was revised and corrected throughout the whole course of Wordsworth's life, and was published after his death.)

1807.—(Aged 37.) Publishes poems in two volumes.

1813.—(Aged 43.) Removes to Rydal Mount. Appointed Distributor of Stamps.

1814.—(Aged 44.) Publishes "The Excursion."

1815.—(Aged 45.) Publishes "The White Doe of Rylston."

1819.—(Aged 49.) Publishes "Peter Bell," and "The Waggoner."

1820.—(Aged 50.) Publishes "Sonnets on the River Duddon."

1822.—(Aged 52.) Publishes "Ecclesiastical Sonnets."

1839.—(Aged 69.) The University of Oxford confers upon him the degree of D. C. L.

1842.—(Aged 72.) Receives a pension of £300 per annum.

1843.—(Aged 73.) Poet Laureate.

1850.—(Aged 80.) Dies, April 23d.

WILLIAM WORDSWORTH.

T HE only reminiscence of Wordsworth's boyhood, of any particular interest, is contained
in the following passage from some autobiográphi-
cal notes, published in the "Memoirs":[1] "I was
of a stiff, moody, and violent temper: so much so
that I remember going once into the attics of my
grandfather's house at Penrith, upon some indignity
having been put upon me, with an intention of
destroying myself with one of the foils which I knew
was kept there. I took the foil in hand, but my
heart failed." Thomas De Quincey, in his "Literary
Reminiscences," gives some particulars of Wordsworth's university life, which are of too apocryphal
a nature to merit serious attention. De Quincey
does not claim to speak from personal knowledge
in this instance, and his observations lack corrobo-
rative evidence.

*Boyhood
and youth.*

Wordsworth was a tall and ungainly man ; with
a grave and severe face, and a manner that indicated

---

[1] Wordsworth (Rev. Christopher). Memoirs of William Wordsworth. Edited by Henry Reed. 2 vols., 16mo. Boston : Ticknor
& Fields, 1851.

tranquillity and independence rather than high breeding.—BRYAN W. PROCTER ("Recollections").[1]

Mr. Wordsworth, in his person, is above the middle size, with marked features, and an air somewhat stately and Quixotic. He reminds one of some of Holbein's heads, grave, saturnine, with a slight indication of sly humor, kept under by the manners of the age, or the pretensions of the person. He has a peculiar sweetness in his smile, and great depth and manliness and a rugged harmony in the tones of his voice.—WILLIAM HAZLITT ("Spirit of the Age").[2]

He was quaintly dressed (according to the costume of that unconstrained period),[3] in a brown fustian jacket and striped pantaloons. There was something of a roll, a lounge in his gait, not unlike his own "Peter Bell." There was a severe, worn pressure of thought about his temples, a fire in his eye (as if he saw something in objects more than the outward appearance), an intense, high, narrow forehead, a Roman nose, cheeks furrowed by strong purpose and feeling, and a convulsive inclination to laughter about the mouth, a good deal at variance with the solemn, stately expression of the rest of the face.—WILLIAM HAZLITT ("My First Acquaintance with Poets").[4]

[1] Procter (Bryan W.). Autobiographical Fragment, and Biographical Notes, with Sketches of Contemporaries, etc. Edited by C. [oventry] P. [atmore]. 12mo. London, 1877.
[2] Hazlitt (William). The Spirit of the Age. 8vo. London, 1825.   [3] About 1798.
[4] Hazlitt (William). Literary Remains. 2 vols., 8vo. London, 1836.

His features were large, and not suddenly expressive ; they conveyed little idea of the " poetic fire " usually associated with brilliant imagination. His eyes were mild and up-looking, his mouth coarse rather than refined, his forehead high rather than broad ; but every action seemed considerate, and every look self-possessed.—SAMUEL C. HALL (" Book of Memories ").[1]

Personal appearance.

His face bore marks of much, not always peaceful, meditation, the look of it not bland or benevolent so much as close, impregnable, and hard : a man *multa tacere loquive paratus*, in a world where he had experienced no lack of contradictions as he strode along. The eyes were not very brilliant, but they had a quiet clearness ; there was enough of brow, and well shaped ; rather too much of cheek (" horse face " I have heard satirists say) ; face of squarish shape, and decidedly longish, as I think the head itself was (its " length " going horizontal) ; he was large-boned, lean, but still firm-knit, tall, and strong-looking when he stood, a right good old steel-gray figure, with rustic simplicity and dignity about him, and a vivacious strength looking through him which might have suited one of those old steel-gray markgrafs whom Henry the Fowler set up to ward the " marches," and do battle with the intrusive heathen in a stalwart and judicious manner.—THOMAS CARLYLE (" Reminiscences ").[2]

---

[1] Hall (Samuel C.). A Book of Memories of Great Men and Women of the Age. 4to. London, 1876.
[2] Carlyle (Thomas). Reminiscences. Edited by J. A. Froude. 8vo. London, 1881.

Feb. 25th, 1831. I am just come home from breakfasting with Henry Taylor to meet Wordsworth ; the same party as when he had Southey— Mill, Eliot, Charles Villiers. Wordsworth may be bordering on sixty ; hard featured, brown, wrinkled, with prominent teeth and a few scattered gray hairs, but nevertheless not a disagreeable countenance.— CHARLES C. F. GREVILLE ("Greville Memoirs ").[1]

Walter Scott said that the eyes of Burns were the finest he ever saw. I cannot say the same of Mr. Wordsworth ; that is, not in the sense of the beautiful, or even of the profound. But certainly I never beheld eyes that looked so inspired or supernatural. They were like fires half burning, half smouldering, with a sort of acrid fixture of regard, and seated at the further end of two caverns. One might imagine Ezekiel or Isaiah to have had such eyes.—LEIGH HUNT ("Autobiography ").[2]

Hampstead, June 4, 1842.—Gurney Hoare brought us the good news that William Wordsworth was staying at old Mrs. Hoare's ; so thither he took us. He is a man of middle height, and not of very striking appearance, the lower part of the face retreating a little ; his eye of a somewhat French diplomatic character, with heavy eyelids, and none of the flash-

---

[1] Greville (Charles C. F.). A Journal of the Reigns of King George IV. and King William IV. Edited by Henry Reed. 3 vols., 8vo. London, 1874.
[2] Hunt (James Henry Leigh). Autobiography and Reminiscences. 3 vols., 16mo. London, 1850.

ing which one connects with poetic genius.—CARO-
LINE FOX (" Memories of Old Friends ").[1]

Wordsworth was, upon the whole, not a well-made
man. His legs were pointedly condemned by all
the female connoisseurs in legs that ever I heard
lecture upon that topic ; not that they were bad in
any way which *would* force itself upon your notice ;
. . . and undoubtedly they had been serviceable
legs beyond the ordinary standard of human requisition ; for I calculate, upon good data, that with
these identical legs Wordsworth must have traversed
a distance of 175 to 180,000 English miles—a mode
of exertion which, to him, stood in the stead of
wine, spirits, and all other stimulants whatsoever
to the animal spirits. . . . But, useful as they
have proved themselves, the Wordsworthian legs
were certainly not ornamental. . . .

*De Quin-
cey's por-
traiture of
Words-
worth.*

But the worst part of Wordsworth's person was
the bust ; there was a narrowness and a droop about
the shoulders which became striking, and had an
effect of meanness when brought into close juxta-
position with a figure of a most statuesque order.
Once on a summer morning, walking in the vale of
Longdale with Wordsworth, his sister, and Mr. J——,
a native Westmoreland clergyman, I remember that
Miss Wordsworth was positively mortified by the
peculiar illustration which was settled upon this
defective conformation. . . . Wordsworth's figure, with all its defects, was brought into powerful

---

[1] Fox (Caroline). Memories of Old Friends. Being Extracts from
the Journals and Letters of Caroline Fox, from 1835 to 1871. Edited by Horace N. Pym. 8vo. London, 1882.

De Quincey's portraiture of Wordsworth.

relief by one which had been cast in a more square and massy mould ; and in such a case it impressed a spectator with a sense of absolute meanness, more especially when viewed from behind, and not counteracted by his countenance ; and yet Wordsworth was of a good height, just five feet ten, and not a slender man ; on the contrary, by the side of Southey his limbs looked thick, almost in a disproportionate degree. But the total effect of Wordsworth's person was always worst in a state of motion ; for, according to the remark I have heard from many country people, "he walked like a cade,"—a cade being some sort of insect which advances by an oblique motion. This was not always perceptible, and in part depended (I believe) upon the position of his arms ; when either of these happened (as was very customary) to be inserted into the unbuttoned waistcoat, his walk had a wry or twisted appearance ; and not appearance only—for I have known it, by slow degrees, gradually to edge off his companion from the middle to the side of the highway.

Meantime, his face—that was one which would have made amends for greater defects of figure ; it was certainly the noblest for intellectual effects that, in actual life, I have seen, or at least have been consciously led to notice. Many such, or even finer, I have seen amongst the portraits of Titian, and, in a later period, amongst those of Van Dyke, from the great era of Charles I., as also from the court of Elizabeth and of Charles II. ; but none which has so much impressed me in my own time. . . . It was a face of the long order, often falsely classed as oval. . . . The head was well filled out ; and there . . . was a great advantage over the head of Charles Lamb, which was absolutely truncated in the posterior region—sawn off, as it were, by no timid sawyer. The forehead was not remarkably lofty. . . . Wordsworth's forehead is . . . liable to caricature misrepresentations in these days of phrenology : but, whatever it may appear to be in any man's fanciful portrait, the real living forehead, as I have been in the habit of seeing it for more than five and twenty years, is not remarkable for its height ; but it *is* perhaps remarkable for its breadth and expansive development.

De Quincey's portraiture of Wordsworth.

Neither are the eyes of Wordsworth "large," as is erroneously stated somewhere in " Peter's Letters ; " on the contrary, they are (I think) rather small ; but *that* does not interfere with their effect, which at times is fine and suitable to his intellectual character. . . . His eyes are not, under any circumstances, bright, lustrous, or piercing : but after a long day's toil in walking, I have seen them assume an appearance the most solemn and spiritual that it is possible for the human eye to wear. The light which resides in them is at no time a superficial light ; but, under favorable accidents, it is a light which seems to come from depths below all depths ; in fact, it is more truly entitled to be held " The light that never was on land or sea," a light radiating from some far spiritual world, than any the most idealizing light that ever yet a painter's hand created.

The nose, a little arched, and large, which, by the way (according to a natural phrenology, existing centuries ago amongst some of the lowest amongst the human species) has always been accounted an

*De Quin-
cey's por-
traiture of
Words-
worth.*

unequivocal expression of animal appetites organi-
cally strong. And that was in fact the basis of
Wordsworth's intellectual power ; his intellectual
passions were fervent and strong, because they
rested upon a basis of animal sensibility superior to
that of most men. . . . The mouth, and the region of the mouth, the whole circumjacencies of the
mouth, were about the strongest feature in Wordsworth's face ; there was nothing specially to be noticed that I know of, in the mere outline of the
lips ; but the swell and protrusion of the parts above
and around the mouth, are both noticeable in themselves, and also because they remind me of a very
interesting fact which I discovered about three
years after this my first visit to Wordsworth.[1]—
THOMAS DE QUINCEY (" Literary Reminiscences ").[2]

*Voice and
conversa-
tion.*

He sat down and began to talk very naturally and
freely, with a mixture of clear gushing accents in
his voice, a deep guttural intonation, and a strong
tincture of the northern *burr*, like the crust on wine.
—WILLIAM HAZLITT ("My First Acquaintance with
Poets ").

---

[1] This discovery (which is enlarged upon at great length) was,
that the best portrait of Wordsworth, according to De Quincey's
judgment, was a certain portrait of Milton, painted by Richardson,
and prefixed to a volume, of which my only knowledge is that De
Q. describes it as "Richardson the painter's thick octavo volume of notes on 'Paradise Lost.'" Wordsworth's family, to whom
this engraving was shown, confirmed the opinion of De Quincey ;
he says, "Not one member of that family but was as much impressed as myself with the accuracy of the likeness."

[2] De Quincey (Thomas). Literary Reminiscences. 2 vols., 16mo.
Ticknor & Fields, Boston, 1851.

His voice was good, frank, and sonorous, though practically clear, distinct, and forcible rather than melodious. . . . The tone of his voice when I got him afloat on some Cumberland or other matter germane to him had a braced rustic vivacity, willingness, and solid precision, which alone rings in my ear when all else is gone.—THOMAS CARLYLE ("Reminiscences"). *Voice and conversation.*

The tone of him business-like, sedately confident ; no discourtesy, yet no anxiety about being courteous. A fine wholesome rusticity, fresh as his mountain breezes, sat well on the stalwart veteran, and on all he said and did. You would have said he was a usually taciturn man ; glad to unlock himself to audience sympathetic and intelligent, when such offered itself.—THOMAS CARLYLE (" Reminiscences ").

My companion (Wordsworth), according to his usual fashion, very soliloquacious, but saying much, of course, that was interesting to hear. . . . In giving me an account of the sort of society he has in his neighborhood in the country, and saying that he rarely went out to dinner, he gave a very intelligible picture of the sort of thing it must be when he *does* go out. "The conversation," he said, " may be called *catechetical ;* for, as they do me the honor to wish to know my opinions on the different subjects, they ask me questions, and I am induced to answer them at great length till I become quite tired." And so he does, I'll warrant him ; nor is it possible, indeed, to edge in a word, at least in a *tête-* *Conversation.*

III.—2

à-tête, till he does get tired.—THOMAS MOORE (Diary, etc., 1835).[1]

Conversation.

He was willing to talk with me in a corner, in noisy, extensive circles, having weak eyes, and little loving the general babble current in such places. One evening, probably about this time, I got him upon the subject of great poets, who, I thought, might be admirable equally to us both ; but was rather mistaken, as I gradually found. Pope's partial failure I was prepared for ; less for the narrowish limits visible in Milton and others. I tried him with Burns, of whom he had sung tender recognition ; but Burns also turned out to be a limited, inferior creature, any genius he had a theme for one's pathos rather ; even Shakspeare himself had his blind sides, his limitations. Gradually it became apparent to me that of transcendent unlimited there was, to this critic, probably but one specimen known—Wordsworth himself! He by no means said so, or hinted so, in words ; but on the whole it was all I gathered from him in this considerable *tête-à tête* of ours ; and it was not an agreeable conquest. New notion as to poetry or poet I had not in the smallest degree got ; but my insight into the depths of Wordsworth's pride in himself had considerably augmented, and it did not increase my love of him ; though I did not in the least hate it either, so quiet was it, so fixed, unappealing, like a dim old lichened crag on the way-side, the private meaning of which, in contrast with any public meaning it had, you

---

[1] Moore (Thomas). Memories, Journal, and Correspondence. Edited by Lord John Russell. 8 vols., 8vo. London, 1853–56.

recognized with a kind of not wholly melancholy grin.

Another and better corner dialogue I afterwards had with him, possibly also about this time, which raised him intellectually some real degrees higher in my estimation than any of his deliverances, written or oral, had ever done, and which I may reckon as the best of all his discoursings or dialogues with me. He had withdrawn to a corner, out of the light and of the general babble, as usual with him. I joined him there, and knowing how little fruitful was the literary topic between us, set him on giving me an account of the notable practicalities he had seen in life, especially of the notable men. He went into all this with a certain alacrity, and was willing to speak whenever able on the terms. . . . In general I forget what men they were, and now remember only the excellent sagacity, distinctness, and credibility of Wordsworth's little biographic portraitures of them. Never, or never but once, had I seen a stronger intellect, a more luminous and veracious power of insight, directed upon such a survey of fellow-men and their contemporary journey through the world. A great deal of Wordsworth lay in the mode and tone of drawing, but you perceived it to be faithful, accurate, and altogether life-like, though Wordsworthian. — THOMAS CARLYLE ("Reminiscences").

Conversation.

Throughout the conversation Wordsworth's manner was animated. . . . His words were very choice; each sentence seemed faultless. No one could have listened to his talk for five minutes, even on ordinary topics, without perceiving that he was an extraordinary man. Not that he was brilliant ; but there was sustained vigor, and that mode of expression which denotes habitual thoughtfulness.—ELLIS YARNALL (quoted in Wordsworth's "Life of Wordsworth ").

When speaking earnestly, his manner and voice become extremely energetic ; and the peculiar emphasis, and even accent, he throws into some of his words, add considerably to their force.   He evidently loves the monologue style of conversation, but shows great candor in giving due consideration to any remarks which others may make.   His manner is simple, his general appearance that of the abstract thinker, whom his subject gradually warms into poetry.   Now for some of these subjects :—

Mamma spoke of the beauty of Rydal, and asked whether it did not rather spoil him for common scenery.   "Oh no," he said, " it rather opens my eyes to see the beauty there is in all ; God is everywhere, and thus nothing is common or devoid of beauty.   No, ma'am, it is the *feeling* that instructs the *seeing*.   Wherever there is a heart to feel, there is also an eye to see ; even in a city you have light and shade, reflections, probably views of the water and trees, and a blue sky above you, and can you want for beauty with all these ?   People often pity me while residing in a city, but they need not, for I can enjoy its characteristic beauties as well as any."—CAROLINE FOX ("Memories of Old Friends").

Very cheerful, merry, courteous, and talkative, much more so than I should have expected from the grave and didactic character of his writings. He held forth on poetry, painting, politics and metaphysics, and with a great deal of eloquence ; *Conversa-* he is more conversible, and with a greater flow of *tion.* animal spirits than Southey. He mentioned that he never wrote down as he composed, but composed walking, riding, or in bed, and wrote down after.—CHARLES C. F. GREVILLE (" Greville Memoirs ").

No one in the habit of conversing with him, but must have been struck with the power, the strength and effectiveness, with which he could argue upon any subject, small or great, provided it was not scientific : he could handle every side of a question, and enforce his own opinion with the energy and tenacity, but with more than the indications of conviction of a lawyer. In the same way, his faculty of observation was capable of employing itself successfully upon objects quite different from those to which he especially consecrated it.—ROBERT P. GRAVES ("Recollections of Wordsworth ").[1]

On a summer morning (let us call it 1840 then) I was apprised by Taylor that Wordsworth had come to town, and would meet a small party of us at a certain tavern in St. James's Street, at breakfast, to which I was invited for the given day and hour. . . . Wordsworth seemed in good tone, and, much to Taylor's satisfaction, talked a great deal ;

[1] Afternoon lectures on English literature and art, delivered in Dublin. 5 vols., 12mo. London, 1863-69.

about "poetic" correspondents of his own (*i.e.*, correspondents for the sake of his poetry; espe-

cially one such who had sent him, from Canton, an excellent chest of tea ; correspondent grinningly applauded by us all) ; then about ruralities and miscellanies. ; . . These were the first topics. Then, finally, about literature, literary laws, prac- tices, observances, at considerable length, and turn- ing wholly on the mechanical part, including even a good deal of shallow enough etymology, from me and others, which was well received. On all this Wordsworth enlarged with evident satisfaction, and was joyfully reverent of the "wells of English un- defiled," though stone-dumb as to the deeper rules and wells of Eternal Truth and Harmony, which you were to try and set forth by said undefiled wells of English, or what other speech you had ! To me a little disappointing, but not much ; though it would have given me pleasure had the robust vet- eran man emerged a little out of vocables into things now and then, as he never once chanced to do. For the rest, he talked well in his way ; with veracity, easy brevity, and force, as a wise tradesman would of his tools and workshop, and as no unwise one could.—THOMAS CARLYLE (" Reminiscences ").

He was a patient and courteous listener, paying the most scrupulous attention to every word, never interrupting, and with a certain fixedness of his clear grey eyes which made one feel that, whatever one's opinion might be, one must be prepared to give a substantial reason for it, and, in doing so, to discard all that might seem fanciful, and not to be readily explained.—Mrs. ALARIC WATTS (" Life of Watts ").[1]

I revert with great delight to a long expedition I one day made with Wordsworth alone. He had heard of the ruins of an old Cistercian abbey, Heisterbach, on the side of the Rhine opposite to that on which we were staying. He asked me, playfully, to join him, in these words :

A country walk.

> "Go with us into the abbey—there ;
> And let us there, at large, discourse our fortunes."

Hitherto I had only seen Wordsworth in the presence of Coleridge ; and had imagined him, constitutionally contemplative and taciturn. To-day I discovered that his reticence was self-imposed, out of consideration for the inordinate loquacity of his brother poet.

Coleridge always speechified or preached,

> " His argument
> Was all too heavy to admit much *talk.*"

Wordsworth chatted naturally and fluently, out of the fulness of his heart, and not from a wish to display his eloquence. . . . Idolatry of nature seemed with Wordsworth both a passion and a principle. . . . On that same stroll of Heisterbach, he pointed out to me such beauty of design in objects I had used to trample under foot, that I felt as if almost every spot on which I trod was holy ground, and that I had rudely desecrated it. His eyes would fill with tears, and his voice falter, as he

[1] Watts (Alaric Alfred). Alaric Watts. A Narrative of his Life. 2 vols., 8vo. London, 1884.

dwelt on the benevolent adaptation of means to ends discernible by reverential observation.'—JULIAN C. YOUNG ("Memoir of C. M. Young ").[2]

Reading aloud.

His reading is very peculiar, but, to my ear, delightful ; slow, solemn, earnest in expression, more than any I have ever heard ; when he reads or recites in the open air, his deep, rich tones seem to proceed from a spirit-voice, and belong to the religion of the place ; they harmonize so fitly with the thrilling tones of woods and waterfalls.—FELICIA D. HEMANS (" Memoir of Mrs. Hemans)." [3]

Hazlitt, in "The Spirit of the Age," says, "His manner of reading his own poetry is particularly imposing." Barry Cornwall also describes his reading, see p. 32.

Lord Cranbrook, in an article published in the *National Review*, April, 1884, reports Wilson as follows : " How strange a contrast there is between Campbell's recitation and Wordsworth's—the former in a thin weak voice, settling now and then the curls of his wig, reciting without power his greatest lyrics ; Wordsworth, with a severe and simple dig-

---

[1] See also pages 73, 74. It is worthy of remark that Southey, who was familiar with all the best talkers of his time, said of Wordsworth, "In conversation he is powerful beyond any of his cotemporaries." These words occur in a letter from Southey to Bernard Barton, in 1814.

[2] Young (Rev. Julian Charles). A Memoir of Charles M. Young, Tragedian, with Extracts from his Son's Journal. 12mo. London and New York, 1871.

[3] Hemans (Felicia D.). Poetical Works. With a Memoir by her Sister, Mrs. Hughes. 7 vols., 12mo. London, 1839.

nity giving a tone to his recitation, which has often after hearing him on a hill-side walk, thrilled me for days after. He has the most remarkable power, in that way, of any man I ever heard. It seemed like inspiration, and I could almost imagine that he spoke by revelation." Lord Cranbrook's interview with "Christopher North," was in 1843, when Campbell and Wordsworth were still alive.

Reading aloud.

In a letter to Wordsworth, Lamb says, " Tell Mrs. W. her postscripts are always agreeable. They are so legible, too. Your manual-graphy is terrible, dark as Lycophron. . . . Well, God bless you, and continue to give you power to write with a finger of power upon our hearts what you fail to impress, in corresponding lucidness, upon our outward eyesight."

Hand-writing.

Wordsworth never wrote, if he could help it ; his wife and his sister were his amanuenses. In a letter of 1803, to Sir George Beaumont, quoted in the " Memoirs," he says "I do not know from what cause it is, but during the last three years I have never had a pen in my hand for five minutes, before my whole frame becomes one bundle of uneasiness ; a perspiration starts out all over me, and my chest is oppressed in a manner which I cannot describe."

Writing painful to him.

Almost all his poems, as I have heard from himself, were composed out of doors, as he either freely traversed hill and vale, or paced some favorite level strip, such as that at Lancrigg, or that in the firgrove consecrated to the memory of his brother, or a terrace in his garden. . . . . And sometimes

Work out-of-doors.

Work out-of-doors.

weeks elapsed before the poems thus composed were committed to paper, a process which was generally performed by the hand of wife, or sister, or daughter.—ROBERT P. GRAVES ("Recollections of Wordsworth").

No musical ear—No sense of smell.

Wordsworth had himself no musical sense, no more than any sense of smell. His sense of hearing, indeed, as well as of sight, was peculiarly keen, but like his friend Elia, he could not distinguish one tune from another.—ROBERT P. GRAVES ("Recollections of Wordsworth").

In speaking of music, and the difference there is between the poetical and musical ear, Wordsworth said that he was totally devoid of the latter, and for a long time could not distinguish one tune from another.—THOMAS MOORE (" Diary").

Impatience.

Wordsworth took down the volume ; unfortunately it was uncut ; fortunately, and by a special providence as to him, tea was proceeding at the time. Dry toast required butter ; butter required knives ; and knives then lay on the table ; but sad it was for the virgin purity of Mr. Burke's yet unsunned pages, that every knife bore upon its blade testimonies of the service it had rendered. Did *that* stop Wordsworth ? Did that cause him to call for another knife ? Not at all ; he

> "Looked at the knife that caus'd his pain ;
> And looked and sighed, and looked and sighed again ;"

and then, after this momentary tribute to regret, he tore his way into the heart of the volume with this knife, that left its greasy honors behind it upon every page : and are they not there to this day ? —THOMAS DE QUINCEY ("Literary Reminiscences ").

At this period (1807) Southey and Wordsworth entertained a mutual esteem, but did not cordially like each other. Indeed, it would have been odd if they had. Wordsworth lived in the open air ; Southey in his library, which Coleridge used to call his wife. Southey had particularly elegant habits (Wordsworth called them finical) in the use of books. Wordsworth, on the other hand, was so negligent, and so indulgent in the same case, that, as Southey laughingly expressed it to me some years afterwards, when I was staying at Greta Hall on a visit—"To introduce Wordsworth into one's library, is like letting a bear into a tulip garden."—THOMAS DE QUINCEY (" Literary Reminiscences ").

Contrast between Words- worth and Southey.

Wordsworth and Dickens did not *take* to each other. Indeed, there was a mutual contempt be- them, although they met only once. This was about the year 1843. Some days after, the gentleman whose guest Wordsworth was, in the suburbs of London, asked the Poet, how he liked the great Novelist ? Wordsworth had a great contempt for young men, and, after pursing up his lips in a fash- ion peculiar to him, and swinging one leg over the other, the bare flesh of his ankles appearing over his socks, slowly answered: "Why, I am not much given to turn critic on people I meet ; but, as you ask me, I will candidly avow that I thought him a very talkative, vulgar young person,—but I dare say he may be very clever. Mind, I don't want to

Mutual antipathies.

Mutual antipathies. say a word against him, for I have never read a line he has written." Some time after this, the same querist guardedly asked Dickens how he had liked the Poet Laureate ?—" Like him ? Not at all. He is a dreadful Old Ass."—R. SHELTON MACKENZIE ("Life of Dickens ").[1]

Impatience of constraint. I do not conceive that Wordsworth could have been an amiable boy ; he was austere and unsocial, I have reason to think, in his habits ; not generous ; and, above all, not self-denying. Throughout his later life, with all the benefits of a French discipline in the lesser charities of social intercourse, he has always exhibited a marked impatience of those par-ticular courtesies of life. Not but he was kind and obliging where his services would cost him no exer-tion ; but I am pretty certain that no consideration would ever have induced Wordsworth to burthen himself with a lady's reticule, parasol, shawl, or any thing that was hers. Mighty must be the danger which would induce him to lead her horse by the bridle. Nor would he, without some demur, stop to offer her his hand over a stile.[2] Freedom—un-limited, careless, insolent freedom—unoccupied pos-session of his own arms—absolute control over his own legs and motions—these have always been so essential to his comfort, that in any case where they were likely to become questionable, he would have declined to make one of the party.—THOMAS DE QUINCEY ("Literary Reminiscences ").

---

[1] Mackenzie (Robert Shelton). Life of Charles Dickens. 12mo. Philadelphia, 1870.

[2] For a quite different view, see p. 50.

In the country he would walk with you, talk with you, and seem gratified with your society; but, somehow or other, it seemed to me as if he were ready to relapse, become wrapt up in speculation, and would rather prefer being left to commune with himself. . . . On his visits to town, the recluse of Rydal Mount was quite a different creature. To me it was demonstrated, by his conduct under every circumstance, that De Quincey . . . had done him gross injustice in the character he loosely threw upon the public, viz., that "he was not generous or self-denying . . . ;" and farther, that he was "slovenly and regardless in dress." I must protest that there was no warrant for this caricature; but, on the contrary, that it bore no feature of resemblance to the slight degree of eccentricity discoverable in Cumberland, and was utterly contradicted by the life in London. In the mixed society of the great Babylon, Mr. Wordsworth was facile and courteous; dressed like a gentleman, and with his tall, commanding figure—no mean type of the superior order, well trained by education and accustomed to good manners—shall I reveal that he was often sportive, and could even go the length of strong (whatever invidiousness might say, not vulgar) expressions in the off-hand mirth of his observations and criticisms?—WILLIAM JERDAN (" Men I have Known ").[1]

Town manners.

Among convivial spirits no one could be more joyous than Wordsworth; no one could enter more heartily and readily into the humors of the passing

[1] Jerdan (William). Men I have Known. 8vo. London, 1866.

Social and genial.

hour ; and among eminent authors no one could ever be found more willing than he was to make allowances for the faults of others, or to afford instruction whenever he met with a pupil whose attachment to literature was not founded on vanity or affectation.—ROBERT P. GILLIES' (" Memoirs of a Literary Veteran ").

Alone in a crowd.

The light was always afflictive to his eyes ;[2] he carried in his pocket something like a skeleton brass candlestick, in which, setting it on the dinner table, between him and the most afflictive or nearest of the chief lights, he touched a little spring, and there flirted out, at the top of his brass implement, a small vertical green circle which prettily enough threw his eyes into shade, and screened him from that sorrow. In proof of his equanimity as lion, I remember, in connection with this green shade, one little glimpse which shall be given presently as finis. . . . Dinner was large, luminous, sumptuous. I sat a long way from Wordsworth ; dessert I think had come in, and certainly there reigned in all quarters a cackle as of Babel (only politer, perhaps), which, far up in Wordsworth's quarter (who was leftward on my side of the table), seemed to have taken a sententious, rather louder, logical, and quasi-

[1] Gillies (Robert Pearce). Memoirs of a Literary Veteran. 3 vols., 12mo. London, 1854.
[2] In a letter to Caroline Bowles, Southey says of Wordsworth, " for many years he has been subject to frequent and severe inflammation of the lids. . . . Any emotion immediately affects the diseased parts ; the excitement of conversation is sufficient for the evil."

scientific turn, heartily unimportant to gods and men, so far as I could judge of it and of the other babble reigning. I look upwards, leftwards, the coast being luckily for a moment clear ; then, far off, beautifully screened in the shadow of his vertical green circle, which was on the farther side of him, sat Wordsworth, silent, slowly but steadily gnawing some portion of what I judged to be raisins, with his eye and attention placidly fixed on these and these alone. The sight of whom, and of his rock-like indifference to the babble, quasi-scientific and other, with attention turned on the small practical alone, was comfortable and amusing to me, who felt like him, but could not eat raisins.—THOMAS CARLYLE ("Reminiscences ").

Alone in a crowd.

The shake of hand he gives you is feckless, egotistical. . . . The languid way in which he gives you a handful of numb, unresponsive fingers, is very significant.—THOMAS CARLYLE (from a letter quoted in Froude's " Carlyle ").[1]

Manner of shaking hands.

He is more simple in his manners than his friend Mr. Coleridge ; but at the same time less cordial or conciliating. . . . There is an air of condescension in his civility. With a tall, loose figure, a peaked austerity of countenance, and no inclination to *embonpoint*, you would say he has something puritanical, something ascetic in his appearance.—WILLIAM HAZLITT (" Spirit of the Age ").

Austerity.

[1] Froude (James A.). Thomas Carlyle. A History of his Life in London. 2 vols., 8vo. London, 1884.

An ungenial coldness of manner has been often ascribed to him. And, indeed, when a friend entered *An apology for his cold- ness* his room he might often be disappointed by an apparently uninterested recognition and a want of cordiality. The fact was, that the earnestness with which his intellect worked rendered it impossible for him quickly to turn from one object of thought to another: never was a man of less versatility or mobility: yet just for this very reason the friend might be perfectly assured that if he gave the poet time to pass out from the train of reflection which had engaged him, the habitual feeling of friendship would gradually more and more brighten his countenance, and the old cordiality warm the tones of his voice.— ROBERT P. GRAVES ("Recollections of Wordsworth").

I have a vivid recollection of Wordsworth, who was a very grave man, with strong features and a deep voice. . . . He was fond (perhaps too *Solemnity— A touch of humor.* fond) of reciting his own poetry before friends and strangers. I was not attracted by his manner, which was almost too solemn, but I was deeply impressed by some of the weighty notes in his voice, when he was delivering out his oracles. . . . I remembered the reading long afterwards, as one recollects the roll of the spent thunder. . . .

Hazlitt says that Wordsworth's face, notwithstanding his constitutional gravity, sometimes revealed indications of dry humor. And once, at a morning visit, I heard him give an account of his having breakfasted in company with Coleridge, and allowed him to expatiate to the extent of his lungs. "How could you permit him to go on and weary himself?"

said Rogers ; "why, you are to meet him at dinner this evening." "Yes," replied Wordsworth ; "I know that very well ; but we like to take the *sting* out of him beforehand." [1]—BRYAN W. PROCTER ("Charles Lamb ; a Memoir").[2]

Solemnity— A touch of humor. .

At a friend's house, after dinner, the conversation turned upon wit and humor. The author of Lalla Rookh, who was present, gave some illustrations from Sheridan's saying, doings, and writings. Starting from his reverie, Wordsworth said that he did not consider himself to be a witty poet : "Indeed," continued he, "I do not think I was ever witty but once in my life." A great desire was naturally expressed by all to know what this special drollery was. After some hesitation, the old poet said, "Well, well, I will tell you. I was standing some time ago at the entrance of my cottage at Rydal Mount. A man accosted me with the question, 'Pray, sir, have you seen my wife pass by ?' Whereupon I said, 'Why, my good friend, I didn't know till this moment that you had a wife !'" The company stared, and finding that the old bard had discharged his entire stock, burst into a roar of laughter, which the facetious Wordsworth, in his simplicity, accepted as a genuine compliment to the brilliancy of his wit.—SAMUEL A. ALLIBONE ("Dictionary").[3]

An example of Wordsworth's wit.

---

[1] This is the only instance which has been recorded of a joke from Wordsworth.

[2] Procter (Bryan Waller). Charles Lamb ; a Memoir. 8vo. London, 1866.

[3] Allibone (Samuel Austin). Critical Dictionary of English Literature, and British and American Authors. 3 vols., 8vo. Philadelphia, 1859–71.

III.—3

Incapable of a joke. He is moral, grave, good-natured, and of kindly intercourse. He does not understand a joke, but requires it to be explained ; after which he looks uneasy. It is not his point. He sees nothing in it. The thing is not, and cannot be made Wordsworth-ian.—RICHARD H. HORNE ("New Spirit of the Age").[1]

"He had a frugal mind." After the trio[2] had left Gedsburgh, and were returning homewards via Amsterdam and Rotterdam, they paid a visit to Haarlem. Mrs. Aders received a letter from Coleridge, dated from that place, in which he told her that they had not arrived many minutes at their hotel before one of the principal waiters of the establishment entered the room, and asked them if they would like to accompany a few other persons in the house to hear the celebrated organ played, as a party was then in the act of forming.

"Oh," said Wordsworth, "we meant to hear the organ ! but why, Coleridge, should we go with strangers ?" "I beg your pardon," interrupted the waiter, who understood and spoke English well, "but it is not every one who is willing to pay twelve guilders (1*l.*) ; and as the organist will never play privately for less, it is customary for persons to go in parties, and share the expense between them." "Ah, then I think I will not go : I am tired," said Wordsworth. "Then you and I will go together, Dora," said Coleridge. Off they went, arm-in-arm, leaving Wordsworth behind them.

---

[1] Horne (Richard Hengist). A New Spirit of the Age. 2 vols., 8vo. London, 1844.
[2] Wordsworth, his daughter, and Coleridge.

They had not been long in the Church of St. Bavon, listening to the different stops which the organist was trying to display to the greatest advantage—the solo stops, the bell stops, the trumpet stop, the vox humana stop—before Coleridge was made sensible of the unwelcome intrusion of a strong current of air throughout the building. He turned his head to see the cause ; ·and, to his amusement, descried his gentle friend, noiselessly closing the door, and furtively making his way behind one of the pillars, from whence he could hear without being seen, and thus escape payment. Before the organist had concluded his labors, Wordsworth had quietly withdrawn. On the return of his friend and his daughter, he asked them how they had enjoyed their visit to St. Bavon, but said nothing of his own ![1]—JULIAN C. YOUNG ("Memoir of C. M. Young ").

"He had a frugal mind."

He told me I should find visitors a great expense, and that I must promise him,—(and he laid his hand on my arm to enforce what he said) I must promise him to do as he and his sister had done, when, in their early days, they had lived at Grasmere.

Household economy.

"When you have a visitor," said he, "you must do as we did ;—you must say 'if you like to have a cup of tea with us, you are very welcome : but if you want any meat,—you must pay for your board.'

[1] Caroline Fox, in her "Memories of Old Friends," tells of a conversation with Hartley Coleridge, in which he said that Wordsworth was "a most unpleasant companion in a tour, from his terrible fear of being cheated."

Now promise me that you will do this." Of course, I could promise nothing of the sort. . . . He insisted : I declined promising; and changed the subject. The mixture of odd economies and neighborly generosity was one of the most striking things in the old poet. At tea there, one could hardly get a drop of cream with any ease of mind, while he was giving away all the milk that the household did not want to neighboring cottages.'—HARRIET MARTINEAU ("Autobiography ").[2]

Mr. Wordsworth is not only a man of principle and integrity, according to the severest standard of such a character, but even a man, in many respects, of amiable manners. Still there are traits of character about him, and modes of expressing them in his manners, which make a familiar or neighborly intercourse with him painful and mortifying. Pride, in its most exalted form, he was entitled to feel ; but something there was, in the occasional expression of this pride, which was difficult to bear. Upon ground where he was really strong, Wordsworth was not arrogant. In a question of criticism, he was open to any man's suggestions. But there *were* fields of thought or of observation which he seemed to think locked up and sacred to himself ; and any alien entrances upon those fields he treated almost as intrusions and usurpations.

---

[1] Wordsworth's manner of living was always extremely plain. He was a water-drinker ; and there is no record of his having made use of any kind of stimulants.

[2] Martineau (Harriet). Autobiography. Edited by M. W. Chapman. 2 vols., 8vo. Boston : Houghton, Mifflin, & Co. 1877.

One of these, and which naturally occurred the most frequently, was the whole theory of picturesque beauty, as presented to our notice every minute by the bold, mountainous scenery amongst which we lived, and as it happened to be modified by the seasons of the year, by the time of day, or by the accidents of light and shade. Now Wordsworth and his sister really had ' . . . a peculiar depth of organic sensibility to the effects of form and color; and to *them* I was willing to concede a vote, such as in ancient Rome was called " a prerogative vote," upon such questions. But, not content with this, Wordsworth virtually claimed the same precedence for all who were connected with himself, though merely by affinity, and therefore standing under no colorable presumption (as blood relations might have done) of inheriting the same constitutional gifts of organization. To everybody, standing out of this sacred and privileged pale, Wordsworth behaved with absolute insult in cases of this nature; he did not even appear to listen; but, as if what they said on such a theme must be childish prattle, turned away with an air of perfect indifference; began talking, perhaps, with another person on another subject; or, at all events, never noticed what we said by an apology for an answer. I, very early in our connection, having observed this inhuman arrogance, took care never afterwards to lay myself under the possibility of such an insult. Systematically I avoided saying anything, however tempted into any expression of my feelings, upon the natural appearances, whether in the sky or upon the earth. Thus I evaded one cause of quarrel; and

Pride and arrogance.

so far Wordsworth was not aware of the irritation and disgust which he had founded in the minds of his friends. But there were other manifestations of the same ungenial and exclusive pride, even still more offensive and of wider application.

Unwilling to hear argument.

With other men, upon finding or thinking oneself ill-used, all one had to do was to make an explanation. . . . Not so with Wordsworth; he had learned . . . a vulgar phrase for all attempts at reciprocal explanations—he called them contemptuously *"fending and proving."* And you might lay your account with being met *in limine*, and further progress barred, by a declaration to this effect— " Mr. X. Y. Z., I will have nothing to do with fending and proving." This amounted, in other words, to saying, that he conceived himself to be liberated from those obligations of justice and courtesy by which other men are bound. . . . Never after the first year or so from my first introduction, had I felt much possibility of drawing the bonds of friendship tight with a man of Wordsworth's nature. He seemed to me too much like his own Pedlar in the " Excursion ;" a man so diffused amongst innumerable objects of equal attention, that he had no calls left in his heart for strong individual attachments.— THOMAS DE QUINCEY (" Literary Reminiscences ").

Emerson's visit.

He led me out into his garden, and showed me the gravel walk in which thousands of his lines were composed. . . . He had just returned from a visit to Staffa, and within three days had made three sonnets on Fingal's Cave, and was composing a fourth, when he was called in to see me. He said,

"If you are interested in my verses, perhaps you will like to hear these lines." I gladly assented ; and he recollected himself for a few moments, and then stood forth and repeated, one after the other, the three entire sonnets with great animation. . . . This recitation was so unlooked-for and surprising—he, the old Wordsworth, standing apart, and reciting to me in a garden-walk, like a school-boy declaiming,—that I at first was near to laugh ; but recollecting myself, that I had come thus far to see a poet, and he was chanting poems to me, I saw that he was right and I was wrong, and gladly gave myself up to hear.—RALPH WALDO EMERSON ("English Traits ").[1]

Emerson's visit.

Knowing that he had no objection to be talked to about his works, I told him that I thought it might interest him to hear which of his poems was Dr. Channing's favorite. I told him that I had not been a day in Dr. Channing's house when he brought me "The Happy Warrior,"—(a choice which I thought very characteristic also). "Ay," said Wordsworth : "that was not on account of the *poetic conditions* being best fulfilled in that poem ; but because it is " (solemnly) "a chain of extremely *valooable* thoughts.—You see,—it does not best fulfil the conditions of poetry ; but it is " (solemnly) "a chain of extremely valooable thoughts."—HARRIET MARTINEAU ("Autobiography ").

Literary egotism.

He asked me what I thought the finest elegiac composition in the language ; and when I diffidently

---

[1] Emerson (Ralph Waldo). **English Traits.** 12mo. Boston, 1856.

suggested "Lycidas," he replied, "You are not far
wrong. It may, I think, be affirmed that Milton's
'Lycidas,' and my 'Laodamia' are twin immortals."
—MRS. ALARIC WATTS (" Life of Watts ").

Some one having observed that the next Waverley
novel was to be " Rob Roy," Wordsworth took down
his volume of Ballads, and read to the company
"Rob Roy's Grave ; " then, returning it to the
shelf, observed—"I do not know what more Mr.
Scott can have to say upon the subject." . . .
Mr. James T. Fields, in his delightful volume of
" Yesterdays with Authors," has an amiable record
of his interview with Wordsworth ; yet he has the
following casual remark, "I thought he did not
praise easily those whose names are indissolubly
connected with his own in the history of literature.
It was languid praise, at least, and I observed that
he hesitated for mild terms which he could apply
to names almost as great as his own."—CHARLES
COWDEN CLARKE (*Gentleman's Magazine*, February,
1874).

I could not forbear the impression that his sympathies were rather with his predecessors than his
contemporaries in the gentle art. I observed that
he rarely left a commendation of the latter wholly
unqualified ; so that the effect of his criticism seemed
to be rather to qualify mercy with justice than, as I
should rather have preferred, to temper justice with
mercy.—MRS. ALARIC WATTS (" Life of Watts ").

After a while he (Professor Wilson) digressed
to Wordsworth and Southey, and asked me if I was

going to return by the Lakes. I proposed doing so. "I will give you letters to both, if you haven't them. I lived a long time in that neighborhood, and know Wordsworth perhaps as well as any one. Many a day I have walked over the hills with him, and listened to his repetition of his own poetry." . . .

Christopher North on his egotism.

"Did Wordsworth repeat any other poetry than his own?"

"Never in a single instance to my knowledge. He is remarkable for the manner in which he is wrapped up in his own poetical life." . . .

"Was the story true that was told in the papers of his seeing, for the first time, in a large company some new novel of Scott's, in which there was a motto taken from his works; and that he went immediately to the shelf and took down one of his own volumes and read the whole poem to the party, who were waiting for a reading of the new book?"

"Perfectly true. It happened in this very house." —NATHANIEL P. WILLIS ("Famous Persons and Places").[1]

Hare[2] says that notwithstanding his greatness he really and heartily admires very few poets. Milton and Spenser—these he loves and appreciates—scarcely any other. Hare doubts his hearty admiration of Shakespeare. Now, as Hare loves Wordsworth, respects him, and thinks we have had no such poet for ages, I feel quite confident in what he says about him, that he does not misunderstand or mis-

Slight appreciation of other poets.

---

[1] Willis (Nathaniel Parker). Famous Persons and Places. 12mo. New York: Charles Scribner. 1854.

[2] Julius (Archdeacon) Hare.

represent him.—DANIEL MACMILLAN (Letter of 1842, in Hughes's " Memoir of Macmillan ").[1]

A personal confession.

I presented myself at Rydal Mount . . . and found the poet walking in his garden. . . . He welcomed me very courteously, and asked me to excuse him for receiving me out of doors, as he preferred the open air. . . . He suddenly said, I thought somewhat ungraciously,—" I am told that you write poetry. I never read a line of your poems and don't intend." I suppose I looked surprised at the apparent rudeness of this, for he went on to say, —" You must not be offended with me ; the truth is, I never read anybody's poetry but my own." Again I suppose my face must have expressed what I certainly felt—a slight degree of wonder at a declaration which I thought so very gratuitous. "You must not be surprised," he added ; "for it is not vanity which makes me say this. I am an old man, and little time is left me in the world. I use that little as well as I may, to revise all my poems carefully, and make them as perfect as I can before I take my final departure."

It was quite evident from the frankness of this explanation, that the old gentleman did not mean to wound my self-love while explaining and vindicating his own. . . . Desiring to turn the conversation, I stopped a moment in our walk to admire the outline of the picturesque mountain across the lake, and pointing to it, asked him its name. " Dear me ! " he replied, " that's Nab Scaur. Have you

---

[1] Hughes (Thomas). Memoir of Daniel Macmillan. 12mo. London, 1882.

never read my poems?" It was on the tip of my tongue to retort, that I never read anybody's poems but my own ; but I reflected that he was old enough to be my grandfather. . . . So I refrained, and listened attentively as he spoke. "I have described Nab Scaur more than once in my poems. Don't you remember the following ?" (And here he recited, in a deep base voice, a passage of twenty or thirty lines, which was entirely new to me, though I did not like to tell him so.)—CHARLES MACKAY ("Forty Years' Recollections ").[1]

A personal confession.

It chanced one night, when I was there,[2] that there was a resplendent arch across the zenith, from the one horizon to the other. . . . Well, when word came into the room of the splendid meteor, we all went out to view it ; and, on the beautiful platform at Mount Rydal we were all walking, in twos and threes, arm in arm, talking of the phenomenon, and admiring it. Now, be it remembered that Wordsworth, Professor Wilson, Lloyd, De Quincey, and myself were present, besides several other literary gentlemen, whose names I am not certain that I remember aright. Miss Wordsworth's arm was in mine, and she was expressing some fears that the splendid stranger might prove ominous, when I, by ill luck, blundered out the following remark, thinking that I was saying a good thing :—"Hout, me'm ! it is neither mair nor less than joost a tree-

"Where are they?"

---

[1] Mackay (Charles). Forty Years' Recollections, from 1830 to 1870. 2 vols., 8vo. London, 1877.

[2] At Wordsworth's house.

umphal airch, raised in honor of the meeting of the poets."

"That's not amiss,—eh? eh?—that's very good," said the Professor, laughing. But Wordsworth, *"Where are they?"* who had De Quincey's arm, gave a grunt, and turned on his heel, and leading the little opium-chewer aside, he addressed him in these disdainful and venomous words:—"Poets? Poets?—what does the fellow mean?—Where are they?"

Who could forgive this? For my part I never can and never will. . . . The *"Where are they?"* was too bad! I have always some hopes that De Quincey was *leeing,* for I did not myself hear Wordsworth utter the words.—JAMES HOGG ("Reminiscences").[1]

Two apologists. He did not intrude his own poetry or himself, but he did not decline to talk about either; and he spoke about both simply, unboastingly, and yet with a manly consciousness of their worth. It was clear he thought he had achieved a high place among poets: it had been the aim of his life, humanly speaking; and he had taken worthy pains to accomplish and prepare himself for the enterprise.—JOHN T. COLERIDGE (quoted in Wordsworth's "Life of Wordsworth").

May 8th, 1812. A visit from Wordsworth, who stayed with me from between twelve and one till past three. I then walked with him to Newman Street. His conversation was long and interesting. He spoke

---

[1] Hogg (James). Poetical Works. With Autobiography. 5 vols., 16mo. Glasgow, 1838–1840.

of his own poems with the just feeling of confidence which a sense of his own excellence gives him.
He is now convinced that he never can derive emol-
ument from them ; but, being independent, he willingly gives up all ideas of doing so.

June 21st, 1820. Wordsworth was very pleasant.
Indeed, he is uniformly so now. And there is absolutely no pretence for what was always an exaggerated charge against him, that he could talk only of
his own poetry, and loves only his own works. He
is more indulgent than he used to be of the works
of others, even contemporaries and rivals.—HENRY
CRABB ROBINSON ("Diary").[1]

October 27th, 1820. We talked of Wordsworth's
exceedingly high opinion of himself; and Lady
Davy mentioned that one day, in a large party, *Self-esteem.*
Wordsworth, without anything having been previously said that could lead to the subject, calling
out suddenly from the top of the table to the bottom, in his most epic tone, "Davy !" and on Davy's
putting forth his head in awful expectation of what
was coming, said, "Do you know the reason why I
published the 'White Doe' in quarto ?" "No,
what was it ?" "To show the world my own opinion of it."—THOMAS MOORE (" Memoirs," edited by
Lord J. Russell).

Wordsworth's attention was arrested by the prepossessing looks of a little girl, who was sitting on
the grass alone. He stopped and talked to her, and

---

[1] Robinson (Henry Crabb). Diary, Reminiscences, and Correspondence. Edited by T. Sadler. 3 vols., 8vo. London, 1869.

*"The cele-
brated
W. W."*

asked her of her parents, her home, whether she went to school, &c., and being well pleased with the ingenuous answers that she gave him, he put one hand on her head, and with the other dived down into the recesses of his coat pocket, and drew forth a little copy of his minor poems, telling her to look at him well, and note his person ; to be sure also to observe well the time of day, and the spot ; and to recollect that this little book had been given to her by the author, the celebrated William Wordsworth![1] —Julian C. Young ("Memoir of C. M. Young").

*Milton's
watch.*

Landor, always generous, says that he never praised anybody. A gentleman in London showed me a watch that once belonged to Milton, whose initials are engraved on its face. He said, he once showed this to Wordsworth, who took it in one hand, then drew out his own watch, and held it up with the other, before the company, but no one making the expected remark, he put back his own in silence. — Ralph Waldo Emerson (" English Traits ").

*Unwar-
ranted
criticism of
his contem-
poraries.*

He often gave an opinion on authors which he never had read, and on some which he could not read ; Plato, for instance. . . . He spoke contemptuously of the Scotch. The first time I ever met him, and the only time I ever conversed with him longer than a few minutes, he spoke contemptuously of Scott, and violently of Byron. He

[1] This story was told by Samuel Rogers, who was walking with Wordsworth when the scene occurred.

chatted about them incoherently and indiscrimi-
nately.—WALTER SAVAGE LANDOR (from a letter to
Emerson).

Dr. Charles Mackay, in his "Forty Years' Recollections," reports the following talk of Samuel Rog-
ers, about Wordsworth : " He lives too much alone. *Too much alone.*
He does not associate with his fellow men. He
has shut himself up for years among the mountains
and the lakes, and worshipped them ; he has ended
by worshipping himself. He has so continually
brooded over his own genius in his darling soli-
tudes, that he has come to consider himself the
centre of the universe. . . . I should not call
him a vain man, or even a conceited man, by nature
or original disposition, but he has become conceited
for want of intercourse with his fellows. He sees
nobody at Grasmere who is not inferior to himself,
and he comes to the conclusion, unconsciously I
have no doubt, that everybody, everywhere else, is
inferior to him. If he would spend six months of
every year in London this idea would be rubbed out
of him by the wholesome friction of society."

I remember Mr. Wordsworth saying that, at a
particular stage of his mental progress, he used to
be frequently so rapt into an unreal transcendental *Mental abstraction.*
world of ideas that the external world seemed no
longer to exist in relation to him, and he had to
reconvince himself of its existence by clasping a
tree, or something that happened to be near him.
—ROBERT P. GRAVES (quoted in Wordsworth's
" Life of Wordsworth ").

April 6th, 1837. At Nismes I took Wordsworth to see the exterior of both the Maison Carrée and *A contrast.* the Arena. He acknowledged their beauty, but expected no great pleasure from such things. He says, "I am unable, from ignorance, to enjoy these sights. I receive an impression, but that is all. I have no science, and can refer nothing to principle." He was, on the other hand, delighted by two beautiful little girls playing with flowers near the Arena ; and I overheard him say to himself, "Oh, you darlings ! I wish I could put you in my pocket, and carry you to Rydal Mount !"—HENRY CRABB ROBINSON ("Diary").

Politics. In his youth Wordsworth was an ardent republican ; but his political opinions changed very materially as he grew older. The character of his conservatism, in his mature years, may be estimated from the fact that he seriously considered the wisdom of seeking a home in some other country in consequence of the alarm with which he viewed the success of the Reform Bill in 1832.

Home life. No one could enjoy anything beyond the most cursory admission into the home of Wordsworth, without feeling that he was breathing there a moral atmosphere singularly pure and healthful. The stamp of truth and genuineness was on everything. Persons and events, theories and projects, were estimated by a standard which was intended to determine, not their conventional and temporary, but their real and permanent value. One would have said that to wear any mask would have been impossible in the presence of a family so truthful and so sensitive, so quick to recognize every genuine emotion, so sure to give instinctive yet not ungentle indication of their sense of what was false or exaggerated. But all this was the action of no polemically critical spirit : kindness and human-heartedness reigned in full concord with truth, the sacred recesses of feeling were carefully respected, and holy things touched with reverence. All around corresponded : an exquisite nature looked in at the windows, or was looked out upon—flowers and books, prints, paintings, and sculptured figures, all loved with something of a personal love, adorned the rooms, which were pervaded by a homely elegance, and one saw that everything was for use or for enjoyment, nothing for ostentation. I need not say that all these things indicated essential characteristics of the poet himself.—ROBERT P. GRAVES (" Recollections of Wordsworth ").

Home life.

There is an almost patriarchal simplicity about him—an absence of all pretension. All is free, unstudied—

" The river winding at its own sweet will "—

in his manner and conversation. There is more of impulse about them than I had expected ; but in other respects I see much that I should have looked for in the poet of meditative life : frequently his head droops, his eyes half close, and he seeems buried in quiet depths of thought.—FELICIA D. HEMANS (" Memoir of Mrs. Hemans ").

III.—4

Home life. I am charmed with Mr. Wordsworth, whose kindness to me has quite a soothing influence over my spirits. . . . "There is a daily beauty in his life," which is in such lovely harmony with his poetry, that I am thankful to have witnessed and *felt* it. He gives me a good deal of his society, reads to me, walks with me, leads my pony when I ride ; and I begin to talk with him as with a sort of paternal friend.—FELICIA D. HEMANS ("Memoir of Mrs. Hemans ").

In his garden. In an article entitled "The English Lakes and their Genii," published in *Harper's Magazine*, December, 1880, Mr. M. D. Conway gives the following description, which he received from Isaac Walker, an old man, who had once been in Wordsworth's service, and who still remembered his master's habits :

"He liked to be out of doors whenever he could. Sometimes he was picking up things to look at them, and then he was talking to things in a very queer way. I can see him now, following a bumble-bee all over the garden ; he puts his hands behind him, this way, and then bends over towards the bee, and wherever it went he followed, making a noise like it—'Boom-oom-oom-oom.' . . . He would stick to that bee long and long, until it went away ; you might go away and come back, and still you would see him striding after that bee, with his mouth down toward it, and hear his ' Boom-oom-oom.' But there was nothing he did n't take notice of."

When one came in contact with himself it was his strength above all things which impressed one.

Here was no merely amiable, no merely simple, or
reverential, or imaginative man, but one eminently
masculine and strong : a man of strong intellect, of *Intellectual strength.*
strong feelings, of sturdy, massive individuality.
If I do not apply to him the epithet "intense," it
is because I conceive it to belong more properly to
a weaker type of man in a state of strain ; but I
never met with a mind which to me seemed to work
constantly with so much vigor, or with feelings so
constantly in a state of fervor : the strong intellect
was, to use his own expression, "*steeped in*" the
strong feeling, but the man was always master of
both : so broad was the basis of his mental constitution, so powerful the original will which guided and
controlled his emotions.—ROBERT P. GRAVES (" Recollections of Wordsworth ").

In intercourse with him it was my delight to witness abundant proofs that the wide and deep benevo-
lence expressed in his poetry was no mere theoretic *Practical benevolence.*
philanthropy, but an active principle.   It showed it-
self toward dependants and neighbors as well as in
the sacred circle of his home, and I remember touching instances, when I have joined him in a walk, of
his putting aside all interest in conversation or ulte-
rior object, if we met with any human being . . .
in trouble or distress, and making with persistency
any needful effort to bring relief or comfort.   And
as with benevolence, so with affection.—ROBERT P.
GRAVES (" Recollections of Wordsworth ").[1]

---

[1] Mr. Graves became the resident clergyman of the parish of
Windermere in 1835, and held that position for nearly thirty years.
His reminiscences of Wordsworth are contained in a lecture deliv-
ered in Dublin in 1868, and published in 1869.

A sister's praise.

In his volume upon Wordsworth, in the " English Men of Letters " series, Mr. F. W. H. Myers[1] quotes as follows from a letter written by Dorothy Wordsworth, in 1792. In the course of a comparison of her brothers, she says :—" Christopher is steady and sincere in his attachments, William has both these virtues in an eminent degree, and a sort of violence of affection, if I may so term it, which demonstrates itself every moment of the day, when the objects of his affection are present with him, in a thousand almost imperceptible attentions to their wishes, in a sort of restless watchfulness which I know not how to describe, a tenderness that never sleeps, and at the same time such a delicacy of manner as I have observed in few men."

Treatment of Hartley Coleridge.

In no aspect did Wordsworth appear to more advantage than in his conduct to poor Hartley Coleridge, who lived in his neighborhood. The weakness, —the special vice,[2]— of that poor, gentle, hopeless being is universally known by the publication of his life ; and I am therefore free to say that, as long as there was any chance of good from remonstrance and rebuke, Wordsworth administered both, sternly and faithfully : but, when nothing more than pity and help was possible, Wordsworth treated him as gently as if he had been,—(what indeed he was in our eyes)—a sick child.—HARRIET MARTINEAU (" Autobiography ").

---

[1] Myers (Frederick W. H.). Wordsworth. 12mo. London and New York, 1881. (English Men of Letters. Edited by John Morley.)

[2] Intemperance.

Upon the publication of two volumes of his poems, in 1807, Wordsworth wrote as follows to his friend Lady Beaumont. We lose sight of egotism in this calm assertion of lofty and unselfish aims. There is something grand in the poet's prophetic assurance of ultimate triumph, at a time when all his admirers could have been gathered together in his own parlor. The letter is to be found in Wordsworth's "Life of Wordsworth." *The scope of his ambition.*

"It is impossible that any expectations can be lower than mine concerning the immediate effect of this little work upon what is called the public. I do not here take into consideration the envy and malevolence, and all the bad passions which always stand in the way of a work of any merit from a living poet ; but merely think of the pure, absolute, honest ignorance in which all worldlings of every rank and condition must be enveloped, with respect to the thoughts, feelings, and images, on which the life of my poems depends. . . .

"Trouble not yourself upon their present reception ; of what moment is that compared with what I trust is their destiny ?—to console the afflicted, to add sunshine to daylight, by making the happy happier ; to teach the young and the gracious of every age to see, to think, and feel, and therefore, to become more actively and securely virtuous ; this is their office ; which I trust they will faithfully perform, long after we (that is, all that is mortal of us) are mouldered in our graves. . . . To conclude, my ears are stone-dead to this idle buzz, and my flesh as insensible as iron to these petty stings ; and, after what I have said, I am sure yours will be the same.   I doubt not that you will share with me an invincible confidence that my writings (and among them these little poems) will co-operate with the benign tendencies in human nature and society, wherever found ; and that they will, in their degree, be efficacious in making men wiser, better, and happier."

SAMUEL TAYLOR COLERIDGE.

1772—1834.

INTRODUCTORY NOTE.

" COLERIDGE'S face, when he repeats his
verses, hath its ancient glory; an archangel
a little damaged "—thus, with good-humored pleas-
antry, wrote Lamb to Wordsworth in 1818. Like
most of Lamb's sayings, these words are suggestive,
beyond their author's original intention. It would
be unjust to the kindly humorist to suppose that he
had any thought of satirizing the character of his
honored friend; yet he could scarcely have suggested more aptly the mingled strength and weakness of Coleridge.

It is impossible to decide how far the comparative failure of Coleridge's life was due to the malign
influence of opium, and how far it was the natural
result of his constitution and temperament. Inac-
tivity, procrastination, vacillating purposes, an irresolute will—from whatever sources they may have
sprung—prevented him from doing justice to the
powers with which he was gifted.

Eulogy, testimony to his great qualities of mind
and heart, is not wanting. Many eminent men
have celebrated his virtues: yet, to some readers,
the strongest and most convincing evidence of his
personal worth will be the fact that he inspired last-

ing affection and reverence in one mind of unusual acuteness and sincerity ; that he was the life-long friend of sensitive, clear-sighted Charles Lamb.

A large, perhaps an unduly large space has been devoted to the various accounts and estimates of Coleridge's conversation. Here it seemed safer to err by excess than by deficiency. Many will be glad to examine all the evidence which can be obtained upon this subject ; for Coleridge was the most distinguished talker of his time. In the *New Monthly Magazine* (London), vol. 94, p. 281, there is an anonymous article, entitled " Coleridge the Table-Talker," which contains a clear and comprehensive summary of the best opinions, pro and con, in regard to this matter. It is, unfortunately, too long to be inserted in this volume.

There is no satisfactory biography of Coleridge. Gillman's ill-considered and wholly inadequate work was never finished. The account by Henry Nelson Coleridge, in the biographical supplement to "Biographia Literaria," stops short at the year 1796, and is continued only in the most fragmentary manner by the poet's daughter, Sara Coleridge. Besides these works we have two rambling, immethodical volumes of recollections by Cottle and Allsop ; and this is all. Here is an opportunity for some one to do good work.[1]   In addition to the books al-

---

[1] The recent publication of a volume upon Coleridge, by H. D. Traill, in the English Men of Letters series, demands attention. This work fully justifies the very modest claims of its author, who clearly recognizes the impossibility of producing a comprehensive and adequate biography of Coleridge, under the limitations imposed by the plan of the series.

ready mentioned, the following are worthy of atten-
tion : Talfourd's various editions of letters and
memorials of Lamb ; Mary Cowden Clarke's
"Recollections of Writers ;" De Quincey's "Liter-
ary Reminiscences ;" Carlyle's "Reminiscences ;"
Hazlitt's "My First Acquaintance with Poets ;"
H. N. Coleridge's "Table Talk of S. T. C. ;" W.
Jerdan's "Men I have Known ;" J. C. Young's
"Memoir of C. M. Young ;" and Miss Eliza
Meteyard's "Group of Englishmen."

LEADING EVENTS OF COLERIDGE'S LIFE.

1772.	Born, October 21st, at Ottery St. Mary, Devonshire.
1782.—(Aged 10.)	A scholar at Christ's Hospital school.
1791.—(Aged 19.)	Enters Cambridge University.
1793.—(Aged 21.)	Leaves the University, and enlists as a private in a cavalry regiment, December 3d.
1794.—(Aged 21–22.)	Obtains his discharge from the army, April 1st. Plans a Pantisocrasy with Southey and others, and publishes the "Fall of Robespierre."
1795.—(Aged 23.)	Marries Miss Sarah Fricker.
1796.—(Aged 24.)	Publishes "The Watchman," and his first volume of poems. Preaches occasionally in Unitarian Churches.
1797.—(Aged 25.)	Publishes a volume of poems, the joint production of Lamb, Lloyd, and himself.
1798.—(Aged 26.)	"Lyrical Ballads," the joint work of Wordsworth and himself, containing "The Ancient Mariner," published. Visits the Continent with William and Dorothy Wordsworth.
1799.—(Aged 27.)	Returns to England.
1804.—(Aged 32.)	Visits Malta.

1806.—(Aged 34.) Returns to England.   Resides at Keswick and
          Grasmere.
1812.—(Aged 40.) Publishes " The Friend."
1813.—(Aged 41.) " Remorse" performed at Drury Lane Theatre.
1816.—(Aged 44.) Publishes "Christabel."   Goes to live with
          the Gillmans.
1817.—(Aged 45.) Publishes " Biographia Literaria."
1825.—(Aged 53.) Publishes " Aids to Reflection."
1834.—(Aged 61 years and 9 months.) Dies, July 25th.

SAMUEL TAYLOR COLERIDGE.

FROM October, 1775, to October 1778.[1] . . .
My Father was very fond of me, and I was my
Mother's darling : in consequence whereof I was
very miserable. For Molly, who had nursed my
brother Francis, and was immoderately fond of him,
hated me because my mother gave me now and then
a bit of cake when he had none. . . . So I became fretful and timorous, and a tell-tale ; and the
school-boys drove me from play, and were always
tormenting me. And hence I took no pleasure in
boyish sports, but read incessantly. . . . And I
used to lie by the wall, and mope ; and my spirits
used to come upon me suddenly, and in a flood ;—
and then I was accustomed to run up and down the
churchyard, and act over again all I had been reading on the docks, the nettles and the rank grass.
At six years of age I remember to have read Belisa-
rius, Robinson Crusoe, and Philip Quarles ; and then
I found the Arabian Nights' Entertainments one
tale of which . . . made so deep an impression
on me . . . that I was haunted by spectres,
whenever I was in the dark : and I distinctly recollect the anxious and fearful eagerness with which

Coleridge's own account of his boy-hood.

---

[1] From three to six years of age.

I used to watch the window where the book lay, and when the sun came upon it, I would seize it, carry it by the wall, and bask, and read. . . .

So I became a dreamer, and acquired an indisposition to all bodily activity ; and I was fretful and inordinately passionate ; and as I could not play at anything, and was slothful, I was despised and hated by the boys ; and because I could read and spell, and had, I may truly say, a memory and understanding forced into almost unnatural ripeness, I was flattered and wondered at by all the old women. And so I became very vain, and despised most of the boys that were at all near my own age, and before I was eight years old I was a *character*. Sensibility, imagination, vanity, sloth, and feelings of deep and bitter contempt for almost all who traversed the orbit of my understanding, were even then prominent and manifest.—SAMUEL T. COLERIDGE (Letter quoted in supplement to " Biographia Literaria ").[1]

From October, 1779, to 1781.[2] I had asked my mother one evening to cut my cheese entire, so that I might toast it. This was no easy matter, it being a *crumbly* cheese. My mother however did it. I went into the garden for something or other, and in the meantime my brother Frank minced my cheese, to "disappoint the favorite." I returned, saw the exploit, and in an agony of passion flew

[1] Coleridge (Samuel T.). Biographia Literaria. Edited, with biographical supplement, by H. N. and Sara Coleridge. 2 vols., 12mo. London, 1847.
[2] From seven to nine years of age.

at Frank. He pretended to have been seriously hurt by my blow, flung himself on the ground, and there lay with outstretched limbs. I hung over him mourning and in a great fright ; he leaped up, and with a hoarse laugh gave me a severe blow in the face. I seized a knife, and was running at him, when my mother came in and took me by the arm. I expected a flogging, and, struggling from her, I ran away to a little hill or slope, at the bottom of which the Otter flows, about a mile from Ottery. There I stayed, my rage died away, but my obstinacy vanquished my fears, and taking out a shilling book, which had at the end morning and evening prayers, I very devoutly repeated them—thinking at the same time with a gloomy inward satisfaction —how miserable my mother must be ! . . . It grew dark, and I fell asleep. It was towards the end of October, and it proved a stormy night. I felt the cold in my sleep, and dreamed that I was pulling the blanket over me, and actually pulled over me a dry thorn-bush which lay on the ground near me. . . . I awoke several times, and finding myself wet, and cold, and stiff, closed my eyes again that I might forget it.'—S. T. COLERIDGE (Letter to T. Poole).

Coleridge's own account of his boyhood.

At first I thought him very plain,[2] that is, for about three minutes ; he is pale, thin, has a wide mouth, thick lips, and not very good teeth, longish,

---

[1] The sequel was that he was found, more dead than alive, in the morning, and carried home to his parents.

[2] Coleridge was about twenty-four years old, when Miss Wordsworth wrote this description.

Personal appearance. loose-growing, half-curling, rough, black hair. But, if you hear him speak for five minutes you think no more of them.   His eye is large and full, and not very dark, but grey, such an eye as would receive from a heavy soul the dullest expression ; but it speaks every emotion of his animated mind : it has more of "the poet's eye in a fine frenzy rolling" than I ever witnessed.   He has fine dark eyebrows, and an overhanging forehead.—Dorothy Words-worth (from a letter of 1797).

Coleridge has a grand head, but very ill balanced, and the features of the face are coarse—although, to be sure, nothing can surpass the depth of mean-ing in his eyes, and the unutterable dreamy luxury in his lips.—John G. Lockhart ("Peter's Letters to His Kinsfolk," 1819).[1]

I am able, by female aid, to communicate a pretty close description of Samuel Taylor Coleridge as he was in the year 1796. In stature . . . he was exactly five feet ten inches in height ; with a bloom-ing and healthy complexion ; beautiful and luxu-riant hair, falling in natural curls over his shoulders. . . . He grew fat and corpulent towards Water-loo ; but he was then slender and agile as an antelope.—Thomas De Quincey ("Coleridge and Opium-Eating ").[2]

[1] Lockhart (John Gibson).   Peter's Letters to His Kinsfolk. 3 vols., 8vo.   Edinburgh, 1819.
[2] De Quincey (Thomas).   Narrative and Miscellaneous Papers. 2 vols., 16mo.   Boston, 1853.

His complexion was at that time (1798) clear, and even bright—

> " As are the children of yon azure sheen."

His forehead was broad and high, light as if built of ivory, with large projecting eyebrows, and his eyes rolling beneath them, like a sea with darkened lustre. "A certain tender bloom his face o'er-spread," a purple tinge as we see it in the pale thoughtful complexions of the Spanish portrait-painters, Murillo and Velasquez. His mouth was gross, voluptuous, open, eloquent; his chin good-humored and round; but his nose, the rudder of the face, the index of the will, was small, feeble, nothing—like what he has done. . . . Coleridge, in his person, was rather above the common size, inclining to the corpulent. . . . His hair (now, alas! gray) was then black and glossy as a raven's, and fell in smooth masses over his forehead.— WILLIAM HAZLITT (" My First Acquaintance with Poets ").

Coleridge was as little fitted for action as Lamb, but on a different account. His person was of a good height, but as sluggish and solid as the other's was light and fragile. He had, perhaps, suffered it to grow old before its time, for want of exercise. His hair was white at fifty; and as he generally dressed in black, and had a very tranquil demeanor, his appearance was gentlemanly, and for several years before his death was reverend. Nevertheless, there was something invincibly young in the look of his face. It was round and fresh-colored, with agreeable features, and an open, indolent, good-natured mouth.   This boy-like expression was very becoming in one who dreamed and speculated as he did when he was really a boy, and who passed his life apart from the rest of the world, with a book, and his flowers.   His forehead was prodigious—a great piece of placid marble ; and his fine eyes, in which all the activity of his mind seemed to concentrate, moved under it with a sprightly ease, as if it was pastime to them to carry all that thought.—LEIGH HUNT ("Autobiography").

In his mature age (when I knew him) Coleridge had a full, round face, a fine, broad forehead, rather thick lips, and strange, dreamy eyes, which were often lighted up by eagerness, but wanted concentration, and were adapted apparently for musing or speculation, rather than for precise or rapid judgment.—BRYAN W. PROCTER ("Charles Lamb; a Memoir").

When years had blanched his hair to a silvery white, his tendency to obesity increased, his countenance was tinged with a slight florid flush, and his large, soft, gray eye beamed with an extraordinary mingled expression of tenderness and splendor, for it was like molten fire, with its fitful force abated by the concomitant signs of thoughtfulness and feeling.—WILLIAM JERDAN ("Men I have Known").

There was rarely much change of countenance ; his face, when I knew him, was overladen with flesh, and its expression impaired ; yet to me it was so tender, and gentle, and gracious, and loving, that I could have knelt at the old man's feet almost in adoration.—Samuel C. Hall ("Book of Memories").

I have seen many curiosities ; not the least of them I reckon Coleridge, the Kantian metaphysician and quondam Lake poet. I will tell you all about our interview when we meet. Figure a fat, flabby, incurvated personage, at once short, rotund, and relaxed, with a watery mouth, a snuffy nose, a pair of strange brown, timid, yet earnest-looking eyes, a high tapering brow, and a great bush of gray hair ; and you have some faint idea of Coleridge. He is a kind, good soul, full of religion and affection and poetry and animal magnetism. His cardinal sin is that he wants *will*. He has no resolution. He shrinks from pain or labor in any of its shapes. His very attitude bespeaks this. He never straightens his knee-joints. He stoops with his fat, ill-shapen shoulders, and in walking he does not tread, but shovels and slides. My father would call it ' skluiffing.' He is also always busied to keep by strong and frequent inhalations, the water of his mouth from overflowing, and his eyes have a look of anxious impotence.—Thomas Carlyle (Letter of 1824).[1]

Personal appearance —Lack of will.

The good man, he was now getting old, toward sixty perhaps ; and gave you the idea of a life that had been full of sufferings ; a life heavy-laden, half-vanquished, still swimming painfully in seas of

---

[1] Froude (James Anthony). Thomas Carlyle. A History of the First Forty Years of his Life. 2 vols., 8vo. London and New York, 1882.

Personal appearance. manifold physical and other bewilderment. Brow and head were round, and of massive weight, but the face was flabby and irresolute. The deep eyes, of a light hazel, were as full of sorrow as of inspiration ; confused pain looked mildly from them, as in a kind of mild astonishment. The whole figure and air, good and amiable otherwise, might be called flabby and irresolute ; expressive of weakness under possibility of strength. He hung loosely on his limbs, with knees bent, and stooping attitude ; in walking, he rather shuffled than decisively stept ; and a lady once remarked, he never could fix which side of the garden-walk would suit him best, but continually shifted, in corkscrew fashion, and kept trying both. A heavy-laden, high-aspiring, and surely much-suffering man. — THOMAS CARLYLE ("Life of Sterling ").[1]

The upper part of Coleridge's face was excessively fine. His eyes were large, light gray, prominent, and of liquid brilliancy, which some eyes of fine character may be observed to possess, as though the orb itself retreated to the innermost recesses of the brain. The lower part of his face was somewhat dragged, indicating the presence of habitual pain ; but his forehead was prodigious, and like a smooth slab of alabaster.—MARY COWDEN CLARKE (" Recollections of Writers ").[2]

In a collection of letters of Lamb, Southey, and Coleridge, to Matilda Betham, published in *Fraser's*

---

[1] Carlyle (Thomas). Life of John Sterling. London, 1851.
[2] Clarke (Charles Cowden and Mary Cowden). Recollections of Writers. 12mo. London, 1878.

Magazine, July, 1878, there is a letter written by Southey, in 1808, in which he thus describes Coleridge: "His countenance is the most variable that I have ever seen; sometimes it is kindled with the brightest expression, and sometimes all its light goes out, and is utterly extinguished. Nothing can convey stronger indications of power than his eye, eyebrow, and forehead. Nothing can be more imbecile than all the rest of the face; look at them separately, you would hardly think it possible that they could belong to one head; look at them together, you wonder how they came so, and are puzzled what to expect from a character whose outward and visible signs are so contradictory."[1]

Personal appearance.

Whatever might have been his habits in boyhood, in manhood he was scrupulously clean in his person, and especially took great care of his hands. . . . In his dress also he was as cleanly as the liberal use of snuff would permit, though the clothes-brush was often in requisition to remove the wasted snuff. "Snuff," he would facetiously say, "was the final cause of the nose, though troublesome and expensive in its use."—JAMES GILLMAN ("Life of Coleridge").[2]

Careful of his personal appearance. —Snuff.

At one period of his life, at least, Coleridge smoked. On July 31st, 1795, he wrote as follows: "Dear Cottle, by the thick smoke that precedes the volcanic eruptions of Etna, Vesuvius, and Hecla, I

A smoker.

---

[1] See pp. 93, 94.
[2] Gillman (James). Life of S. T. Coleridge. (Only one volume was published.) Vol. I., 8vo. London, 1838.

A smoker.

feel an impulse to fumigate, at (now) 25 College Street, one pair of stairs room ; yea, with our Oronoko, and if thou wilt send me by the bearer, four pipes, I will write a panegyrical epic poem upon thee, with as many books as there are letters in thy name." This letter was published in Cottle's " Reminiscences." [1] As there is no record of Coleridge's having ever forsworn the kindly plant, it may be assumed, with reasonable probability, that he continued " to fumigate."

Voice—Pronunciation.

His voice was deep and musical, and his words followed each other in an unbroken flow, yet free from monotony.   There was indeed a peculiar charm in his utterance.   His pronunciation was remarkably correct ; in some respects pedantically so.   He gave the full sound of the *l* in *talk*, and *should*, and *would.*—CHARLES R. LESLIE (" Autobiographical Recollections ").[2]

The benignity of his manner befitted the beauty of his disquisitions ; his voice rose from the gentlest pitch of conversation to the height of impassioned eloquence without effort, as his language expanded from some common topic of the day to the loftiest abstractions.—THOMAS N. TALFOURD (" Final Memorials of Charles Lamb ").[3]

---

[1] Cottle (Joseph). Reminiscences of S. T. Coleridge and R. Southey.   Crown 8vo.   London, 1847.
[2] Leslie (Charles Robert).   Autobiographical Recollections. Edited by Tom Taylor.   2 vols., 12mo.   London, 1860.
[3] Talfourd (Thomas Noon).   Final Memorials of Charles Lamb. 2 vols., 12mo.   London, 1848.

His voice, naturally soft and good, had contracted itself into a plaintive snuffle and sing-song;[1] he spoke as if preaching,—you would have said, preaching earnestly and also hopelessly the weightiest things. I still recollect his "object" and "subject," terms of continual recurrence in the Kantian province; and how he sung and snuffled them into "om-m-mject," and "sum-m-mject," with a kind of solemn shake or quaver, as he rolled along.— THOMAS CARLYLE ("Life of Sterling").

Voice—Pronunciation.

In some of the smaller pieces, as the conclusion of the "Kubla Khan," for example, not only the lines by themselves are musical, but the whole passage sounds all at once as an outburst or crash of harps in the still air of autumn. The verses seem as if *played* to the ear upon some unseen instrument. And the poet's manner of reciting verse is similar. It is not rhetorical, but musical; so very near recitative, that for any one else to attempt it would be ridiculous; and yet it is perfectly miraculous with what exquisite searching he elicits and makes sensible every particle of the meaning, not leaving a a shadow of a shade of the feeling, the mood, the degree, untouched. . . . A chapter of Isaiah from his mouth involves the listener in an act of exalted devotion. We have mentioned this, to show how the whole man is made up of music; and yet Mr. Coleridge has no *ear* for music, as it is technically called. Master as he is of the intellectual recitative, he could not *sing* an air to save his life. But his delight in music is intense and unweari-

Reading aloud and recitation.

---

[1] This was during Coleridge's last years, at Highgate.

able, and he can detect good from bad with unerring discrimination.—ANON. (*Quarterly Review*, August, 1834).

1810.—"Coleridge kept me on the stretch of attention and admiration from half-past three till twelve o'clock. On politics, metaphysics, and poetry, more especially on the Regency, Kant, and Shakespeare, he was astonishingly eloquent. But I cannot help remarking that although he practises all sorts of delightful tricks, and shows admirable skill in riding his hobby, yet he may be easily unsaddled. I was surprised to find how one may obtain from him concessions which lead to gross inconsistencies. Though an incomparable declaimer and speech-maker, he has neither the readiness nor the acuteness required by a colloquial disputant; so that, with a sense of inferiority which makes me feel humble in his presence, I do not feel in the least afraid of him."—*Extract from a Letter.*

As a disputant.

This I wrote when I knew little of him; I used afterwards to compare him as a disputant to a serpent—easy to kill, if you assume the offensive, but if you let him attack, his bite is mortal. Some years after this, when I saw Madame de Staël in London, I asked her what she thought of him: she replied, "He is very great in monologue, but he has no idea of dialogue."—HENRY CRABB ROBINSON ("Diary").

In a conversation with Lord Cranbrook in 1843, Wilson said: "Coleridge's weakness was an extreme love of sympathy. . . . It was this weakness, and not pride or vanity, which led him to delight in talking; and when he had an attentive hearer he would enlarge on every subject with enthusiasm; but if there were the slightest apathy or carelessness displayed, it was curious to see how his voice died away at once. And yet I am convinced that this was not love of display, but of having other minds in communion, as it were, with his own; and when he felt that they were so, he would impart to every object of conversation a hue and tinge of beauty which could not be surpassed." Lord Cranbrook reports this conversation in an article published in the "National Review," April, 1884.

"Christopher North" upon Coleridge's conversation.

I observed that, as a rule, Wordsworth allowed Coleridge to have all the talk to himself; but once or twice Coleridge would succeed in entangling Wordsworth in a discussion on some abstruse metaphysical question; when I would sit by, reverently attending, and trying hard to look intelligent, though I did not feel so; for at such times a leaden stupor weighed down my faculties. I seemed as if I had been transported by two malignant genii into an atmosphere too rarefied for me to live in. I was soaring, as it were, 'twixt heaven and the lower parts of the earth. . . . When, however, these potent spirits descended to a lower level, and deigned to treat of history or politics, theology or belles lettres, I breathed again; and, imbibing fresh ideas from them, felt invigorated.

Coleridge and Wordsworth in conversation.

I must say I never saw any manifestation of small jealousy between Coleridge and Wordsworth; which, considering the vanity possessed by each, I

Coleridge and Wordsworth in conversation.

thought uncommonly to the credit of both. I am sure they entertained a thorough respect for each other's intellectual endowments.—JULIAN C. YOUNG (" Memoir of C. M. Young ").

Preparatory to talk.

" What do you think of Dr. Channing, Mr. Coleridge ? " said a brisk young gentleman to the mighty discourser, as he sat next him at a small tea-party. " Before entering upon that question, sir," said Coleridge, opening upon his inquirer those " noticeable gray eyes," with a vague and placid stare, and settling himself in his seat for the night, "I must put you in possession of my views, *in extenso*, on the origin, progress, present condition, future likelihoods, and absolute essence of the Unitarian controversy, and especially the conclusions I have, upon the whole, come to on the great question of what may be termed the philosophy of religious difference."—DR. JOHN BROWN (" Horæ Subsecivæ ").[1]

A contrast.

If Wordsworth condescended to converse with me, he spoke to me as if I were his equal in mind, and made me pleased and proud in consequence. If Coleridge held me by the button, for lack of fitter audience, he had a talent for making me feel *his* wisdom and my own stupidity ; so that I was miserable and humiliated by the sense of it.—JULIAN C. YOUNG (" Memoir of C. M. Young ").

Eminent literary men have often been remarkable for the fertility of their conversation, and their powers in this respect have not unfrequently been

[1] Brown (John, M.D.). Horæ Subsecivæ. 2 vols., 12 mo. Edinburgh, 1858–61. (Reprinted in Boston, as " Spare Hours," 1866.)

used without due restraint and discrimination. Coleridge was no exception to this rule ; he would con-
tinue to talk on in an unbroken flow, and connect *Discursive conversation.*
his arguments and observations so adroitly that un-
til you had left him you could not detect their fallacy. Mr. Harness called on him one day with Milman, on their return from paying a visit to Joanna
Baillie. The poet seemed unusually inspired, and
rambled on, raising his hands and his head in the
manner which Charles Matthews so cleverly carica-
tured ; and asserting, among other strange theories,
that Shakespeare was a man of too pure a mind to
be able to depict a really worthless character. "All
his villains," he said, "were bad upon good principles ; even Caliban had something good in him."
Coleridge, in his old age, became a characteristic
feature in Highgate. He was the terror and amusement of all the little children who bowled their
hoops along the poplar avenue. Notwithstanding
his fondness for them—he called them "Kingdom-
of-Heavenites"—his Cyclopean figure and learned
language caused them indescribable alarm. Sometimes he would lay his hand on the shoulders of one
of them, and walk along discoursing metaphysics to
the trembling captive, while the rest fled for refuge
and peeped out with laughing faces from behind
the trees. "I never," he exclaimed one day to the
baker's boy—"I never knew a man good because he
was religious, but I have known one religious because he was good."—A. G. L'ESTRANGE ("Life of
W. Harness").[1]

[1] L'Estrange (Rev. A. G.). The Literary Life of the Rev. William Harness. London, 1870.

In the fog. When he confined himself to his "judgments, analytic and synthetic," I had a glimmering conception of his meaning ; but when he gave tongue on "a priori knowledge and a posteriori knowledge," and spake of "modality," and of the "paralogism of pure reason," my feeble brain reeled, and I gasped for escape from the imaginary and chimerical to the material and practical.—JULIAN C. YOUNG ("Memoir of C. M. Young ").

A suspicion. *July 16th*, 1825.—I think I never heard Coleridge so very eloquent as to-day, and yet it was painful to find myself unable to recall any part of what had so delighted me, *i.e.* anything which seemed worthy to be noted down. So that I could not but suspect some illusion arising out of the impressive tone and the mystical language of the orator. He talked on for several hours without intermission.—HENRY CRABB ROBINSON ("Diary ").

Dean Milman's opinion about his conversation. The Dean[1] used often to see and hear S. T. Coleridge, but his wonderful talk was far too unvaried from day to day ; also, there were some absolute deficiencies in it, such as the total absence of wit ; still it was very remarkable. "But," he added, "I used to be wicked enough to divide it into three parts : one-third was admirable, beautiful in language and exalted in thought ; another third was sheer absolute nonsense ; and of the remaining third, I knew not whether it were sense or nonsense."—CAROLINE FOX ("Memories of Old Friends ").

---

[1] Milman.

"Wordsworth and myself," said Rogers, "had walked to Highgate to call on Coleridge, when he was living at Gillman's. We sat with him two hours, he talking the whole time without intermission. When we left the house, we walked for some time without speaking. 'What a wonderful man he is!' exclaimed Wordsworth. 'Wonderful, indeed,' said I. 'What depth of thought, what richness of expression!' continued Wordsworth. 'There's nothing like him that ever I heard,' rejoined I,—another pause. 'Pray,' inquired Wordsworth, 'did you precisely understand what he said about the Kantian philosophy?' *R.* 'Not precisely.' *W.* 'Or about the plurality of worlds?' *R.* 'I can't say I did. Indeed, if the truth must out, I did not understand a syllable from one end of his monologue to the other.' *W.* 'No more did I.'"—ANON. (*Edinburgh Review*, July, 1856).

It was only when his "philosophy" (with which he abounded on all occasions) betrayed him into abstruse paradoxes and metaphysical refinements that his rich colloquialism took the shape of dissertation, and was delivered with a fervid eloquence, most powerful in lecture, but subversive of conversation ; and these bursts were so admirable that there was seldom any disposition to interrupt him. When it did occur that they went wandering into all cognate matters and consonant sentiments, it was the easiest thing possible, by throwing in some absurd remark or irrelevant question, to divert the current into quite a different channel, and enjoy and re-enjoy the versatility and depths of an inex-

Much puzzled.

Not always oratorical— Easily turned aside.

haustible mind.—WILLIAM JERDAN ("Men I have Known ").

His benignity of manner placed his auditors entirely at their ease ; and inclined them to listen delighted to the sweet, low tone in which he began to discourse on some high theme. Whether he had won for his greedy listener only some raw lad, or charmed a circle of beauty, rank, and wit, who hung breathless on his words, he talked with equal eloquence ; for his subject, not his audience, inspired him. At first his tones were conversational ; he seemed to dally with the shallows of the subject and with fantastic images which bordered it ; but gradually the thought grew deeper, and the voice deepened with the thought ; the stream gathering strength, seemed to bear along with it all things which opposed its progress, and blended them with its current ; and stretching away into regions tinted with ethereal colors, was lost at airy distance in the horizon of fancy. His hearers were unable to grasp his theories, which were indeed too vast to be exhibited in the longest conversation ; but they perceived noble images, generous suggestions, affecting pictures of virtue, which enriched their minds and nurtured their best affections. . . . He usually met opposition by conceding the point to the objector, and then went on with his high argument as if it had never been raised : thus satisfying his antagonist, himself, and all who heard him ; none

Various accounts of his conversation.[1]

---

[1] The space which has been given to accounts of Coleridge's conversation may seem disproportionately large: Readers who find the subject uninteresting are counselled to turn to p. 91.

of whom desired to hear his discourse frittered into points, or displaced by the near encounter even of the most brilliant wits.—THOMAS N. TALFOURD (" Letters of Charles Lamb ").[1]

Coleridge is the only person who can talk to all sorts of people, on all sorts of subjects, without caring a farthing for their understanding one word he says—and *he* talks only for admiration and to be listened to, and accordingly the least interruption puts him out. I firmly believe he would make just the same impression on half his audiences, if he purposely repeated absolute nonsense with the same voice and manner and inexhaustible flow of undulating speech !—WILLIAM HAZLITT (" Conversation of Authors ").[2]

During the whole of his residence in Bristol, there was, in the strict sense, little of the true, interchangeable conversation in Mr. C. On almost every subject on which he essayed to speak, he made an impassioned harangue of a quarter, or half an hour.—JOSEPH COTTLE (" Reminiscences of Coleridge and Southey ").

After dinner he got up, and began pacing to and fro, with his hands behind his back, talking and walking, as Lamb laughingly hinted, as if qualifying for an itinerant preacher; now fetching a simile from Loddige's garden, at Hackney; and

---

[1] Talfourd (Thomas N.). Letters of Charles Lamb, with a Sketch of his Life. 2 vols., 12mo. London, 1837.

[2] Hazlitt (William). The Plain Speaker; Opinions on Books, Men, and Things. 2 vols., 8vo. London, 1826.

Conversa-
tion.

then driving off for an illustration to the sugar-making in Jamaica. With his fine, flowing voice, it was glorious music, of the "never-ending, still-beginning" kind : and you did not wish it to end. It was rare flying, as in the Nassau Balloon ; you knew not whither, nor did you care. Like his own bright-eyed Marinere, he had a spell in his voice that would not let you go. To describe my own feeling afterward, I had been carried, spiralling, up to heaven by a whirlwind intertwisted with sun-beams, giddy and dazzled, but not displeased, and had then been rained down again with a shower of mundane stocks and stones that battered out of me all recollection of what I had heard, and what I had seen !—THOMAS HOOD ("Literary Reminiscences").[1]

One day, when dining with some lawyers, he had been more than usually eloquent and full of talk. His perpetual interruptions were resented by one of the guests, who said to his neighbor, "I'll stop this fellow ;" and thereupon addressed the master of the house with "G——, I've not forgotten my promise to give you the extract from 'The Pandects.' It was the ninth chapter that you were alluding to. It be-gins : 'Ac veteres quidam philosophi.'" "Pardon me, sir," interposed Coleridge, "there I think you are in error. The ninth chapter begins in this way, 'Incident sæpe causæ, etc.'" It was in vain to re-fer to anything on the supposition that the poet was ignorant, for he really had some acquaintance with every subject.—BRYAN W. PROCTER ("Recollections of Men of Letters").

---

[1] Hood (Thomas). Works. 4 vols., 12mo. New York, 1852-53.

Coleridge was prodigal of his words, which in fact he could with difficulty suppress ; but he seldom talked of himself or of his affairs.—B. W. PROCTER *Conversa-tion.* ("Recollections of Men of Letters").

In illustration of his unfailing talk, I will give an account of one of his days, when I was present. He had come from Highgate to London, for the sole purpose of consulting a friend about his son Hartley ("our dear Hartley"), towards whom he expressed, and I have no doubt felt, much anxiety. He arrived about one or two o'clock, in the midst of a conversation, which immediately began to interest him. He struck into the middle of the talk very soon, and "held the ear of the house" until dinner made its appearance about four o'clock. He then talked all through dinner, all the afternoon, all the evening, with scarcely a single interruption. He expatiated on this subject and on that ; he drew fine distinctions ; he made subtle criticisms. He descended to anecdotes, historical, logical, rhetorical ; he dealt with law, medicine, and divinity, until, at last, five minutes before eight o'clock, the servant came in and announced that the Highgate stage was at the corner of the street, and was waiting to convey Mr. Coleridge home. Coleridge immediately started up oblivious of all time, and said in a hurried voice, "My dear Z——, I will come to you some other day, and talk to you about our dear Hartley." He had quite forgotten his son and everybody else, in the delight of having such an enraptured audience.—B. W. PROCTER ("Recollections of Men of Letters").

III.—6

Coleridge was not without what talkers call wit, and there were touches of prickly sarcasm in him, contemptuous enough of the world and its idols and popular dignitaries; he had traits even of poetic humor: but in general he seemed deficient in laughter ; or indeed in sympathy for concrete human beings either on the sunny or the stormy side.   One right peal of concrete laughter at some convicted flesh-and-blood absurdity, one burst of noble indignation at some injustice or depravity, rubbing elbows with us on this solid Earth, how strange would it have been in that Kantean haze-world, and how infinitely cheering amid its vacant air-castles and dim-melting ghosts and shadows ! None such ever came.   His life had been an ab-stract thinking and dreaming, idealistic, passed amid the ghosts of defunct bodies and of unborn ones.   The moaning sing-song of that theosophico-metaphysical monotony left on you, at last, a very dreary feeling.—THOMAS CARLYLE (" Life of Ster-ling ").

I have heard Coleridge talk, with eager musical energy, two stricken hours, his face radiant and moist, and communicate no meaning whatsoever to any individual of his hearers,—certain of whom, I for one, still kept eagerly listening in hope ; the most had long before given up, and formed (if the room were large enough) secondary humming groups of their own.   He began anywhere : you put some question to him ; made some suggestive observation ; instead of answering this, or decidedly setting out towards answer of it, he would accumulate formidable apparatus, logical swim-bladders, transcendental life-preservers, and other precaution- ary and vehiculatory gear, for setting out ; perhaps did at last get under way,—but was swiftly solicited, turned aside by the glance of some radiant new game on this hand or that, into new courses ; and ever into new ; and before long into all the Uni- verse, where it was uncertain what game you would catch, or whether any.

His talk, alas, was distinguished, like himself, by irresolution : it disliked to be troubled with con- ditions, abstinences, definite fulfillments ;—loved to wander at its own sweet will, and make its auditor and his claims and humble wishes a mere passive bucket for itself! He had knowledge about many things and topics, much curious reading ; but gen- erally all topics led him, after a pass or two, into the high seas of theosophic philosophy, the hazy infinitude of Kantean transcendentalism, with its " sum-m-mjects " and " om-m-mjects." Sad enough ; for with such indolent impatience of the claims and ignorances of others, he had not the least talent for explaining this or any thing unknown to them ; and you swam and fluttered in the mistiest wide unin- telligible deluge of things, for the most part in a rather profitless uncomfortable manner.

Glorious islets, too, I have seen rise out of the haze ; but they were few, and soon swallowed in the general element again. Balmy, sunny islets, islets of the blest and the intelligible ;—on which occa- sions those secondary humming groups would all cease humming, and hang breathless upon the elo- quent words ; till once your islet got wrapt in the

Conversa- tion.

*Conversa-
tion.*

mist again, and they could recommence humming. Eloquent artistically expressive words you always had ; piercing radiances of a most subtle insight came at intervals ; tones of noble pious sympathy, recognizable as pious, though strangely colored, were never wanting long : but in general you could not call this aimless, cloud-capt, cloud-based, lawlessly meandering human discourse of reason by the name of "excellent talk," but only of "surprising" ; and were reminded bitterly of Hazlitt's account of it : " Excellent talker, very,—if you let him start from no premises and come to no conclusion."— THOMAS CARLYLE ("Life of Sterling ").

Nothing could be more copious than his talk ; and furthermore it was always virtually or literally, of the nature of a monologue ; suffering no interruption, however reverent ; hastily putting aside all foreign additions, annotations, or most ingenious devices for elucidation, as well-meant superfluities which would never do.   Besides, it was talk not flowing anywhither like a river, but spreading everywhither in inextricable currents and regurgitations like a lake or sea ; terribly deficient in definite goal or aim, nay often in logical intelligibility ; *what* you were to believe or do, on any earthly or heavenly thing, obstinately refusing to appear from it.   So that, most times, you felt logically lost ; swamped near to drowning in this tide of ingenious vocables, spreading out boundless as if to submerge the world.—THOMAS CARLYLE (" Life of Sterling ").

My impressions of the man and of the place are conveyed faithfully enough in the " Life of Sterling ;" that first interview in particular, of which I had expected very little, was idle and unsatisfactory, and yielded me nothing. Coleridge, a puffy, anxious, obstructed-looking, fattish old man, hobbled about with us, talking with a kind of solemn emphasis on matters which were of no interest (and even *reading* pieces in proof of his opinions thereon). I had him to myself once or twice, in various parts of the garden walks, and tried hard to get something about *Kant* and Co. from him, about "reason" versus "understanding" and the like, but in vain. Nothing came from him that was of use to me that day, or in fact any day. The sight and sound of a sage who was so venerated by those about me, and whom I too would willingly have venerated, but could not—this was all. Several times afterward, Montague, on Coleridge's "Thursday evenings," carried Irving and me out, and returned blessing Heaven (I not) for what he had received. Irving and I walked out more than once on mornings too, and found the Dodona oracle humanly ready to act, but never to me, or Irving either I suspect, explanatory of the question put. Good Irving strove always to think that he was getting priceless wisdom out of this great man, but must have had his misgivings. Except by the Montague-Irving channel, I at no time communicated with Coleridge. I had never on my own strength had much esteem for him, and found slowly in spite of myself that I was getting to have less and less. Early in 1825 was my last sight of him ; a print of Porson brought some trifling utterance : "Sensuality such a *dissolution* of the features of a man's face ;" and I remember

Conversation.

nothing more.—THOMAS CARLYLE (" Reminiscences ").

Conversation.

In a letter written in 1824, published by Mr. Froude, Carlyle says: "The conversation of the man is much as I anticipated—a forest of thoughts, some true, many false, more *part* dubious, all of them ingenious in some degree, often in a high degree. But there is no method in his talk: he wanders like a man sailing among many currents, whithersoever his lazy mind directs him; and, what is more unpleasant, he preaches, or rather soliloquizes. He cannot speak, he can only *tal-k* (so he names it). Hence I found him unprofitable, even tedious."

Coleridge led me to a drawing-room, rang the bell for refreshments, and omitted no point of a courteous reception. He told me that there would be a very large dinner party on that day, which, perhaps, might be disagreeable to a perfect stranger; but, if not, he could assure me of a most hospitable welcome from the family. I was too anxious to see him under all aspects to think of declining the invitation. And these little points of business being settled—Coleridge, like some great river, the Orellana, or the St. Lawrence, which had been checked and fretted by rocks or thwarting islands, and suddenly recovers its volume of waters, and its mighty music, swept at once, as if returning to his natural business, into a continuous strain of eloquent dissertation, certainly the most novel, the most finely illustrated, and traversing the most spacious fields of thought, by transitions the most just and logical, that it was possible to conceive.

What I mean by saying that his transitions were "just," is by way of contradistinction to that mode of conversation which courts variety by means of *verbal* connections. Coleridge, to many people, and often I have heard the complaint, seemed to wander; and he seemed then to wander the most, when in fact his resistance to the wandering instinct was greatest,—viz., when the compass, and huge circuit, by which his illustrations moved, travelled farthest into remote regions, before they began to revolve. Long before this coming-round commenced, most people had lost him, and naturally enough supposed that he had lost himself. They continued to admire the separate beauty of the thoughts, but did not see their relations to the dominant theme. Had the conversation been thrown upon paper, it might have been easy to trace the continuity of the links. . . . I can assert, upon my long and intimate knowledge of Coleridge's mind, that logic, the most severe, was as inalienable from his modes of thinking, as grammar from his language.—THOMAS DE QUINCEY ("Literary Reminiscences").

Conversation.

He (Wordsworth) said that the liveliest and truest image he could give of Coleridge's talk was, "that of a majestic river, the sound or sight of whose course you caught at intervals, which was sometimes concealed by forests, sometimes lost in sand, then came flashing out broad and distinct, then again took a turn which your eye could not follow, yet you knew and felt that it was the same river: so," he said, "there was always a train, a stream, in Coleridge's discourse, always a connection between its parts in his own mind, though one not always perceptible to the minds of others."—Mrs. Davy (Quoted in Wordsworth's " Life of Wordsworth ").

His ordinary manner was plain and direct enough ; and even when, as sometimes happened, he seemed to ramble from the road, and to lose himself in a wilderness of digressions, the truth was, that at that very time he was working out his foreknown conclusion through an almost miraculous logic, the difficulty of which consisted precisely in the very fact of its minuteness and universality.   He took so large a scope, that, if he was interrupted before he got to the end, he appeared to have been talking without an object ; although, perhaps, a few steps more would have brought you to a point, a retrospect from which would show you the pertinence of all he had been saying.   I have heard persons complain that they could get no answer to a question from Coleridge.   The truth is, he answered, or meant to answer, so fully, that the querist should have no second question to ask.   In nine cases out of ten the saw he question was short or misdirected ; and knew that a mere yes or no answer could not embrace the truth—that is, the whole truth, and might, very probably, by implication, convey error.   Hence that exhaustive, cyclical mode of discoursing in which he frequently indulged. . . .

Mr. Coleridge's conversation at all times required attention, because what he said was so individual and unexpected.   But when he was dealing deeply with a question, the demand upon the intellect of the hearer was very great ; not so much for any hardness of language, for his diction was always simple and easy ; nor for the abstruseness of the thoughts, for they generally explained, or appeared to explain, themselves ; but pre-eminently on account of the seeming remoteness of his associations, and the exceeding subtlety of his transitional links. —HENRY N. COLERIDGE ("Table-Talk of S. T. C.").[1]

Conversation.

The manner of Coleridge was rather *emphatic* than *dogmatic*, and thus he was generally and satisfactorily listened to. There was neither the *bow-wow* nor the growl which seemed usually to characterize Johnson's method of speaking ; and his periods were more lengthened and continuous. . . . Coleridge was a *mannerist.* It was always the same tone—in the same style of expression—not quick and bounding enough to diffuse instant and general vivacity. . . . There was always *this* characteristic feature in his multifarious conversation—it was delicate, reverend, and courteous. —THOMAS F. DIBDIN (" Reminiscences of a Literary Life ").[2]

His eloquence threw a new and beautiful light on most subjects, and when he was beyond my comprehension, the melody of his voice, and the impressiveness of his manner held me a willing lis-

---

[1] Coleridge (Henry N., *Eaitor*). Specimens of the Table-Talk of S. T. Coleridge. 2 vols., 16mo. New York, 1835.
[2] Dibdin (Thomas Frognall). Reminiscences of a Literary Life. 8vo. London, 1836.

tener, and I was flattered at being supposed capable of understanding him. Indeed, men far advanced beyond myself in education might have felt as children in his presence.—CHARLES R. LESLIE ("Autobiographical Recollections ").

Those who remember him in his more vigorous days can bear witness to the peculiarity and transcendant power of his conversational eloquence. It was unlike anything that could be heard elsewhere; the kind was different, the degree was different, the manner was different. The boundless range of scientific knowledge, the brilliancy and exquisite nicety of illustration, the deep and ready reasoning, the strangeness and immensity of bookish lore—were not all ; the dramatic story, the joke, the pun, the festivity, must be added—and with these the clerical-looking dress, the thick waving silver hair, the youthful colored cheek, the indefinable mouth and lips, the quick yet steady and penetrating greenish gray eye, the slow and continuous enunciation, and the everlasting music of his tones,—all went to make up the image and to constitute the living presence of the man. He is now no longer young. . . . His natural force is indeed abated; but his eye is not dim, neither is his mind yet enfeebled. . . . Mr. Coleridge's conversation, it is true, has not now all the brilliant versatility of his former years; yet we know not whether the contrast between his bodily weakness and his mental power does not leave a deeper and a more solemnly affecting impression, than his most brilliant displays in youth could ever have done. To see the pain-stricken countenance relax, and the contracted frame dilate under the kindling of intellectual fire alone—to watch the infirmities of the flesh shrinking out of sight, or glorified and transfigured in the brightness of the awakening spirit—is an awful object of contemplation ; and in no other person did we ever witness such a distinction,—nay, alienation of mind from body,— such a mastery of the purely intellectual over the purely corporeal, as in the instance of this remarkable man. Even now his conversation is characterized by all the essentials of its former excellence ; there is the same individuality, the same unexpectedness, the same universal grasp ; nothing is too high, nothing too low for it : it glances from earth to heaven, from heaven to earth, with a speed and a splendor, an ease and a power, which almost seem inspired.—ANON. (*Quarterly Review*, 1834).

Conversation.

Dec. 5th, 1811. Accompanied Mrs. Rutt to Coleridge's lecture. In this he surpassed himself in the art of talking in a very interesting way, without speaking at all on the subject announced. According to advertisement, he was to lecture on "Romeo and Juliet" and Shakespeare's female characters. Instead of this he began with a defence of school-flogging, in preference at least to Lancaster's mode of punishing, without pretending to find the least connection between that topic and poetry. Afterwards he remarked on the character of the age of Elizabeth and James I. as compared with that of Charles I.; distinguished not very clearly between wit and fancy ; referred to the different languages of Europe ; attacked the fashionable notion concern-

As a lecturer.

As a lecturer.

ing poetic diction : ridiculed the tautology of Johnson's line, "If observation with extensive view," etc. ; and warmly defended Shakespeare against the charge of impurity. While Coleridge was commenting on Lancaster's mode of punishing boys, Lamb whispered, "It is a pity he did not leave this till he got to 'Henry VI.,' for then he might say he could not help taking part against the Lancastrians." Afterwards, when Coleridge was running from topic to topic, Lamb said, "This is not much amiss. He promised a lecture on the Nurse in 'Romeo and Juliet,' and in its place he has given us one in the *manner* of the Nurse."

Dec. 13th, 1811.—(To Mrs. Clarkson.) He confined himself to "Romeo and Juliet" for a time, treated of the inferior characters, and delivered a most eloquent discourse on love, with a promise to point out how Shakespeare has shown the same truths in the persons of the lovers. Yesterday we were to have a continuation of the theme. Alas ! Coleridge began with a parallel between religion and love, which, though one of his favorite themes, he did not manage successfully. Romeo and Juliet were forgotten. And in the next lecture we are really to hear something of these lovers. Now this will be the fourth time that his hearers have been invited expressly to hear of this play. There are to be only fifteen lectures altogether (half have been delivered), and the course is to include Shakespeare and Milton, the modern poets, etc. ! ! ! Instead of a lecture on a definite subject, we have an immethodical rhapsody, very delightful to you and me, and only offensive from the certainty that it may and ought to offend those who come with other expectations. Yet, with all this, I cannot but be charmed with these *splendida vitia*, and my chief displeasure is occasioned by my being forced to hear the strictures of persons infinitely below Coleridge, without any power of refuting or contradicting them.—HENRY CRABB ROBINSON ("Diary").

As a lecturer.

I had received directions for finding out the house where Coleridge was visiting; and in riding down a main street of Bridgewater, I noticed a gateway corresponding to the description given me. Under this was standing, and gazing about him, a man whom I shall describe. In height he might seem to be about five feet eight (he was in reality about an inch and a half taller, but his figure was of an order which drowns the height); his person was broad and full, and tended even to corpulence; his complexion was fair, though not what painters technically style fair, because it was associated with black hair; his eyes were large and soft in their expression, and it was from the peculiar appearance of haze or dreaminess, which mixed with their light, that I recognized my object. This was Coleridge. I examined him steadfastly for a minute or more, and it struck me that he saw neither myself nor any other object in the street. He was in a deep reverie, for I had dismounted, made two or three trifling arrangements at an inn door, and advanced close to him, before he had apparently become conscious of my presence. The sound of my voice, announcing my own name, first awoke him; he started, and, for a moment, seemed at a loss to understand my pur-

De Quincey's first interview with Coleridge.

pose or his own situation ; for he repeated rapidly a number of words which had no relation to either of us.　There was no *mauvaise honte* in his manner, but simple perplexity, and an apparent difficulty in recovering his position among daylight realities. This little scene over, he received me with a kindness of manner so marked that it might be called gracious.—THOMAS DE QUINCEY ("Literary Reminiscences ").

De Quincey's first interview with Coleridge.

I had scarcely entered the room, and was trying to improve a bad sketch I had made the day before, when an old gentleman entered, with a large quarto volume beneath his arm.　.　.　.　As he entered, I rose and bowed.　Whether he was conscious of my well-intentioned civility I cannot say, but at all events he did not return my salutation.　He appeared preoccupied with his own cogitations.　I began to conjecture what manner of man he was. His general appearance would have led me to suppose him a dissenting minister.　His hair was long, white, and neglected ; his complexion was florid, his features were square, his eyes watery and hazy, his brow broad and massive, his build uncouth, his deportment grave and abstracted.　He wore a white starchless neckcloth tied in a limp bow, and was dressed in a shabby suit of dusky black.　His breeches were unbuttoned at the knee, his sturdy limbs were encased in stockings of lavender-colored worsted, his feet were thrust into well-worn slippers much trodden down at heel.　In this ungainly attire he paced up and down, and down and up, and round and round a saloon sixty feet square, with

An unexpected meeting.

head bent forward, and shoulders stooping, absently musing, and muttering to himself, and occasionally clutching to his side his ponderous tome, as if he feared it might be taken from him.   I confess my young spirit chafed under the wearing quarter-deck monotony of his promenade, and, stung by the cool manner in which he ignored my presence, I was about to leave him in undisputed possession of the field, when I was diverted from my purpose by the entrance of another gentleman, whose kindly smile, and courteous recognition of my bow, encouraged me to keep my ground, and promised me some compensation for the slight put upon me by his precursor.

Coleridge and Words- worth on a jaunt.

He was dressed in a brown holland blouse ; he held in his left hand an alpenstock (on the top of which he had placed the broad-brimmed "wide-awake" he had just taken off), and in his right hand a sprig of apple blossom overgrown with lichen. His cheeks were glowing with the effects of recent exercise.   So noiseless had been his entry, that the peripatetic philosopher, whose back was turned to him at first, was unaware of his presence.   But no sooner did he discover it than he shuffled up to him, grasped him by both hands, and backed him bodily into a neighboring arm-chair.   Having secured him there, he "made assurance doubly sure," by hanging over him, so as to bar his escape, while he delivered his testimony on the fallacy of certain of Bishop Berkeley's propositions, in detecting which, he said, he had opened up a rich vein of original reflection. Not content with cursory criticism, he plunged profoundly into a metaphysical lecture, which, but for

*Coleridge
and Words-
worth on a
jaunt.*

the opportune intrusion of our fair hostess and her young lady friend, might have lasted until dinner time. It was then, for the first time, I learned who the party consisted of ; and I was introduced to Samuel Taylor Coleridge, William Wordsworth, and his daughter Dora (1828).—JULIAN C. YOUNG ("Memoir of C. M. Young ").

*An infirm
will.*

Southey and Wordsworth, both well qualified to form a correct judgment of the case, thus speak of Coleridge's want of moral firmness. Southey writes to John Rickman, in 1804, " He is worse in body than you seem to believe ; but the main cause lies in his own management of himself, or, rather, want of management. His mind is in a perfect St. Vitus's dance—eternal activity without action. At times he feels mortified that he should have done so little ; but this feeling never produces any exertion. ' I will begin to-morrow,' he says, and thus he has been all his life-long letting to-day slip." Wordsworth is quoted, in Rev. C. Wordsworth's Memoir of him, as follows :—" Of all men whom I have ever known, Coleridge had the most of passive courage in bodily trial, but no one was so easily cowed when moral firmness was required in miscellaneous conversation, or in the daily intercourse of social life."

*Indecision
and lack of
energy.*

Coleridge had a weighty head, dreaming gray eyes, full, sensual lips, and a look and manner which were entirely wanting in firmness and decision. His motions also appeared weak and undecided, and his voice had nothing of the sharpness or ring of a resolute man. When he spoke his words were thick and slow, and when he read poetry his utterance was altogether a chant.— BYRAN W. PROCTER (" Recollections of Men of Letters ").

Indecision and lack of energy.

In all, he was physically of an enervated nature— I mean the reverse of muscular. His action was most quiet and subdued, even when most energetically declaiming : and his hand . . . was as velvety as the sheathed paw of cat or mole, and might have manifested the veriest Sybarite that ever lived for luxury alone. — WILLIAM JERDAN (" Men I have Known ").

Mr. Harness used occasionally to visit Coleridge when the latter was staying with Mr. Gillman, the apothecary-doctor, at Highgate. The poet originally went there to recover his health, which he had broken down by over-indulgence in opium. He placed himself there under a sort of voluntary restraint, and strict orders were given by Mr. Gillman that no drugs of any kind were to be allowed him. Coleridge, missing the stimulant to which he had been long accustomed, pined and languished under the restriction ; he abandoned his pen and sank into utter despondency. One day a large roll of papers came to the poet from the publisher, and on Mr. Gillman's visiting him in the evening, he found him an altered man ; Coleridge was himself again, full of animation and energy, and busily employed in writing an article for the forthcoming " Review." The change was so sudden and remarkable that the doctor's suspicions were aroused. He

Opium.

III.—7

Opium.

instituted inquiries and found that a roll of opium had, at the poet's entreaty, been inclosed in the packet which had arrived that morning from the publisher.—A. G. L'ESTRANGE (" Life of W. Harness ").

The passion for the intoxicating drug, which he shared in common with his friend the famous "Opium-Eater," grew into so pernicious a habit that it could hardly be restrained within bounds consistent with rational life. All that could be achieved was to procure temporary respites from a condition which would otherwise have been utterly visionary, and close upon insanity. . . . . Irregularities injurious to self-interest were ever produced by these tempting flights into dreamland. Abstraction took the place of literary employment ; procrastination marred the most feasible projects ; and engagements, however important, gave way to the rainbow illusions in which the senses could be tranced.— WILLIAM JERDAN (" Men I have Known ").

Coleridge *began* the use of opium from bodily pain (rheumatism), and for the same reason *continued* it, till he had acquired a habit too difficult under his own management to control.—JAMES GILLMAN " Life of Coleridge ").

*A safe-
guard.*

He went so far at one time in Bristol, to my knowledge, as to hire a man for the express purpose, and armed with the power of resolutely interposing between himself and the door of any druggist's shop ; . . . a man shrinks from exposing to another that infirmity of will which he might else have but a feeble motive for disguising to himself; and the delegated man, the external conscience, as it were, of Coleridge, though destined—in the final resort, if matters came to absolute rupture, and to an absolute duel, as it were, between himself and his principal—in that extremity to give way, yet might have long protracted the struggle, before coming to that sort of *dignus vindice nodus;* and in fact, I know, upon absolute proof, that, before reaching that crisis, the man showed fight; and, faithful to his trust, and comprehending the reasons for it, he declared that if he must yield, he would "know the reason why."—THOMAS DE QUINCEY ("Literary Reminiscences").

A safe-guard.

Joseph Cottle gives a very full and painful record of his observation of Coleridge's subjection to opium. It has not seemed desirable to reproduce any portion of this record; for Cottle, in common with other friends of Coleridge, shows an utter inability to comprehend the physical aspect of the case, and hence his conclusions are illogical and unjust. The simple truth is, that the miserable victim of the opium-habit is rather a subject for the most skilful medical treatment, than for exhortation and reproof.

Opium.

It was a remarkable quality in Mr. Coleridge's mind that edifices excited little interest in him. On his return from Italy, and after having resided for some time in Rome, I remember his describing to me the state of society; the characters of the Pope and Cardinals; the gorgeous ceremonies, with the

Indiffer-ence to ar-chitecture.

superstitions of the people ; but not one word did he utter concerning St. Peter's, the Vatican, or the numerous antiquities of the place.—JOSEPH COTTLE ("Reminiscences of Coleridge and Southey ").

Criticism of pictures. He knew little or nothing of the art of painting ; yet I have heard him discuss the merits and defects of a picture of the poorest class, as though it had sprung from the inspiration of a Raffaelle. He would advert to certain parts, and surmise that it had been touched upon here and there ; would pronounce upon its character and school, its *chiaroscuro,* the gradations, the handling, etc., when in fact it had no mark or merit or character about it. It became transfigured, sublimated, by the speaker's imagination, which far excelled both the picture and its author.—BRYAN W. PROCTER ("Recollections of Men of Letters ").

Hours. At two or three o'clock in the afternoon he would make his first appearance ; through the silence of the night, when all other lights had long disappeared, in the quiet cottage of Grasmere *his* lamp might be seen invariably by the belated traveller, as he descended the long steps from Dun-mail-raise ; and at five or six o'clock in the morning, when man was going forth to his labor, this insulated son of reveries was retiring to bed.—THOMAS DE QUINCEY ("Literary Reminiscences ").

Unmusical. The melody of Coleridge's verse had led me, as in the case of Scott, to credit him with the possession of the very soul of song ; and yet, either from defective ear, or from the intractability of his vocal organs, his pronunciation of any foreign language but his own was barbarous; and his inability to follow the simplest melody, quite ludicrous. The German tongue he knew *au fond.* He had learned it grammatically, critically, and scientifically at Göttingen; yet so unintelligible was he when he tried to speak it, that I heard Schlegel say to him one evening, "Mein lieber Herr, would you speak English? I understand it; but your German I cannot follow." Whether he had ever been before enlightened on his malpronunciation of German, I know not; but he was quite conscious that his pronunciation of French was execrable, for I heard him avow as much.—JULIAN C. YOUNG (" Memoirs of C. M. Young ").

Unmusical.
—Bad pro-nunciation of foreign tongues.

He was a man of violent prejudices, and had conceived an insuperable aversion for the *grande nation*, of which he was not slow to boast. "I hate," he would say, "the hollowness of French principles; I hate the republicanism of French politics; I hate the hostility of the French people to revealed religion; I hate the artificiality of French cooking; I hate the acidity of French wines; I hate the flimsiness of the French language:—my very organs of speech are so anti-Gallican that they refuse to pronounce intelligibly their insipid tongue."—JULIAN C. YOUNG ("Memoir of C. M. Young ").

Prejudices.

Coleridge often spoiled a book; but in the course of doing this, he enriched that book with so many and so valuable notes, tossing about him, with such lavish profusion, from such a cornucopia of discur-

Treatment of books.

sive reading, and such a fusing intellect, commen-
taries, so many-angled and so many-colored, that I
have envied many a man whose luck has placed him
in the way of such injuries.—THOMAS DE QUINCEY
("Literary Reminiscences").

Treatment of books.

Reader, if haply thou art blessed with a moderate
collection, be shy of showing it ; or if thy heart over-
floweth to lend them, lend thy books ; but let it be
to such a one as S. T. C.—he will return them (generally anticipating the time appointed) with usury ;
enriched with annotations, tripling their value.   I
have had experience. Many are these precious MSS.
of his—(in *matter* oftentimes, and almost in *quantity* not unfrequently, vying with the originals)—in
no very clerkly hand—legible in my Daniel ; in old
Burton ; in Sir Thomas Browne ; and those abstruser
cogitations of the Greville, now, alas ! wandering
in Pagan lands.—I counsel thee, shut not thy heart,
nor thy library, against S. T. C.—CHARLES LAMB
("Essay on the Two Races of Men").[1]

Humor.

I have not yet noticed a vein of sportive humor
which he occasionally displayed, and which was exceedingly amusing when it accompanied the relation
of any whimsical anecdote.   The lustre of his large
eye, the gravity of his look, the silvery tone of his
voice, and the slightly drawling manner in the delivery of his narrative, gave a peculiar significance to
these little stories, of which no idea can be formed
from the matter, divorced from the accessories of

---

[1] Lamb (Charles).   Elia.   Essays which have appeared under
that Signature in the London Magazine.   12mo. London, 1823.

person, emphasis, and playful action.—WILLIAM JERDAN (" Men I have Known ").

Dr. Clement Carlyon, in his " Early Years and Late Reflections," [1] says that Coleridge " was never above a pun when it crossed his mind opportunely." Dr. C. gives some specimens of the Coleridgean puns, of a peculiarly atrocious character.

Puns.

Not many months before his death, when alluding to his general health, he told me that he never in his life knew the sensation of headache ; adding, in his own peculiarly vivid manner of illustration, that he had no more internal consciousness of possessing a head than he had of having an eye.—MARY COWDEN CLARKE (" Recollections of Writers ").

Freedom from headache.

Marked gifts are often attended by marked deficiencies even in the intellect : those best acquainted with my Father are well aware that there was in him a special *intellectual* flaw ; Archdeacon Hare has said that his memory was " notoriously irretentive ; " and it is true that, on a certain class of subjects, it was extraordinarily confused and inaccurate ; matter of fact, as such, laid no hold upon his mind ; of all he heard and saw, he readily caught and well retained the spirit, but the *letter* escaped him ; he seemed incapable of paying the due regard to it.—SARA COLERIDGE (Introduction to " Biographia Literaria ").

Memory.

---

[1] Carlyon (Clement, M. D.). Early Years and Late Reflections. 3 vols., 12mo. London, 1856.

Memory.

The Rev. Robert Tennant . . . had a great reverence and admiration for Mr. Coleridge, and used occasionally to call upon him. During one of these visits, Mr. C. spoke of a book . . . in which there were some valuable remarks bearing upon the subject of their conversation. Mr. Tennant immediately purchased the book upon this recommendation, but on reading it was surprised to find no such passages as Mr. C. had referred to. Some time after he saw the same book at the house of a friend, and mentioned the circumstance to him ; upon which his friend directed him to the margin of the volume before him, and there he found the very remarks in Mr. C.'s own writing, which he had written in as marginalia, and forgotten that they were his own and not the author's.[1]—SARA COLERIDGE (Introduction to " Biographia Literaria ").

Unfulfilled plans.

His mind was in a singular degree distinguished for the habit of projecting. New projects and plans . . . followed each other in rapid succession, and while the vividness of the impression lasted, the very completion could scarcely have afforded more satisfaction than the vague design. To project, with him was commonly sufficient. . . . I remember him once to have read to me, from his pocket-book, a list of eighteen different works which he had resolved to write, and several of them in quarto, not one of which he ever effected. . . . Another prominent feature in Mr. Coleridge's mind was procrastination. It is not to be supposed that

[1] See p. 146.

he ever made a promise or entered on an engage-
ment without intending to fulfil it, but none who
knew him could deny that he wanted much of that *Unfulfilled plans.*
steady, persevering determination which is the precursor of success.—JOSEPH COTTLE (" Reminiscences
of Coleridge and Southey ").

Nobody who knew him ever thought of depend-
ing on any appointment he might make ; spite of
his uniformly honorable intentions, nobody attached *Lack of punctuality.*
any weight to his assurances *in re futura :* those who
asked him to dinner or any other party, as a matter
of course sent a carriage for him, and went person-
ally or by proxy to fetch him ; and, as to letters, unless the address was in some female hand that com-
manded his affectionate esteem, he tossed them all
into one general *dead-letter bureau,* and rarely, I believe, opened them at all.—THOMAS DE QUINCEY
(" Literary Reminiscences ").

I remember once meeting him in Paternoster Row ;
he was inquiring his way to Bread Street, Cheapside,
and, of course, I endeavored to explain to him that *A delusive "Bump of Locality."*
if he walked on about two hundred yards, and took
the fourth turning to the right, it would be the
street he wanted. I noted his expression, so vague
and unenlightened, that I could not help expressing
my surprise as I looked earnestly at his forehead,
and saw the organ of "locality" unusually prominent above the eyebrows. He took my meaning,
laughed, and said, " I see what you are looking at :
why, at school my head was beaten into a mass of
bumps, because I could not point out Paris in a

map of France."—SAMUEL C. HALL ("Book of Memories").

In old age.

Coleridge was fat, and began to lament, in very
delightful verses, that he was getting infirm. There
was no old age in his verses. I heard him one day,
under the Grove at Highgate, repeat one of his
melodious lamentations, as he walked up and down,
his voice undulating in a stream of music, and his
regrets of youth sparkling with visions ever young.
. . . It is no secret that Coleridge lived in the
Grove at Highgate with a friendly family,[1] who had
sense and kindness enough to know that they did
themselves honor by looking after the comforts of
such a man. His room looked upon a delicious
prospect of wood and meadow, with colored gardens under the window, like an embroidery to the
mantle. I thought, when I first saw it, that he had
taken up his dwelling-place like an abbot. Here
he cultivated his flowers, and had a set of birds for
his pensioners, who came to breakfast with him.
He might have been seen taking his daily stroll up
and down, with his black coat and white locks, and
a book in his hand, and was a great acquaintance of
the little children. His main occupation, I believe,
was reading.—LEIGH HUNT ("Autobiography").

*Religious
views.*

In his youth, Coleridge was for some time a
Unitarian preacher. Later in life he joined the
Established Church. His mature opinions may be
gathered from the following extract from a letter,
which he wrote to his godson, a few days before

---

[1] The Gillmans.

his own death : "I have known what the enjoy-ments and advantages of this life are, and what the more refined pleasures which learning and intellec-tual power can bestow ; and with all the experience which more than threescore years can give, I now, on the eve of my departure, declare to you (and earnestly pray that you may hereafter live and act on the conviction), that health is a great blessing—competence obtained by honorable industry is a great blessing—and a great blessing it is to have kind, faithful, honest relatives ; but that the great-est of all blessings, as it is the most ennobling of all privileges, is to be, indeed, a Christian. But I have been likewise, through a large portion of my later life, a sufferer, sorely afflicted with bodily pains, languors, and bodily infirmities, and for the last three or four years have, with few and brief in-tervals, been confined to a sick room, and at this moment, in great weakness and heaviness, write from a sick-bed, hopeless of a recovery ; and I thus, on the very brink of the grave, solemnly bear wit-ness to you that the Almighty Redeemer, most gracious in His promises to them that truly seek Him, is faithful to perform what He hath promised, and hath preserved, under all my pains and infirmi-ties, the inward peace that passeth all understand-ing, with the supporting assurance of a reconciled God, who will not withdraw His Spirit from me in the conflict, and in His own time will deliver me from the evil one."

Religious views.

Caroline Fox, in her "Memories of Old Friends," tells of Mary Coleridge's account of Coleridge :

A pleasant glimpse.

"When in the midst of the highest talk he would turn to her, smoothe her hair, look into her face, and say,—'God bless you, my pretty child, my pretty Mary!' He was most tender and affectionate, and always treated her as if she were six years old."

Surpassing expectation.

Of all celebrated persons I ever saw, Coleridge alone surpassed the expectation created by his writings; for he not only was, but appeared to be, greater than the noblest things he had written.— Thomas N. Talfourd ("Final Memorials of Charles Lamb").

The last tribute of a friend.

A few months after the death of Coleridge, and only a few weeks before his own death, Lamb wrote these memorable words:[1]

"When I heard of the death of Coleridge, it was without grief. It seemed to me that he long had been on the confines of the next world—that he had a hunger for eternity. I grieved then that I could not grieve. But since, I feel how great a part he was of me. His great and dear spirit haunts me. I cannot think a thought, I cannot make a criticism on men or books, without an ineffectual turning and reference to him. He was the proof and touchstone of all my cogitations. He was a Grecian (or in the first form) at Christ's Hospital,

---

[1] First published by John Forster, in an article upon Lamb, in the New Monthly Magazine, 1835. Republished in Mr. Babson's Eliana. (Babson (J. E.). Eliana: Being the hitherto Uncollected Writings of Charles Lamb. 8vo. New York and Boston, 1864.)

where I was deputy Grecian ; and the same subordination and deference to him I have preserved through a life-long acquaintance.   Great in his writings, he was greatest in his conversation.   In him was disproved that old maxim, that we should allow every one his share of talk.   He would talk from morn to dewy eve, nor cease till far midnight ; yet who ever would interrupt him—who would obstruct that continuous flow of converse, fetched from Helicon or Zion ?   He had the tact of making the unintelligible seem plain.   Many who read the abstruser parts of his ' Friend ' would complain that his works did not answer to his spoken wisdom. They were identical.   But he had a tone in oral delivery, which seemed to convey sense to those who were otherwise imperfect recipients.   He was my fifty years' old friend without a dissension.   Never saw I his likeness, nor probably the world can see again.   I seem to love the house he died at more passionately than when he lived.   I love the faithful Gillmans more than while they exercised their virtues toward him living.   What was his mansion is consecrated to me a chapel.

The last
tribute of a
friend.

Edmondton, November, 21, 1834."

CHARLES LAMB.

1775–1834.

INTRODUCTORY NOTE.

O F Charles Lamb it may be said, more truly than of almost any other man, that his own works are his best biography. Familiarity with his writings is indispensable to any adequate knowledge of his character. No man was ever more truly autobiographic. He constantly portrays himself, although seldom with deliberate intention. It would not be quite practicable to reprint the "Essays of Elia" in this volume ; but, fortunately, there remain other and more available sources of knowledge.

The two authors of chief authority are Talfourd and Procter ("Barry Cornwall"), both of whom wrote from personal knowledge. There is a pleasant, discursive book, by Percy Fitzgerald, entitled "Charles Lamb ; his Friends, his Haunts, and his Books," and there is a valuable, although carelessly edited volume, not free from serious inaccuracies— "Charles and Mary Lamb," by W. C. Hazlitt. The latest work is Mr. Ainger's well-considered biography in the "English Men of Letters" series. The ideal life of Lamb is yet to be written ; but it will not be the work of any ordinary book-maker. It is reserved for some man of high genius to make the most attractive biography in the language ; and he may well be deemed fortunate, who shall thus link his name with that of the best beloved of English authors.

Among those who have written of him, a remarkable unanimity of sentiment prevails. Harsh critics grow tender, and cynics[1] speak gently, when they tell of Charles Lamb. Some of the most valuable of the many contemporary notices of him are to be found in the following works : P. G. Patmore's " My Friends and Acquaintance ; " Charles and Mary Cowden Clarke's " Recollections of Writers ; " Hazlitt's " Spirit of the Age," and various essays ; Leigh Hunt's "Autobiography ; " De Quincey's "Biographical Essays," and " Literary Reminiscences ; " C. R. Leslie's " Autobiographical Recollections ; " and Hood's " Literary Reminiscences."

Many years ago Walter Savage Landor wrote these lines ; to-day they are as fresh as ever :

> " Once, and once only have I seen thy face,
> Elia ! once only has thy tripping tongue
> Run o'er my breast, yet never has been left
> Impression on it stronger or more sweet.
> Cordial old man ! what youth was in thy years,
> What wisdom in thy levity, what truth
> In every utterance of that purest soul !
> Few are the spirits of the glorified
> I'd spring to earlier at the gate of Heaven."

---

[1] Thomas Carlyle furnishes the one exception.

LEADING EVENTS OF LAMB'S LIFE.

1775.   Born, February 10th, in London.
1782.—(Aged 7.)   At Christ's Hospital School.
1789.—(Aged 14.)   Leaves Christ's Hospital, and enters the service
                         of the South Sea House.
1792.—(Aged 17.)   Enters the service of the East India Company.
1796.—(Aged 21.)   Mary Lamb becomes insane.
1797.—(Aged 22.)   Publishes a volume of poems, the joint produc-
                         tion of Coleridge, Lloyd, and himself.
1798.—(Aged 23.)   Publishes "Rosamond Gray."
1802.—(Aged 27.)   Publishes "John Woodvil."
1806.—(Aged 31.)   "Mr. H——," a farce, performed at Drury
                         Lane Theatre.
1807.—(Aged 32.)   Publishes "Tales from Shakespeare."
1808.—(Aged 33.)   Publishes "Specimens of Dramatic Authors."
1818.—(Aged 43.)   Publishes two volumes of his writings in prose
                         and verse.
1820.—(Aged 45.)   Contributes to the *London Magazine*.
1823.—(Aged 48.)   Publishes "Essays of Elia."
1825.—(Aged 50.)   Retires from the service of the East India
                         Company, with a pension of four hundred
                         and fifty pounds per annum.
1833.—(Aged 58.)   Publishes "Last Essays of Elia."
1834.—(Aged 59 years and 10 months.) Dies, December 27th.

CHARLES LAMB.

O NE of his school-fellows, of whose genial qualities he has made affectionate mention in his
"Recollections of Christ's Hospital," Charles V. Le *School-
days.*
Grice, . . . has supplied me with some particulars of his school-days, for which friends of a later
date will be grateful. "Lamb," says Mr. Le Grice,
"was an amiable, gentle boy, very sensible and keenly observing, indulged by his school-fellows and by
his master on account of his infirmity of speech.
His countenance was mild; his complexion clear
brown, with an expression which might lead you to
think that he was of Jewish descent. His eyes were
not each of the same color, one was hazel, the other
had specks of gray in the iris, mingled as we see red
spots in the blood-stone. His step was plantigrade,
which made his walk slow and peculiar, adding to
the staid appearance of his figure. I never heard
his name mentioned without the addition of Charles,
although, as there was no other boy of the name of
Lamb, the addition was unnecessary ; but there was
an implied kindness in it, and it was a proof that his
gentle manners excited that kindness. His delicate
frame and his difficulty of utterance, which was increased by agitation, unfitted him for joining in any

boisterous sport."—THOMAS N. TALFOURD ("Final
Memorials of Charles Lamb ").

Personal appearance.

Mr. Lamb's personal appearance was remarkable.
It quite realized the expectations of those who think
that an author and a wit should have a distinct air,
a separate costume, a particular cloth, something
positive and singular about him.   Such unquestionably had Mr. Lamb.   Once he rejoiced in snuff-color,
but latterly his costume was inveterately black—
with gaiters which seemed longing for something
more substantial to close in.   His legs were remarkably slight ; so indeed was his whole body, which
was of short stature, but surmounted by a head of
amazing fineness.   His face was deeply marked and
full of noble lines—traces of sensibility, imagination, suffering, and much thought.   His wit was in
his eye, luminous, quick, and restless.   The smile
that played about his mouth was ever cordial and
good-humored ; and the most cordial and delightful
of its smiles were those with which he accompanied
his affectionate talk with his sister, or his jokes
against her.—JOHN FORSTER (*New Monthly Magazine*,
1835).

Charles Lamb was about forty years of age when
I first saw him ; and I knew him intimately for the
greater part of twenty years.   Small and spare in
person, and with small legs ("immaterial legs"
Hood called them), he had a dark complexion, dark,
curling hair, almost black, and a grave look, lighten-
ing up occasionally, and capable of sudden merriment.   His laugh was seldom excited by jokes merely

ludicrous ; it was never spiteful ; and his quiet smile was sometimes inexpressibly sweet ; perhaps it had a touch of sadness in it. His mouth was well-shaped ; his lip tremulous with expression ; his brown eyes were quick, restless, and glittering, and he had a grand head, full of thought.—BRYAN W. PROCTER ("Charles Lamb ; a Memoir").

Personal appearance.

Very often Charles Lamb was one of the party, . . . with his gentle, sweet, yet melancholy countenance ; for I can recall it only as bearing the stamp of mournfulness, rather than of mirth.—S. C. HALL ("Retrospect of a Long Life ").[1]

A light frame, so fragile that it seemed as if a breath would overthrow it, clad in clerk-like black, was surmounted by a head of form and expression the most noble and sweet. His black hair curled crisply about an expanded forehead ; his eyes, softly brown, twinkled with varying expression, though the prevalent feeling was sad ; and the nose slightly curved, and delicately carved at the nostril, with the lower outline of the face regularly oval, completed a head which was finely placed on the shoulders, and gave importance, and even dignity, to a diminutive and shadowy stem. Who shall describe his countenance —catch its quivering sweetness—and fix it forever in words? There are none alas! to answer the vain desire of friendship. Deep thought, striving with humor ; the lines of suffering wreathed into cordial mirth ; and a smile of painful sweetness, present an

---

[1] Hall (Samuel Carter). Retrospect of a Long Life. 8vo. London and New York, 1883.

image to the mind it can as little describe as lose.—
THOMAS N. TALFOURD ("Letters of Charles Lamb ").

The first time I saw and spoke with Charles Lamb
was where he was most at home—in Fleet Street.
He was of diminutive and even ungraceful appearance, thin and wiry, clumsily clad, and with a shuf-
fling gait, more than awkward ; though covered, it
was easy to perceive that the head was of no common order, for the hat fell back as if it fitted better
there than over a large intellectual forehead, which
overhung a countenance somewhat expressive of
anxiety and even pain. His wit was in his eye—
luminous, quick, and restless ; and the smile that
played about his mouth was cordial and good-humored.—SAMUEL C. HALL ("Book of Memories ").

I was sitting one morning beside our editor, busily
correcting proofs, when a visitor was announced,
whose name, grumbled by a low ventriloquial voice,
like Tom Pipes calling down the hold through the
hatchway, did not resound distinctly on my tym-
panum. However, the door opened, and in came a
stranger,—a figure remarkable at a glance, with a
fine head, on a small spare body, supported by two
almost immaterial legs. He was clothed in sables,
of a by-gone fashion, but there was something wanting, or something present about him, that certified
he was neither a divine, nor a physician, nor a
school-master : from a certain neatness and sobriety
in his dress, coupled with his sedate bearing, he
might have been taken, but that such a costume
would be anomalous, for a *Quaker* in black. He

looked still more (what he really was) a literary Modern Antique, a New Old Author, a living Anachronism, contemporary at once with Burton the Elder and Colman the Younger.   Meanwhile he advanced with rather a peculiar gait, his walk was plantigrade, and with a cheerful " How d'ye," and one of the blandest, sweetest smiles, that ever brightened a manly countenance, held out two fingers to the editor. *Personal appearance.*

The two gentlemen in black soon fell into discourse ; and whilst they conferred, the Lavater principle within me set to work upon the interesting specimen thus presented to its speculations.   It was a striking intellectual face, full of wiry lines, physiognomical quips and cranks, that gave it great character.   There was much earnestness about the brows, and a great deal of speculation in the eyes, which were brown and bright, and "quick in turning ;" the nose, a decided one, though of no established order ; and there was a handsome smartness about the mouth.   Altogether, it was no common face—none of those *willow-pattern* ones, which Nature turns out by thousands at her potteries ;—but more like a chance specimen of the Chinese ware, one to the set—unique, quaint.   No one who had once seen it could pretend not to know it again.   It was no face to lend its countenance to any confusion of persons in a Comedy of Errors.   You might have sworn to it piecemeal—a separate affidavit for every feature.—THOMAS HOOD ("Literary Reminiscences").

I do not know whether Lamb had any oriental blood in his veins, but certainly the most marked

*Personal
appearance.*

complexional characteristic of his head was a *Jewish*
look, which pervaded every portion of it, even to
the sallow and uniform complexion, and the black
and crispy hair standing off loosely from the head,
as if every single hair was independent of the rest.
The nose, too, was large and slightly hooked, and
the chin rounded and elevated to correspond. There
was altogether a *Rabbinical* look about Lamb's head,
which was at once striking and impressive.

Thus much of form chiefly. In point of intellectual character and expression, a finer face was never
seen, nor one more fully, however vaguely, corresponding with the mind whose features it inter-
preted. There was the gravity usually engendered
by a life passed in book-learning, without the
slightest tinge of that assumption and affectation
which almost always attend the gravity *so* engendered ; the intensity and elevation of general expression that mark high genius, without any of its
pretension and its oddity : the sadness waiting on
fruitless thoughts and baffled aspirations, but no
evidences of that spirit of scorning and contempt
which these are apt to engender. Above all, there
was a prevading sweetness and gentleness which
went straight to the heart of every one who looked
on it ; and not the less so, perhaps, that it bore
about it an air, a something, seeming to tell that it
was not *put on*—for nothing would be more unjust
than to tax Lamb with assuming anything, even a
virtue, which he did not possess—but preserved and
persevered in, spite of opposing and contradictory
feelings within, that struggled in vain for mastery.
It was a thing to remind you of that painful smile

which bodily disease and agony will sometimes put on, to conceal their sufferings from the observation of those they love.

His head might have belonged to a full-sized person, but it was set upon a figure so *petite* that it took an appearance of inappropriate largeness by comparison. This was the only striking peculiarity in the *ensemble* of his figure ; in other respects it was pleasing and well formed, but so slight and delicate as to bear the appearance of extreme spareness, as if of a man air-fed, instead of one rejoicing in a proverbial predilection for "roast pig." The only defect of the figure was that the legs were too slight even for the slight body.—PETER G. PATMORE ("My Friends and Acquaintance").[1] *Personal appearance.*

He was the leanest of mankind, tiny black breeches buttoned to the knee-cap, and no further, surmounting spindle-legs, also in black, face and head fineish, black, bony, lean, and of a Jew type rather ; in the eyes a kind of smoky brightness or confused sharpness ; spoke with a stutter ; in walking tottered and shuffled.—THOMAS CARLYLE ("Reminiscences").

Charles Lamb had three striking personal peculiarities ; his eyes were of different colors, one being grayish blue, the other brownish hazel ; his hair was thick, retaining its abundance and its dark-brown hue with scarcely a single gray hair among it until even the latest period of his life ; and he had a

---

[1] Patmore (Peter George).   My Friends and Acquaintance. 3 vols., 8vo.   London, 1854.

smile of singular sweetness and beauty.—MARY
COWDEN CLARKE ("Recollections of Writers").

Persons who had been in the habit of traversing
Covent Garden at that time (seven and forty years
ago) might, by extending their walk a few yards
into Russell Street, have noted a small, spare man,
clothed in black, who went out every morning and
returned every afternoon, as regularly as the hands
of the clock moved toward certain hours. You
could not mistake him. He was somewhat stiff in
his manner, and almost clerical in dress; which indicated much wear. He had a long, melancholy
face, with keen, penetrating eyes; and he walked,
with a short, resolute step, city-wards. He looked
no one in the face for more than a moment, yet
contrived to see everything as he went on. No
one who ever studied the human features could
pass him by without recollecting his countenance :
it was full of sensibility, and it came upon you like
a new thought, which you could not help dwelling
upon afterwards; it gave rise to meditation, and
did you good. This small, half-clerical man was—
Charles Lamb.—BRYAN W. PROCTER ("Charles
Lamb; a Memoir").

Lamb . . . was always dressed in black. "I
take it," he says, "to be the proper costume of an
author." When this was once objected to, at a
wedding, he pleaded the raven's apology in the
fable, that "he had no other." His clothes were
entirely black ; and he wore long black gaiters, up
to the knees. His head was bent a little forward,
like one who had been reading ; and, if not standing

or walking, he generally had in his hand an old book, a pinch of snuff, or, later in the evening, a pipe. He stammered a little, pleasantly, just enough to prevent his making speeches; just enough to make you listen eagerly for his words, always full of meaning, or charged with a jest; or referring (but this was rare) to some line or passage from one of the old Elizabethan writers, which was always ushered in with a smile of tender reverence.—BRYAN W. PROCTER ("Charles Lamb; a Memoir ").

Costume—various characteristics.

His speech was brief and pithy; not too often humorous; never sententious nor didactic. Although he sometimes talked whilst walking up and down the room (at which time he seldom looked at the person with whom he was talking), he very often spoke as if impelled by the necessity of speaking—suddenly, precipitately. If he could have spoken very easily, he might possibly have uttered long sentences, expositions or orations; such as some of his friends indulged in, to the utter confusion of their hearers.

Conversation.

But he knew the value of silence; and he knew that even truth may be damaged by too many words. When he did speak, his words had a flavor in them beyond any that I have heard elsewhere. His conversation dwelt upon persons or things within his own recollection, or it opened (with a startling doubt, or a question, or a piece of quaint humor) the great circle of thought.—BRYAN W. PROCTER ("Charles Lamb; a Memoir ").

There was L—— himself, the most delightful, the most provoking, the most witty and sensible of men.

He always made the best pun, and the best remark in the course of the evening. His serious conversation, like his serious writing, is his best. No one ever stammered out such fine, piquant, deep, eloquent things in half a dozen half-sentences as he does. His jests scald like tears : and he probes a question with a play upon words. . . . There was no fuss or cant about him ; nor were his sweets or his sours ever diluted with one particle of affectation.—WILLIAM HAZLITT ("Conversation of Authors ").

Many of Lamb's witty and curious sayings have been repeated since his death, which are worthy to be held in undying remembrance ; but they give no idea of the general tenor of his conversation, which was far more singular and delightful in the traits, which could never be recalled, than in the epigrammatic terms which it is possible to quote. It was fretted into perpetual eddies of verbal felicity and happy thought, with little tranquil intervals reflecting images of exceeding elegance and grace.—THOMAS N. TALFOURD ("Letters of Charles Lamb ").

He has an affectionate heart, a mind *sui generis ;* his taste acts so as to appear like the unmechanic simplicity of an instinct—in brief, he is worth an hundred men of *mere* talents. Conversation with the latter tribe is like the use of leaden bells—one warms by exercise, Lamb every now and then *irradiates,* and the beam, though single and fine as a hair, is yet rich with colors, and I both see and feel it.—SAMUEL T. COLERIDGE (from a Letter to God-win, in C. K. Paul's " W. Godwin ").[1]

In miscellaneous gatherings Lamb said little un-less an opening arose for a pun. And how effectual that sort of small shot was from *him*, I need not say to anybody who remembers his infirmity of stammering, and his dexterous management of it for purposes of light and shade. He was often able to train the roll of stammers into settling upon the words immediately preceding the effective one, by which means the keynote of the jest or sarcasm, benefiting by the sudden liberation of his embar-goed voice, was delivered with the force of a pistol-shot. That stammer was worth an annuity to him as an ally of his wit. Firing under cover of that ad-vantage he did triple execution ; for, in the first place, the distressing sympathy of the hearers with *his* distress of utterance won for him unavoidably the silence of deep attention ; and then, whilst he had us all hoaxed into attitude of mute suspense by an appearance of distress that he perhaps did not really feel, down came a plunging shot into the very thick of us, with ten times the effect it would else have had.—THOMAS DE QUINCEY (" Biographical Essays ").[2]

Artful stammer-ing.

Lamb read remarkably well. There was rather a defect of vigor in his style of reading ; and it was a

[1] Paul (Rev. Charles Kegan). William Godwin ; his Friends and Contemporaries. 2 vols., 8vo. London, 1876.
[2] De Quincey (Thomas). Biographical Essays. 16mo. Boston, 1851.

style better suited to passages of tranquil or solemn movement, than to those of tumultuous passion. But his management of the pauses was judicious, his enunciation very distinct, his tones melodious and deep, and his cadences well executed.—THOMAS DE QUINCEY (" Literary Reminiscences ").

When he read aloud it was with a slight tone, which I used to think he had caught from Coleridge ; Coleridge's recitation, however, rising to a chant.—BRYAN W. PROCTER (" Charles Lamb ; a Memoir ").

Lamb was entirely destitute of what is commonly called " a taste for music." A few old tunes ran in his head ; now and then the expression of a sentiment, though never of song, touched him with rare and exquisite delight. . . . But usually music only confused him, and an opera—to which he once or twice tried to accompany Miss Isola—was to him a maze of sound in which he almost lost his wits.— THOMAS N. TALFOURD (" Letters of Lamb ").

The Rev. Joseph H. Twichell, in an interesting article—" Concerning Charles Lamb "—published in *Scribner's Monthly*, March, 1876, gives some valuable information about Lamb's commercial life. In a railway carriage in England, Mr. Twichell had the good luck to meet a gentleman who had been a fellow-clerk of Lamb's : " Lamb's handwriting, he said, was for commercial purposes (alas !) faulty : he was neither a neat nor an accurate accountant ; he made frequent errors, which he was in the habit of wiping out with his little finger. (All of which Mr. Ogilvie

illustrated with a pencil on the margin of a news-
paper.) . . . He further stated that for all Lamb
so ruefully bewails, in his letters, the hardship of his
India House task, he hardly ever used to do what
would be called a full day's work : he often came
late (we know for certain he did once), and generally
stood around and talked a good deal."

*Recollec-
tions of a
fellow-
clerk.*

Much injustice has been done to Lamb by accus-
ing him of excess in drinking. The truth is, that a
very small quantity of any strong liquid (wine, etc.)
disturbed his speech, which at best was but an eloquent stammer. The distresses of his early life made
him ready to resort to any remedy which brought for-
getfulness ; and he himself, frail in body and excitable, was very speedily affected. During all my intimacy with him, I never knew him drink immoderately, except once. . . . Lamb's mode of life was
temperate, his dinners consisting of meat, with veg-
etables and bread only. . . . He was himself a
small and delicate eater at all times ; and he entertained something like aversion toward great feeders.
—BRYAN W. PROCTER ("Charles Lamb ; a Memoir").

*Temper-
ance.*

With respect to Lamb's personal habits, much has
been said of his intemperance ; and his biographer
justly remarks, that a false impression prevails upon
this subject. In eating he was peculiarly temperate ;
and, with respect to drinking, though his own admirable wit (as in that delightful letter to Mr. Carey,
where he describes himself, when confided to the
care of some youthful protector, as "as an old rep-
robate Telemachus consigned to the guidance of a

*Mistake
about his
intemper-
ance.*

III.—9

Mistake about his intemper- ance.

wise young Mentor ")—though, I say, his own admirable wit has held up too bright a torch to the illumination of his own infirmities, so that no efforts
of pious friendship could now avail to disguise the
truth, yet it must not be forgotten—1st, that we are
not to imagine Lamb's frailty in this respect habitual or deliberate—he made many powerful resist-
ances to temptation ; 2dly, he often succeeded for long
seasons in practising entire abstinence ; 3dly, when
he *did* yield to the mingled temptation of wine, social
pleasure, and the expansion of his own brotherly
heart, that prompted him to entire sympathy with
those around him (and it cannot be denied that, for
any one man to preserve an absolute sobriety
amongst a jovial company, wears too much the
childish air of playing the spy upon the privileged
extravagances of festive mirth),—whenever this *did*
happen, Lamb, never, to my knowledge, passed the
bounds of an agreeable elevation.   He was joyous,
radiant with wit and frolic, mounting with the sudden motion of a rocket into the highest heaven of
outrageous fun and absurdity ; then bursting into a
fiery shower of puns, chasing syllables with the agil-
ity of a squirrel bounding amongst the trees, or a
cat pursuing its own tail ; but, in the midst of all this
stormy gayety, he never said or did anything that
could by possibility wound or annoy.   The most noticeable feature in his intoxication was the sudden-
ness with which it ascended to its meridian.   Half a
dozen glasses of wine taken during dinner—for
everybody was encouraged by his sunshiny kindness,
to ask *him* to take wine—these, with perhaps one or
two after dinner, sufficed to complete his inebriation

to the crisis of sleep ; after waking from which, so far as I know, he seldom recommenced drinking. This sudden consummation of the effects was not, perhaps, owing to a weaker (as Sergeant Talfourd supposes), but rather to a more delicate and irritable system, than is generally found amongst men. The sensibility of his organization was so exquisite, that effects which travel by separate stages with most other men, in him fled along the nerves with the velocity of light.—THOMAS DE QUINCEY ("Literary Reminiscences ").

Mistake about his intemperance.

The reader must not for a moment suppose . . . that Charles Lamb was in the habit of indulging in that "inordinate cup," which is so justly said to be "unblest, and its ingredient a devil." My very object and excuse in alluding to the subject has been to show that precisely the reverse was the case—that the cup in which *he* indulged was a blessing one, no less to himself than to others, and that for both parties " its ingredient " was an angel. —PETER G. PATMORE (" My Friends and Acquaintance ").

Julius Hare told Daniel Macmillan that "two glasses of wine made Lamb quite light—not tipsy but elevated." So Daniel Macmillan wrote in a letter published in his memoir by Thomas Hughes.

Perhaps the pipe was the only thing in which Lamb really exceeded. He was fond of it from the very early years when he was accustomed to smoke "Orinooko" at the "Salutation and Cat," with Coleridge in 1796. He attempted on several occasions

Tobacco.

to give it up, but his struggles were overcome by counter-influences. "Tobacco," he says, "stood in its own light." At last, in 1805, he was able to conquer and abandon it—for a time. His success, like desertion from a friend, caused some remorse and a great deal of regret. In writing to Coleridge about his house, which was "smoky," he inquires, "Have you cured it? It is hard to cure anything of smoking."—BRYAN W. PROCTER ("Charles Lamb; a Memoir").

Tobacco.

It was curious to note the gradations in Lamb's manner to his various guests, although it was courteous to all. With Hazlitt he talked as though they met the subject in discussion on equal terms; with Leigh Hunt he exchanged repartees; to Wordsworth he was almost respectful; with Coleridge he was sometimes jocose, sometimes deferring; with Martin Burney fraternally familiar; with Manning affectionate; with Godwin merely courteous; or if friendly, then in a minor degree.—BRYAN W. PROCTER ("Charles Lamb; a Memoir").

Manners to different friends.

Charles Lamb had a head worthy of Aristotle, with as fine a heart as ever beat in human bosom, and limbs very fragile to sustain it. . . . There never was a true portrait of Lamb. His features were strongly yet delicately cut; he had a fine eye as well as forehead; and no face carried in it greater marks of thought and feeling. . . . As his frame, so was his genius. It was as fit for thought as could be, and equally as unfit for action; and this rendered him melancholy, apprehensive, humor-

A strong mind in a weak body.

ous, and willing to make the best of every thing as it was, both from tenderness of heart, and abhorrence of alteration. His understanding was too great to admit an absurdity ; his frame was not strong enough to deliver it from a fear. His sensibility to strong contrasts was the foundation of his humor, which was that of a wit at once melancholy and willing to be pleased. He would beard a superstition, and shudder at the old phantasm while he did it. One could have imagined him cracking a jest in the teeth of a ghost, and then melting into thin air himself, out of a sympathy with the awful.—LEIGH HUNT (" Autobiography ").

A strong mind in a weak body.

Finding no footing in certainty, he delighted to confound the borders of theoretical truth and falsehood. He was fond of telling wild stories to children, engrafted on things about them ; wrote letters to people abroad, telling them that a friend of theirs had come out in genteel comedy ; and persuaded George Dyer that Lord Castlereagh was the author of " Waverley !" . . . He wrote . . . two lives of Liston and Munden, which the public took for serious, and which exhibit an extraordinary jumble of imaginary facts and truth of by-painting. Munden he made born at Stoke Pogis, the very sound of which was like the actor speaking and digging his words. He knew how many false conclusions and pretensions are made by men who profess to be guided by facts only, as if facts could not be misconceived, or figments taken for them ; and therefore, one day, when somebody was speaking of a person who valued himself on being a matter-

Love of paradox and extravagance.

of-fact man, "Now," said he, "I value myself on being a matter-of-lie man."—LEIGH HUNT ("Autobiography").

Love of paradox and extravagance.

Lamb, in a letter to Southey, dated August ninth, 1815, more than seven years after the event, thus alludes to his having been present: "I was at Hazlitt's marriage, and had like to have been turned out several times during the ceremony. Anything awful makes me ·laugh."—WILLIAM C. HAZLITT ("Memoirs of W. Hazlitt").[1]

" Do you remember ?"

In the words of our dear departed friend, Charles Lamb, "you good-for-nothing old Lake Poet," what has become of you? Do you remember his saying that at my table in 1819, with "Jerusalem" towering behind us in the painting room, and Keats and your friend Monkhouse of the party? Do you remember Lamb voting me absent, and then making a speech descanting on my excellent port, and proposing a vote of thanks? Do you remember his then voting me present? I had never left my chair—and informing me ·of what had been done during my retirement, and hoping I was duly sensible of the honor? Do you remember the Commissioner (of Stamps and Taxes) who asked you if you did not think Milton a great genius, and Lamb getting up and asking leave with a candle to examine his phrenological development? Do you remember poor dear Lamb, whenever the Commissioner was equally profound, saying: "My son John

---

[1] Hazlitt (William Carew). Memoirs of William Hazlitt. 2 vols., 12mo. London, 1867.

went to bed with his breeches on," to the dismay of the learned man ? Do you remember you and I and Monkhouse getting Lamb out of the room by force, and putting on his great-coat, he reiterating his earnest desire to examine the Commissioner's skull ? . . . Ah! my dear old friend, you and I shall never see such days again ! The peaches are not so big now as they were in our days.—BENJAMIN R. HAYDON (Letter to Wordsworth, 1842, published in Haydon's "Correspondence ").[1]

"Do you re-member ?"

Charles was frequently merry ; but ever at the back of his merriment, there reposed a grave depth, in which rich colors and tender lights were inlaid. For his jests sprang from his sensibility ; which was as open to pleasure as to pain. This sensibility, if it somewhat impaired his vigor, led him into curious and delicate fancies, and taught him a liking for things of the highest relish, which a mere robust jester never tastes.—BRYAN W. PROCTER (" Charles Lamb ; a Memoir ").

Character of his humor

I once said something in his presence which I thought possessed smartness. He commended me with a stammer : "Very well, my dear boy, very well ; Ben (taking a pinch of snuff) Ben Jonson has said worse things than that—and b-b-better."

To Coleridge : " Bless you, old sophist, who next to human nature taught me all the corruption I was capable of knowing."

Specimens of his humor.

---

[1] Haydon (Frederick W.). Benjamin Robert Haydon. Corre-spondence and Table-talk, with a Memoir. 2 vols., 8vo. Lon-don, 1876.

Specimens of his humor.

To Mr. Gilman . . . he writes, "Coleridge is very bad, but he wonderfully picks up, and his face, when he repeats his verses, hath its ancient glory —an archangel's a little damaged."

To Wordsworth (who was superfluously solemn) he writes : "Some d——d people have come in, and I must finish abruptly. By d——d, I only mean deuced."

"Charles," said Coleridge to Lamb, " I think you have heard me preach?" "I n-n-never heard you do anything else," replied Lamb.

Mrs. K., after expressing her love for her young children, added, tenderly, "And how do *you* like babies, Mr. Lamb ?" His answer, immediate, almost precipitate, was " Boi-boi-boiled, ma'am."

An old lady, fond of her dissenting minister, wearied Lamb by the length of her praises. " I speak because I *know* him well," said she. "Well, I don't ;" replied Lamb, " I don't ; but d——n him, at a venture."—BRYAN W. PROCTER ("Charles Lamb : a Memoir ").

At home and in society.

The fact is, that in ordinary society, if Lamb was not an ordinary man, he was only an odd and strange one—displaying no superior knowledge or wit or wisdom or eloquence, but only that invariable accompaniment of genius, a moral incapacity to subside into the conventional cant or the flat commonplace of every-day life. He would do anything to gratify his guests but that. He would joke, or mystify, or pun, or play the buffoon ; but he could not bring himself to prose, or preach, or play the philosopher. He could not be *himself* (for others, I mean) except when something out of himself made him so ; but he could not be anything at variance with himself to please a king.

The consequence was, that to those who did not know him, or, knowing, did not or could not appreciate him, Lamb often passed for something between an imbecile, a brute, and a buffoon ; and the first impression he made on ordinary people was always unfavorable—sometimes to a violent and repulsive degree. . . . The truth is, that the Elia of private life could be known and appreciated only by his friends and intimates, and even by them only at home. He shone, and was answerable to his literary and social reputation, only in a *tête-à-tête*, or in those unpremeditated colloquies over his own table, or by his own fireside, in which his sister and one or two more friends took part, and in which every inanimate object about him was as familiar as the "household words" in which he uttered his deep and subtle thoughts, his quaint and strange fancies, and his sweet and humane philosophy. Under these circumstances, he was perfectly and emphatically a *natural* person, and there was not a vestige of that startling oddity and extravagance, which subjected him to the charge of affecting to be "singular" and "original" in his notions, feelings, and opinions.

In any other species of "company" than that to which I have just referred, however cultivated or intellectual it might be, Lamb was unquestionably liable to the charge of seeming to court attention by the strangeness and novelty of his opinions, rather than by their justness and truth—he was *liable* and open to this charge, but as certainly he did not *de-*

serve it ; for affection supposes a something assumed, put on, pretended—and of this Lamb was physically as well as morally incapable.   His strangeness and oddity under the one set of circumstances, was as natural to him as his naturalness and simplicity under the other.—PETER G. PATMORE (" My Friends and Acquaintance ").

At home and in society.

There were but two persons whom Lamb avowedly did not wish to encounter beneath his roof, and those two, merely on account of private and family differences.   For the rest, they left all their hostilities at the door, with their sticks.   This forbearance was due to the truly tolerant spirit of the host, which influenced all within its sphere.   Lamb, while he willingly lent a crutch to halting humility, took delight in tripping up the stilts of pretension.   Anybody might trot out his hobby : but he allowed nobody to ride the high horse. . . .   He hated anything like cock-of-the-walk-ism ; and set his face and his wit against all ultraism, transcendentalism, sentimentalism, conventional mannerism, and above all, separatism.   In opposition to the exclusives, he was emphatically an inclusive.—THOMAS HOOD (" Literary Reminiscences ").

An inclusive.

If he was intolerant of anything, it was of intolerance. . . .   He hated evil-speaking, carping, and petty scandal.   On one occasion having slipped out an anecdote to the discredit of a literary man, during a very confidential conversation, the next moment, with an expression of remorse for having impaired even my opinion of the party, he bound me

A hater of scandal.

solemnly to bury the story in my own bosom. In another case he characteristically rebuked the back-biting spirit of a censorious neighbor. Some Mrs. Candor telling him, in expectation of an ill-natured comment, that Miss ——, the teacher at the Ladies' School, had married a publican. " Has she so ? " said Lamb, " then I'll have my beer there ! "— THOMAS HOOD (" Literary Reminiscences ").

A hater of scandal.

Lamb, from the dread of appearing affected, some-times injured himself by his behavior before persons who were slightly acquainted with him. With the finest and tenderest feelings ever possessed by man, he seemed carefully to avoid any display of senti-mentality in his talk.—CHARLES R. LESLIE (" Auto-biographical Recollections ").

Anti-senti-mentality.

Mary Cowden Clarke, in an article published in the *Gentleman's Magazine*, December, 1873, tran-scribes a whimsical letter which Lamb sent to her husband in 1829. In this letter Lamb says, " I am called the Black Shepherd—you shall be Cowden with the Tuft ; " whereupon Mrs. Clarke observes ; " The latter name ('Cowden with the Tuft') slyly implies the smooth baldness with scant curly hair distinguishing the head of the friend addressed, and which seemed to strike Charles Lamb so forcibly that one evening, after gazing at it for some time, he suddenly broke forth with the exclamation, ' Gad, Clarke ! what whiskers you have behind your head ! ' He was fond of trying the dispositions of those with whom he associated by an odd speech such as this ; and if they stood the test pleasantly and took it in

Testing his friends.

good part he liked them the better ever after.   One time that the Novellos and Cowden Clarkes went down to see the Lambs at Enfield, and he was standing by his book-shelves talking with them in his usual delightful cordial way, showing them some precious volume lately added to his store, a neighbor chancing to come in to remind Charles Lamb of an appointed ramble, he excused himself by saying :— ' You see I have some troublesome people just come down from town, and I must stay and entertain them ; so we'll take our walk together to-morrow.' "

Testing his friends.

His style of playful bluntness when speaking to his intimates was strangely pleasant—nay, welcome : it gave you the impression of his liking you well enough to be rough and unceremonious with you : it showed you that he felt at home with you.   It accorded with what you knew to be at the root of an ironical assertion he made—that he always gave away gifts, parted with presents, and *sold* keepsakes. It underlay in sentiment the drollery and reversed truth of his saying to us, " I always call my sister Maria when we are alone together, Mary when we are with our friends, and Moll before the servants."—MARY COWDEN CLARKE (" Recollections of Writers ").

Whimsicality.

The very basis of Lamb's character was laid in horror of affectation.   If he found himself by accident using a rather fine word, notwithstanding that it might be the most forcible in that place (the word *arrest*, suppose, in certain situations for the word *catch*) he would, if it were allowed to stand, make

Simplicity and hatred of affectation.

merry with his own grandiloquence at the moment ; and, in after-moments, he would continually ridicule that class of words, by others carried to an extreme of pedantry—the word *arride*, for instance, used in the sense of *pleasing or winning the approbation.* . . . Hence—that is, from this intense sincerity and truth of character—Lamb would allow himself to say things that shocked the feelings of the company—shocked sometimes in the sense of startling or electrifying, as by something that was odd ; but also sometimes shocked with the sense of what *was* revolting, as by a Swiftian laying bare of naked, shivering human nature. — THOMAS DE QUINCEY (" Literary Reminiscences ").

Simplicity and hatred of affectation.

Lamb never affected any spurious gravity. Neither did he ever act the Grand *Senior*. He did not exact that common copy-book respect, which some asinine persons would fain command on account of the mere length of their years. . . . There was nothing of Sir Oracle about Lamb. On the contrary, at sight of a solemn visage that " creamed and mantled like the standing pool," he was the first to pitch a mischievous stone to disturb the duck-weed. " He was a boy-man," as he truly said of Elia ; " and his manners lagged behind his years." He liked to herd with people younger than himself. Perhaps, in his fine generalizing way, he thought that, in relation to eternity, we are all contemporaries. However, without reckoning birth-days, it was always " Hail fellow, well met ;" and although he was my elder by a quarter of a century, he never made me feel, in our excursions, that I was " taking a walk

" A boy-man."

with the schoolmaster."—Thomas Hood (" Literary Reminiscences ").

Scorn of pharisaism.

The case of insincerity, above all others, which moved his bile, was where, out of some pretended homage to public decorum, an individual was run down on account of any moral infirmities, such as we all have, or have had, or at least so easily and naturally may have had, that nobody knows whether we have them or not. In such a case, and in this only almost, Lamb could be savage in his manner.

I remember one instance, where many of the leading authors of our age were assembled—Coleridge, Wordsworth, Southey, etc. Lamb was amongst them ; and when —— was denounced as a man careless in the education of his children, and generally reputed to lead a licentious life—" Pretty fellows *we* are," said Lamb, " to abuse him on that last score, when every one of us, I suppose, on going out this night into the Strand, will make up to the first pretty girl he sees." Some laughed—some looked grim—some looked grand—but Wordsworth, smiling, and yet with solemnity, said—" I hope, I trust, Mr. Lamb, you are mistaken ; or, at least, you do not include us all in this sweeping judgment ? " " Oh, as to that," said Lamb, " who knows ? There's no telling : sad Josephs are some of us in this very room."—Thomas De Quincey (" Literary Reminiscences ").

Unaffected —Shy.

Although sometimes strange in manner, he was thoroughly unaffected ; in serious matters thoroughly sincere. He was, indeed (as he confesses), terribly shy ; diffident, not awkward in manner ; with occasionally nervous, twitching motions that betrayed this infirmity. He dreaded the criticisms of servants far more than the observations of their masters. To undergo the scrutiny of the first, as he said to me, when we were going to breakfast with Mr. Rogers one morning, was "terrible." [1]— BRYAN W. PROCTER ("Charles Lamb : a Memoir"). *Unaffected —Shy.*

He was . . . the most humble and unpretending of human beings, the most thoroughly sincere, the most impatient of simulation or dissimulation, and the one who threw himself the most unreservedly for your good opinion upon the plain natural expression of his real qualities, as nature had formed them, without artifice, or design, or disguise, more than you find in the most childlike of children.—THOMAS DE QUINCEY (" Literary Reminiscences "). *Humility and sincerity.*

Among the prominent characteristics of Lamb, I know not how it is that I have omitted to notice the peculiar emphasis and depth of his courtesy. This quality was in him a really chivalrous feeling, springing from his heart, and cherished with the sanctity of a duty.—THOMAS DE QUINCEY ("Literary Reminiscences"). *Courtesy.*

Mr. Lamb has a distaste to new faces, to new books, to new buildings, to new customs. He is shy of all imposing appearances, of all assumptions of self-importance, of all adventitious ornaments, *Love of the past.*

---

[1] Hazlitt also was troubled by this dread of servants. See p. 185.

Love of the past.

of all mechanical advantages, even to a nervous excess. It is not merely that he does not rely upon, or ordinarily avail himself of them ; he holds them in abhorrence, he utterly abjures and discards them, and places a great gulf between him and them. . . . He evades the present, he mocks at the future. His affections revert to, and settle on the past, but then, even this must have something personal and local in it to interest him deeply and thoroughly. —WILLIAM HAZLITT (" Spirit of the Age ").

Love for the old authors.

No one, as I believe, will ever taste the flavor of certain writers as he has done. He was the last true lover of Antiquity. Although he admitted a few of the beauties of modern times, yet in his stronger love he soared backward to old acclivities, and loved to rest there. . . . He had more real knowledge of old English literature than any man whom I ever knew. He was not an antiquarian. He neither hunted after commas, nor scribbled notes which confounded his text. The *Spirit* of the author descended upon him ; and he felt it ! With Burton and Fuller, Jeremy Taylor, and Sir Thomas Browne, he was an intimate. The ancient poets,— chiefly the dramatic poets—were his especial friends. He knew every point and turn of their wit, all the beauty of their characters ; loving each for some one distinguishing particular, and despising none.— BRYAN W. PROCTER (" Charles Lamb : a Memoir ").

Taste in books.

Mr. Lamb's taste in books is . . . fine, and it is peculiar. It is not the worse for a little *idiosyncrasy.* He does not go deep into the Scotch novels, but he is at home in Smollett or Fielding. He is little read in Junius or Gibbon, but no man can give a better account of Burton's Anatomy of Melancholy, or Sir Thomas Browne's Urn-Burial, or Fuller's Worthies, or John Bunyan's Holy War. No one is more unimpressible to a specious declamation ; no one relishes a recondite beauty more. His admiration of Shakespeare and Milton does not make him despise Pope ; and he can read Parnell with patience, and Gay with delight. His taste in French and German is somewhat defective ; nor has he made much progress in the science of Political Economy or other abstruse studies, though he has read vast folios of controversial divinity, merely for the sake of the intricacy of style, and to save himself the pain of thinking.—WILLIAM HAZLITT (" Spirit of the Age ").

Taste in books.

There were few modern volumes in his collection ; and subsequently, such presentation copies as he received were wont to find their way into my own book-case, and often through eccentric channels. A Leigh Hunt, for instance, would come skimming to my feet through the branches of the apple-trees (our gardens were contiguous) ; or a Bernard Barton would be rolled down stairs after me, from the library door. *Marcian Colonna* I remember finding on my window-sill, damp with the night's fog ; and the *Plea of the Midsummer Fairies* I picked out of the strawberry bed.'—THOMAS WESTWOOD (*Notes and Queries*, September, 1866).

Whimsical treatment of modern books.

---

¹ This was during the last years of Lamb's life. Mr. Westwood's story has been made the occasion for a large amount of wire-drawn comment, by some of Lamb's editors, as an evidence of his unsound mental condition !

III.—10

I will here add a note or two of Wordsworth's conversation. Talking of dear Charles Lamb's very strange habit of quizzing, and of Coleridge's *incorrectness* in talk. Wordsworth said that he thought much of this was owing to a *school-habit.* Lamb's veracity was unquestionable in all matters of a serious kind : he never uttered an untruth either for profit or through vanity, and certainly never to injure others. Yet he loved a quizzing lie, a fiction that amused him like a good joke, or an exercise of wit. In Coleridge there was a sort of dreaminess, which would not let him see things as they were. He would talk about his own feelings and recollections and intentions in a way that deceived others, but he was first deceived himself.— HENRY CRABB ROBINSON (" Diary ").

Veracity of Lamb and Coleridge.

In temper he was quick, but easily appeased. He never affected that exemption from sensibility which has sometimes been mistaken for philosophy, and has conferred reputation upon little men. In a word, he exhibited his emotions in a fine, simple, natural manner. Contrary to the usual habit of wits ; no retort or reply by Lamb, however smart in character, ever gave pain.—BRYAN W. PROCTER (" Charles Lamb : a Memoir ").

Quick-tempered and sensitive.

He was restless and fond of walking. I do not think he could ride on horseback ; but he could walk during all the day.—BRYAN W. PROCTER (" Charles Lamb : a Memoir ").

Fond of walking.

Very curious was the antipathy of Charles to objects that are generally so pleasant to other men.

It was not a passing humor, but a life-long dislike. He admired the trees, and the meadows, and murmuring streams in poetry. I have heard him repeat some of Keats's beautiful lines in the Ode to the Nightingale, about the "pastoral eglantine," with great delight. But that was another thing : that was an object in its proper place : that was a piece of art. Long ago he had admitted that the mountains of Cumberland were grand objects "to look at, but" (as he said) "the houses in streets were the places to live in." I imagine that he would no more have received the former as an equivalent for his own modest home, than he would have accepted a portrait as a substitute for a friend. He was, beyond all other men whom I have met, essentially metropolitan. He loved "the sweet security of streets," as he said ; "I would set up my tabernacle there."— BRYAN W. PROCTER ("Charles Lamb : a Memoir ").

Dislike for country life.

"The country" was to Lamb precisely what London is to thoroughly country people born and bred, —who, however they may long to see it for the first time, and are lost in a week's empty admiration of its "sights and wonders,"—would literally die of homesickness if compelled to remain long in it. I remember, when wandering once with Lamb among the pleasant scenery about Enfield shortly after his retirement there, I was congratulating him on the change between these walks and his accustomed ones about Islington, Dalston, and the like. But I soon found that I was treading on tender ground, and he declared. afterwards, with a vehemence of expression extremely unusual with him, and almost with tears in his eyes, that the most squalid garret in the most confined and noisome purlieu of London would be a paradise to him, compared with the fairest dwelling placed in the loveliest scenery of "the country." "I *hate* the country!" he exclaimed, in a tone and with an emphasis which showed not only that the feeling came from the bottom of his soul, but that it was working ungentle and sinister results there, that he was himself almost alarmed at. . . . Away from London, Lamb's spirits seemed to shrink and retire inwards and his body to fade and wither like a plant in an uncongenial soil.—PETER G. PATMORE (" My Friends and Acquaintance ").

Dislike for country life.

When I speak of his extreme liking for London, it must not be supposed that he was insensible to great scenery. After his only visit to the Lake country, and beholding Skiddaw, he writes back to his host, " O ! its fine black head, and the bleak air at the top of it, with a prospect of mountains all about making you giddy. It was a day that will stand out like a mountain in my life ; " adding, however, " Fleet Street and the Strand are better places to live in, for good and all. I could not *live* in Skiddaw. I could spend there two or three years, but I must have a prospect of seeing Fleet Street at the end of that time, or I should mope and pine away." He loved even its smoke, and asserted that it suited his vision.—BRYAN W. PROCTER (" Charles Lamb : a Memoir ").

Town and country.

July 3*rd*, 1814.—A day of great pleasure. Charles Lamb and I walked to Enfield by Southgate, after

an early breakfast in his chambers. . . . After
tea, Lamb and I returned. The whole day delight-
fully fine, and the scenery very agreeable. Lamb
cared for the walk more than the scenery, for the
enjoyment of which he seems to have no great sus-
ceptibility. His great delight, even in preference
to a country walk, is a stroll in London. The shops
and the busy streets, such as Thames Street, Bank-
side, etc., are his great favorites. He, for the same
reason, has no great relish for landscape painting.
But his relish for historic painting is exquisite.—
HENRY CRABB ROBINSON (" Diary ").

Indiffer-
ence to
natural
scenery.

Some of Lamb's admirers, more zealous than dis-
creet, have maintained that he was really an enthusiastic lover of scenery. In view of all the facts,
such an assumption does not seem tenable. Wordsworth, however, appears to have held this view, if
we may judge from Caroline Fox's account of a talk
with him. Wordsworth declared that he himself
enjoyed city life, whereupon Caroline Fox said that
" Lamb's rhapsody on London might not then have
been sent to him in a spirit necessarily ironical.
'Oh, no,' he answered, 'and Lamb's abuse of the
country and his declared detestation of it was all affected ; he enjoyed it and entered into its beauties ;
besides, Lamb had too kindly and sympathetic a nature to detest anything.' "

There was an hereditary taint of insanity in the
family, which caused even Charles himself to be
placed, for a short time, in Hoxton Lunatic Asylum.
" The six weeks that finished last year and began

Insanity.

Insanity.

this (1796), your very humble servant spent very agreeably in a madhouse, at Hoxton." These are his words when writing to Coleridge.—BRYAN W. PROCTER ("Charles Lamb : a Memoir").

This also is to be added to his afflictions—not merely the fear, constantly impending that his fireside (as I said before) might be rendered desolate, and *that* by a sudden blow, as well as for an indefinite duration ; but also, the fear (not equally strong, but equally impending forever) that he himself, with all his splendid faculties, might, as by a flash of lightning, be swallowed up "in darkness infinite."—THOMAS DE QUINCEY ("Literary Reminiscences").

It is not true that he was ever deranged, or subjected to any restraint, shortly before his death. There never was the least symptom of mental disturbance in him after the time (1795–6) when he was placed for a few weeks in Hoxton Asylum, to allay a little nervous irritation.—BRYAN W. PROCTER ("Charles Lamb : a Memoir").

Life at home.

Whilst at home he had no curiosity for what passed beyond his own territory. His eyes were never truant ; no one ever saw him peering out of window, examining the crowds flowing by ; no one ever surprised him gazing on vacancy. "I lose myself," he says, "in other men's minds. When I am not walking I am reading ; I cannot sit and think ; books think for me." If it was not the time for his pipe, it was always the time for an old play, or for a talk with friends. In the midst of this society his own mind grew green again and blos-

somed, or, as he would have said, "burgeoned."—
BRYAN W. PROCTER ("Charles Lamb : a Memoir ").

The room in which he lived was plainly and
almost carelessly furnished. Let us enter it for a
moment. Its ornaments, you see, are principally *A fireside*
several long shelves of ancient books (those are his *glimpse.*
" ragged veterans "). Some of Hogarth's prints,
two after Leonardo da Vinci and Titian, and a portrait of Pope, enrich the walls. At the table sits an
elderly lady (in spectacles) reading ; whilst from an
old-fashioned chair by the fire springs up a little
spare man in black, with a countenance pregnant
with expression, deep lines in his forehead ; quick,
luminous, restless eyes, and a smile as sweet as ever
threw sunshine upon the human face. You see
that you are welcome. He speaks : " Well, boys,
how are you ? What's the news with you ? What
will you take ?"—BRYAN W. PROCTER (*Athenæum*,
January, 1835).

Invited to breakfast with a gentleman in the Temple, to meet Charles Lamb and his sister. . . .
There was a rap at the door at last, and enter a gen- *A breakfast*
tleman in black small-clothes and gaiters, short and *party.*
very slight in his person, his head set on his shoulders with a thoughtful, forward bent, his hair just
sprinkled with gray, a beautiful, deep-set eye, aqui-
line nose, and a very indescribable mouth. Whether
it expressed most humor or feeling, good nature or
a kind of whimsical peevishness, or twenty other
things which passed over it by turns, I cannot in
the least be certain. . . . As there was to be no

one else, we immediately drew round the breakfast table. I had set a large arm-chair for Miss Lamb. "Don't take it, Mary," said Lamb, pulling it away from her very gravely, "it appears as if you were going to have a tooth drawn." . . .

Nothing could be more delightful than the kindness and affection between the brother and the sister, though Lamb was continually taking advantage of her deafness to mystify her with the most singular gravity upon every subject that was started. "Poor Mary," said he, "she hears all of an epigram but the point." "What are you saying of me, Charles?" she asked. "Mr. Willis," said he, raising his voice, "*admires your Confessions of a Drunkard* very much, and I was saying that it was no merit of yours, that you understood the subject." We had been speaking of this admirable essay (which is his own), half an hour before. . . .

Mr. R. spoke of buying a book of Lamb's, a few days before, and I mentioned my having bought a copy of Elia the last day I was in America. . . . "What did you give for it?" said Lamb. "About seven and sixpence." "Permit me to pay you that," said he, and with the utmost earnestness he counted out the money upon the table. "I never yet wrote anything that would sell," he continued. "I am the publisher's ruin. My last poem won't sell a copy. Have you seen it, Mr. Willis?" I had not. "It's only eighteen pence, and I'll give you sixpence toward it;" and he described to me where I should find it sticking up in a shop-window in the Strand.

Lamb ate nothing, and complained in a querulous tone of the veal-pie. There was a kind of potted fish, . . . which he had expected our friend would procure for him. He inquired whether there was not a morsel left perhaps in the bottom of the last pot. Mr. R. was not sure. " Send and see," said Lamb, "and if the pot has been cleaned, bring me the cover. I think the sight of it would do me good." The cover was brought, upon which there was a picture of the fish. Lamb kissed it with a reproach-ful look at his friend, and then left the table, and began to wander round the room with a broken, uncertain step, as if he almost forgot to put one leg before the other. His sister rose after awhile, and commenced walking up and down, very much in the same manner, on the opposite side of the table, and in the course of half an hour they took their leave. —NATHANIEL P. WILLIS (" Pencillings by the Way ").[1]

A breakfast party.

The Lambs had heard of my being in solitary lodgings, and insisted on my coming to dine with them, which more than once I did in the winter of 1821–22. The mere reception by the Lambs was so full of goodness and hospitable feeling, that it kin-dled animation in the most cheerless or torpid of invalids. I cannot imagine that any *memorabilia* occurred during the visit. There were no strangers ; Charles Lamb, his sister, and myself made up the party. Even this was done in kindness. They knew that I should have been oppressed by an effort such as must be made in the society of strangers ; and they placed me by their own fireside where I could

A visit to the Lambs.

[1] Willis (Nathaniel Parker). Pencillings by the Way. 12mo. New York : Charles Scribner. 1853.

say as little or as much as I pleased. We dined about five o'clock, and it was one of the hospitalities inevitable to the Lambs, that any game which they might receive from rural friends in the course of the week, was reserved for the day of a friend's dining with them.

. In regard to wine, Lamb and myself had the same habit—perhaps it rose to the dignity of a principle —viz., to take a good deal *during* dinner—none *after* it. Consequently, as Miss Lamb (who drank only water) retired almost with the dinner itself, nothing remained for men of our principles, the vigor of which we had illustrated by taking rather too much of old port before the cloth was drawn, except taking amœbœan colloquy, or, in Dr. Johnson's phrase, a dialogue of brisk reciprocation. But this was impossible ; over Lamb, at this period of his life, there passed regularly, after taking wine, a brief eclipse of sleep. It descended upon him as softly as a shadow. In a gross person laden with superfluous flesh, and sleeping heavily, this would have been disagreeable ; but in Lamb, thin even to meagreness, spare and wiry as an Arab of the desert, or as Thomas Aquinas, wasted by scholastic vigils, the affection of sleep seemed rather a network of aerial gossamer than of earthly cobweb — more like a golden haze falling upon him gently from the heavens than a cloud exhaling upwards from the flesh. Motionless in his chair as a bust, breathing so gently as scarcely to seem entirely alive, he presented the image of repose midway between life and death like the repose of sculpture ; and to one who knew his history, a repose contrasting with the calamities and internal storms of his life. I have heard more persons than I can now distinctly recall, observe of Lamb when sleeping, that his countenance in that state assumed an expression almost seraphic, from its intellectual beauty of outline, its childlike simplicity, and its benignity. It could not be called a transfiguration that sleep worked in his face ; for his features wore essentially the same expression when waking ; but sleep spiritualized that expression, exalted it, and also harmonised it. Much of the change lay in that last process. The eyes it was that disturbed the unity of effect in Lamb's waking face. They gave a restlessness to the character of his intellect, shifting, like northern lights, through every mode of combination with fantastic playfulness, and sometimes by fiery gleams, obliterating for the moment that pure light of benignity which was the predominant reading on his features. —THOMAS DE QUINCEY (" Biographical Essays ").

A visit to the Lambs.

He took my arm, and we walked to the Temple, Lamb stammering out fine remarks as we walked, and when we reached his staircase, he detained me with an urgency which would not be denied, and we mounted to the top story, where an old petted servant, called Becky, was ready to receive us. We were soon seated beside a cheerful fire ; hot water and its better adjuncts were before us ; and Lamb insisted on my sitting with him while he smoked "one pipe." . . . How often the pipe and the glasses were replenished, I will not undertake to disclose ; but I can never forget the conversation : though the first, it was more solemn, and in higher

An evening in 1815.

mood, than any I ever after had with Lamb through the whole of our friendship. How it took such a turn between strangers, one of them a lad not quite twenty, I cannot tell ; but so it happened. We discoursed then of life and death, and our anticipation of a life beyond the grave. Lamb spoke of these awful themes with the simplest piety, but expressed his own fond cleavings to life—to all well-known accustomed things—and a shivering (not shuddering) sense of that which is to come, which he so finely indicated in his "New Year's Eve," years afterward. It was two o'clock before we parted.—THOMAS N. TALFOURD ("Letters of Charles Lamb ").

I availed myself of Charles Lamb's friendly invitation on Tuesday, August 5, 1834. On reaching his cottage—which stood back from the road (nearly opposite the church), between two houses which projected beyond it, and was screened by shrubs and trees—I found that he was out, taking his morning's stroll. I was admitted into a small, panelled, and agreeably shaded parlor. The modest room was hung round with engravings by Hogarth in dark frames. Books and magazines were scattered on the table and on the old-fashioned window seat. I chatted awhile with Miss Lamb—a meek, intelligent, very pleasant, but rather deaf elderly lady, who told me that her brother had been gratified by parts of my poem (" Emily de Wilton ") and had read them to her. " Elia " came in soon after —a short thin man. His dress was black, and he wore a capacious coat, breeches and gaiters, and a white neck-handkerchief. His dark and shaggy hair, eyebrows, heated face and very piercing jet-black eyes gave to his appearance a singularly wild and striking expression. The sketch of him in *Fraser's Magazine* gives a true idea of his dress and figure, but his portraits fail to represent adequately his remarkably "fine Titian head, full of dumb eloquence," as Hazlitt described it. He grasped me cordially by the hand, sat down, and taking a bottle from a cupboard behind him, mixed some rum and water. On another occasion his sister objected to this operation, and he refrained. Presently after he said, "May I have a little drop now? only a *leetle* drop?" "No," said she; "be a good boy." At last, however, he prevailed, and took his usual draught. On each visit (that of August 5 having been quickly succeeded by another) I found he required to be drawn into conversation. He would throw out a playful remark, and then pause awhile. He spoke by fits and starts, and had a slight impediment in his utterance which made him, so to say, grunt once or twice before he began a sentence; but his tones were loud and rich.

He told me that he knew his letters before he could speak. . . . He hated the country and loved to walk on the London road, because then he would fancy that he was wending thither.[1]—J. F. RUSSEL (*Notes and Queries*, 1882).

He delighted in children, and in telling them strange, wild stories. . . . A daughter of Sheri-

Charles Lamb at home.

---

[1] For further accounts of Lamb at home, see p. 271 *et seq.*

dan Knowles used to tell how, as a very little girl, she had been taken out by Charles Lamb for a day's holiday to see all the shows, and how on meeting a Punch's show, they sat down together on a door-step and saw the entertainment through—not only one, but a whole series, which for him as well as for his little companion seemed to have an inexhaustible charm. . . . Once too—I have heard on the same authority—he saw a group of hungry little faces wistfully looking into the window of a pastry-cook's shop; he went in and came out, and distributed cakes all around. — PERCY FITZGERALD (" Charles Lamb," etc.).[1]

Fondness for children.

He never kept a letter; except a couple or so: and heartily despised " relics," especially of the sentimental sort.   Thus, when a traveller brought him acorns, from Virgil's tomb, he amused himself with throwing them at the hackney coachmen that passed by.—PERCY FITZGERALD ("Charles Lamb," etc.).

Letters and relics.

At Mr. Morgan's house in Berners Street, I first saw Charles Lamb, who was intimate in a literary coterie composed of persons with principles very opposite to those of Coleridge.   Somebody, wishing to give the latter a favorable impression of these people, spoke of Lamb's friendship for them; and Coleridge replied, " Charles Lamb's character is a *sacred* one with me; no associations that he may form can hurt the purity of his mind, but it is not, therefore, necessary that I should see all men with his

Coleridge's tribute.

[1] Fitzgerald (Percy).   Charles Lamb : his Friends, his Haunts, and his Books.   12mo.   London, 1866.

eyes." There can be no doubt that it was of Lamb he spoke in the following passage from the "Table Talk :"—" Nothing ever left a stain on that gentle creature's mind, which looked upon the degraded men and things around him like moonshine on a dunghill, which shines and takes no pollution. All things are shadows to him, except those which move his affections."—CHARLES R. LESLIE (" Autobiographical Recollections ").

Coleridge's tribute.

Hazlitt has alluded *con amore* to these meetings[1] in his Essay " On the Conversation of Authors," and has reported one of the most remarkable discussions which graced them in his Essay " On Persons One would Wish to have Seen." . . . In this was a fine touch of Lamb's pious feeling, breaking through his fancies and his humors, which Hazlitt has recorded, but which cannot be duly appreciated, except by those who can recall to memory the suffused eye and quivering lip with which he stammered out a reference to the name which he would not utter— " There is only one other person I can ever think of after this," said he. " If Shakespeare was to come into the room, we should all rise to meet him ; but if *That Person* were to come into it, we should all fall down and kiss the hem of his garment."— THOMAS N. TALFOURD (" Letters of Charles Lamb ").

Reverence.

When they left off housekeeping and went to reside at Enfield, they boarded for some time in the house of a reputable old couple, to whom they paid, for the plainest possible accommodation, a price al-

Ill-requited kindness.

---

[1] At Lamb's chambers in Inner Temple-lane.

Ill-requited kindness.

most sufficient to keep all the household twice over, but where, nevertheless, they were expected to pay for every extra cup of tea, or any other refreshment, they might offer to any occasional visitor. Lamb soon found out the mistake he had made in connecting himself with these people, and did not fail to philosophize (to his friends) on their blind stupidity, in thus risking what was almost their sole means of support, in order to screw an extra shilling out of his easy temper. . . . Yet this sort of thing Lamb bore patiently, month after month, for years, under the feeling, or rather on the express plea of " What was to become of the poor people if he left them ? " The Protectionists never pleaded harder for their " vested rights " than did Lamb for the claims of these people to continue to live upon him, and affront him every now and then into the bargain, because they had been permitted to begin to do so.—PETER G. PATMORE ("My Friends and Acquaintance ").

A delicacy for a sheep-stealer.

When a young lady, who was staying at his house, had been making some clothes for the child of a poor gypsy woman in the neighborhood, whose husband was afterward convicted of sheep-stealing, he would not allow her (the young lady) to quit the village without going to see and take leave of her unhappy *protégée,*—on the express plea that otherwise the felon's wife might imagine that she had heard of her husband's " misfortune," and was ashamed to go near her. " I have a delicacy for a sheep-stealer," said he. There are many who duly appreciate . . . the beauty and the merits of this delicacy to the personal feelings of others, . . . but I never knew any one who was capable of uniformly, at all costs, *practising* it, except Charles Lamb and William Hazlitt,—both of whom extended it to the lowest and vilest of man and woman kind ; would give the wall to a beggar if it became a question which of the two should cede it, and if they had visited a convicted felon in his cell, would have been on tenterhooks all the time, lest anything might drop from them to indicate that they had less consideration for the object of their visit than if he had been the most "respectable" of men.—PETER G. PATMORE (" My Friends and Acquaintance ").

A delicacy for a sheep-stealer.

From much that I have said of Charles Lamb it will have been gathered that he was little qualified to live in what is called "the world." It may seem paradoxical to say so, but he was quite as little qualified to live out of it. In some sort wedded both to solitude and to society, so far from being able to make himself "happy with either," each was equally incapable of filling and satisfying his affections. The truth is that, deep and yet gentle as those affections were, his daily life gave token that in their early development they had received a sinister bias which never afterwards quitted them—perchance a blow which struck them from the just centre on which they seemed to have been originally destined to revolve, in a circle of the most perfect beauty and harmony.

A character study.

Those of Lamb's friends who felt a real and deep interest in his intellectual character, and its results on his personal happiness, must, I think, have seen

III.—11

this influence at work in almost every movement of his mind and heart, as these developed themselves in his ordinary life and conversation ; for in his published writings the evidences I allude to do not appear, at least in any distinct and tangible form. There, in short, and there only, was Charles Lamb his own man—his early, natural, original self. . . .

It would be a task as difficult as delicate, to adduce detailed evidence of the peculiar condition of mind and heart, in Charles Lamb, to which I have just alluded ; but I think that some, at least, of his intimates, will call to mind such evidence, especially in connection with the last few years of his life. I appeal to those intimates whether they ever saw Lamb wholly at his ease for half an hour together—wholly free from that restlessnesss which is incompatible with mental tranquillity ; whether they ever saw him wrapt in that deep and calm *repose*, in the absence of which there can be no actual, soul-felt satisfaction.

If, indeed, they have seen him alone in his book-room—he unknowing of their presence—hanging in rapt sympathy over the tattered pages of one of his beloved old folios . . . they may have seen him in a condition of mind analagous to that self-centred repose which is the soul of human happiness, but not identical with it.

It is not the less true that Lamb was, for the moment, delighted at the advent of an unlooked-for friend, even though he was thereby interrupted in the midst of one of these beatific communings. But they must have read his character ill, or with little interest, who did not perceive that, after the pleasant excitement of the moment was over, he became restless, uneasy, and "busied about many things"—about anything rather than the settling down quietly into a condition of mind or temper, even analogous to that from which the new arrival had irretrievably roused him, for that day at least. Feeling the unseasonable disturbance *as* such, yet not for a moment admitting it to be such, even to himself, he became *over*-anxious to show you how welcome you were,—doing half a dozen things in a breath, to prove the feeling,—every one of which, if read aright, proved something very like the reverse. If it happened to be about dinner-time, he would go into the kitchen to see if it was ready, or put on his hat and go out to order an additional supply of porter, or open a bottle of wine and pour some out,—taking a glass himself to set you the example, as he innocently imagined,—but, in reality, to fortify himself for the task of hospitality that you had imposed upon him ; anything, in fact, but sit quietly down by the fire, and enjoy your company, or let you enjoy his. And if you happened to arrive when dinner or tea was over, he was perfectly fidgety, and almost cross, till you were fairly seated at the meal which he and his excellent sister insisted on providing for you, whether you would or not.

It is true that, by the time all these preliminaries were over, he had recovered his ease, and was really glad to see you ; and if you had come to stay the night, when the shutters were shut, and the candles came, and you were comfortably seated round the fire, he was evidently pleased and bettered by the

Restless-ness.

Company irksome to him.

Company irksome to him.
occasion thus afforded for a dish of cosey table-talk. But not the less true is it that every knock at the door sent a pang to his heart ; and this without any distinction of persons : whoever it might be, he equally welcomed and wished them away, and all for the same reason—namely, that they called him from the company of his own thoughts, or those still better communings with the thoughts of his dead friends, with whom he could hold an intercourse unclogged by any actual bodily presence.— PETER G. PATMORE (" My Friends and Acquaintance)."

Fondness for animals.
As an instance of Charles Lamb's sympathy with dumb beasts, his two friends here named once saw him get up from table, while they were dining with him and his sister at Enfield, open the street-door, and give admittance to a stray donkey into the front strip of garden, where there was a grass-plot, which he said seemed to possess more attraction for the creature than the short turf of the common on Chase-side, opposite to the house where the Lambs then dwelt. This mixture of the humorous in manner and the sympathetic in feeling always more or less tinged the sayings and the doings of beloved Charles Lamb ; there was a constant blending of the overtly whimsical expression or act with betrayed inner kindness and even pathos of sentiment. Beneath this sudden opening of his gate to a stray donkey that it might feast on his garden grass while he himself ate his dinner, possibly lurked some stung sense of wanderers unable to get a meal they hungered for when others revelled

in plenty,—a kind of pained fancy finding vent in playful deed or speech, that frequently might be traced by those who enjoyed his society.—C. and M. C. CLARKE (" Recollections of Writers ").

A visit of Coleridge was always regarded by Lamb, as an opportunity to afford a rare gratification to a few friends, who, he knew, would prize it ; *Sharing a treat.* and I well remember the flush of prideful pleasure which came over his face as he would hurry, on his way to the India House, into the office in which I was a pupil, and stammer out the welcome invitation for the evening.   This was true self-sacrifice ; for Lamb would have infinitely preferred having his inspired friend to himself.—THOMAS N. TALFOURD (" Final Memorials of Charles Lamb ").

Charles Lamb, William Hazlitt, and Leigh Hunt, formed a remarkable trio of men, each of whom was decidedly different from the others.   Only one *A remarkable trio.* of them (Hunt) cared much for praise.   Hazlitt's sole ambition was to sell his essays, which he rated scarcely beyond their marketable value ; and Lamb saw enough of the manner in which praise and censure were at that time distributed, to place any value on immediate success.   Of posterity neither of them thought.

Leigh Hunt, from temperament, was more alive to pleasant influences (sunshine, freedom for work, rural walks, complimentary words) than the others. Hazlitt cared little for these things ; a fierce argument or a well-contested game at racketts was more to his taste ; whilst Lamb's pleasures (except, perhaps, from his pipe) lay amongst the books of the old English writers. ' His soul delighted in communion with ancient generations, more especially A remarkable trio. with men who had been unjustly forgotten. Hazlitt's mind attached itself to abstract subjects ; Lamb's was more practical, and embraced men. Hunt was somewhat indifferent to persons as well as to things, except in the cases of Shelley and Keats, and his own family ; yet he liked poetry and poetical subjects.

Hazlitt (who was ordinarily very shy) was the best talker of the three. Lamb said the most pithy and brilliant things. Hunt displayed the most ingenuity. All three sympathised often with the same persons or the same books ; and this, no doubt, cemented the intimacy that existed between them for so many years. Moreover, each of them understood the others, and placed just value on their objections when any difference of opinion (not infrequent) arose between them. Without being debaters, they were accomplished talkers. They did not argue for the sake of conquest, but to strip off the mists and perplexities which sometimes obscure truth. These men—who lived long ago—had a great share of my regard. They were all slandered, chiefly by men who knew little of them, and nothing of their good qualities ; or by men who saw them only through the mist of political or religious animosity. Perhaps it was partly for this reason that they came nearer to my heart.—Bryan W. Procter (" Charles Lamb : a Memoir ").

Lamb's charity extended to all things. I never heard him speak spitefully of any author. He thought that every one should have a clear stage, unobstructed. His heart, young at all times, never grew hard or callous during life. There was always in 'it a tender spot, which Time was unable to touch. He gave away *greatly*, when the amount of his means is taken into consideration ; he gave away money —even annuities, I believe—to old impoverished friends whose wants were known to him. I remember that once, when we were sauntering together on Pentonville Hill, and he noticed great depression in me, which he attributed to want of money, he said, suddenly, in his stammering way, " My dear boy, I—I have a quantity of useless things. I have now—in my desk, a—a hundred pounds—that I don't—don't *know* what to do with. Take it." I was much touched ; but I assured him that my depression did not arise from want of money.—BRYAN W. PROCTER (" Charles Lamb : a Memoir ").

Always charitable.

He used to seek out occasions of devoting a part of his surplus to those of his friends whom he believed it would really serve, and almost forced loans, or gifts in the disguise of loans, upon them. If he thought one, in such a position, would be the happier for 50*l.* or 100*l.*, he would carefully procure a note for the sum, and, perhaps, for days before he might meet the object of his friendly purpose, keep the note in his waistcoat pocket, burning in it to be produced, and, when the occasion arrived—" in the sweet of the night—" he would crumple it up in his hand and stammer out his difficulty of disposing of a little money ; " I don't know what to do with it—

Benevolence.

pray take it—pray use it—you will do me a kindness if you will "—he would say ; and it was hard
to disoblige him !

Let any one who has been induced to regard
Lamb as a poor, slight, excitable, and excited being, consider that such acts as these were not infrequent—that he exercised hospitality of a substantial kind, without stint, all his life—that he
spared no expense for the comfort of his sister,
there only lavish—and that he died leaving sufficient
to accomplish all his wishes for survivors—and
think what the sturdy quality of his goodness must
have been amidst all the heart-aches, and head-
aches of his life—and ask the virtue which has
been supported by strong nerves, whether it has
often produced any good to match it ?—THOMAS N.
TALFOURD (" Final Memorials of Charles Lamb ").

As to his kindness and practical benevolence Mr.
Ogilvie [1] declared that it could not be overstated.
His sympathies were so easily won that he was
often imposed upon, yet he never learned to be
suspicious. He had been known to wear a coat six
months longer, that he might spare a little money
to some needy acquaintance. There was hardly
ever a time when he did not have somebody living
upon him. If he was freed from one client, another
would soon arise to take his place. A poor literary aspirant, or vagabond, especially, he could not
resist, and he regularly had one or more on his
hands. He would even take them to his house,

---

[1] A fellow-clerk of Lamb's.

and let them stay there weeks and months together.
—JOSEPH H. TWICHELL (*Scribner's Monthly*, March,
1876).

I knew Lamb, and I know certain cases in which
he was concerned—cases which it is difficult to
publish with any regard to the feelings of persons
now living, but which (if published in all their circumstances) would show him to be the very noblest
of human beings. He was a man in a sense more
eminent than would be conceivable by many people,
princely—nothing short of that—in his beneficence.
Many liberal people I have known in this world—
many who were charitable in the widest sense—
many munificent people, but never any one upon
whom, for bounty, for indulgence and forgiveness,
for charitable construction of doubtful or mixed
actions, and for regal munificence, you might have
thrown yourself with so absolute a reliance as upon
this comparatively poor Charles Lamb.—THOMAS
DE QUINCEY (" Literary Reminiscences ").

*Princely
beneficence.*

Her relapses were not dependent on the seasons;
they came in hot summers and with the freezing
winters. The only remedy seems to have been extreme quiet when any slight symptom of uneasiness
was apparent. Charles (poor fellow) had to live,
day and night, in the society of a person who was
—mad! If any exciting talk occurred, he had to
dismiss his friend with a whisper. If any stupor
or extraordinary silence was observed, then he had
to rouse her instantly. He has been seen to take
the kettle from the fire and place it for a moment

*Constant
care of his
sister.*

on her head-dress, in order to startle her into recollection. He lived in a state of constant anxiety; —and there was no help.—BRYAN W. PROCTER ("Charles Lamb : a Memoir").

Constant care of his sister.

The constant impendency of this giant sorrow saddened to "the Lambs" even their holidays; as the journey which they both regarded as the relief and charm of the year was frequently followed by a seizure; and, when they ventured to take it, a strait-waistcoat, carefully packed by Miss Lamb herself, was their constant companion. Sad experience, at last, induced the abandonment of the annual excursion, and Lamb was contented with walks in and near London, during the interval of labor. Miss Lamb experienced, and full well understood, premonitory symptoms of the attack, in restlessness, low fever, and the inability to sleep; and, as gently as possible, prepared her brother for the duty he must soon perform; and thus, unless he could stave off the terrible separation till Sunday, obliged him to ask leave of absence from the office as if for a day's pleasure—a bitter mockery! On one occasion Mr. Charles Lloyd met them, slowly pacing together a little footpath in Hoxton fields, both weeping bitterly, and found on joining them, that they were taking their solemn way to the accustomed Asylum. —THOMAS N. TALFOURD ("Final Memorials of Charles Lamb").

On the following night, according to his promise, Mr. Lamb honored us with a visit, accompanied by his sister, Mr. and Mrs. Hood, and a few others hastily gathered together for the occasion. On entering the room, Mr. Lamb seemed to have forgotten that any previous introduction had taken place. "Allow me, madam," said he "to introduce to you, my sister Mary; she's a very good woman, but she drinks!" "Charles, Charles," said Miss Lamb, imploringly (her face at the same time covered with blushes), "how can you say such a thing?" "Why," rejoined he, "you know it's a fact; look at the redness of your face. Did I not see you in your cups at nine o'clock this morning?" "For shame, Charles," returned his sister; "what will our friends think?" "Don't mind him, my dear Miss Lamb," said Mrs. Hood, soothingly; "I will answer that the cups were only breakfast-cups full of coffee."—MARY BALMANNO ("Pen and Pencil").[1]

Of middle height, with brown, and rather ruddy complexion, gray eyes expressive of sense and shrewdness, but neither large nor brilliant; his head and features well-shaped, and the general expression of his countenance quiet, kind, and observant, undergoing rapid changes in conversation, as did his manner, variable as an April day, particularly to his sister, whose saint-like good humor and patience were as remarkable as his strange and whimsical modes of trying them. But the brother and sister perfectly understood each other, and "Charles," as she always called him, would not have been the "Charles" of her loving heart without the pranks and oddities which he was continually playing off

---

[1] Balmanno (Mary). Pen and Pencil. 8vo. New York: D. Appleton & Co. 1858.

upon her—and which were only outnumbered by the instances of affection, and evidences of ever watchful solicitude with which he surrounded her. —MARY BALMANNO (" Pen and Pencil ").

Last hours.

On Friday evening Mr. Ryle, of the India House, . . . called on me, and informed me that he was in danger. I went over to Edmonton on the following morning, and found him very weak, and nearly insensible to things passing around him. Now and then a few words were audible, from which it seemed that his mind, in its feebleness, was intent on kind and hospitable thoughts. His last correspondent, Mr. Childs, had sent a present of a turkey, instead of the suggested pig ; and the broken sentences which could be heard, were of some meeting of friends to partake of it. . . . In less than an hour afterwards, his voice gradually grew fainter, as he still murmured the names of Moxon, Procter, and some other old friends, and he sank into death as placidly as into sleep.— THOMAS N. TALFOURD (" Letters of Charles Lamb ").

Heroic life.

The fact that distinguished Charles Lamb from other men was his entire devotion to one grand and tender purpose. There is, probably, a romance involved in every life. In his life it exceeded that of others. In gravity, in acuteness, in his noble battle with a great calamity, it was beyond the rest. Neither pleasure nor toil ever distracted him from his holy purpose. Everything was made subservient to it. He had an insane sister, who, in a moment of uncontrollable madness, had unconsciously destroyed her own mother ; and to protect and save this sister—a gentle woman, who had watched like a mother over his own infancy—the whole length of his life was devoted.   What he endured, through the space of nearly forty years, from the incessant fear and frequent recurrence of his sister's insanity, can now only be conjectured.   In this constant and uncomplaining endurance, and in his steady adherence to a great principle of conduct, his life was heroic.—BRYAN W. PROCTER ("Charles Lamb: a Memoir").

Heroic life.

There was no sadness assumed by the attendants, but we all talked with warm affection of dear Mary Lamb, and that most delightful of creatures, her brother Charles—of all the men of genius I ever knew, the one the most intensely and universally to be loved.—HENRY CRABB ROBINSON ("Diary," etc.).

At Mary Lamb's funeral.

No man, it is my belief, was ever loved or lamented more sincerely than Charles Lamb.—BRYAN W. PROCTER ("Charles Lamb: a Memoir").

WILLIAM HAZLITT.

1778–1830.

yours
W. Hazlitt

INTRODUCTORY NOTE.

EAGER powers, restlessly squandering themselves, for the want of effectual discipline ;
downright sincerity of thought and speech ; persist-
ent adherence to convictions ; enthusiasm blazing
beyond all limits of discretion ; hot and vehement
passions unsubdued by the dictates of judgment or
the mastery of a resolute will ; strong loves, and
bitter hatreds—such are the impressions of character which we receive from the life of Hazlitt.

His convictions had the intensity of passions,
and he never surrendered them.   To him men were
either angels or demons.   Had he been Hamlet he
would have known whether the Ghost's "intents"
were "wicked or charitable," whether he brought
with him "airs from heaven, or blasts from hell ; "
and his mind once made up that the spirit which he
had seen was in truth a devil, the testimony of all the
heavenly band of seraphim could not have shaken
him.

At one period he was driven nearly, if not quite
insane, by his infatuation about a servant girl,
whom his vivid imagination had idealized into a
goddess—nay, rather into a transcendent creature,
combining in her own person the attributes of all

III.—12

the goddesses. His life was feverish and unhappy. How could it have been otherwise, with a nature open to such hallucinations, and subject to such disastrous upheavals ?

Hazlitt's life was written by his grandson, William Carew Hazlitt. This work has no literary quality higher than smartness, and is chiefly remarkable for its want of decent reticence in regard to matters which did not need publicity. It is a pity that there is no better biography of so interesting a man. Alexander Ireland's bibliography of the works of Hazlitt and Leigh Hunt, contains a large amount of information, gathered from the reports of contemporary writers ; and much interesting and valuable matter will be found in P. G. Patmore's "My Friends and Acquaintance," and Barry Cornwall's " Recollections of Writers."

LEADING EVENTS OF HAZLITT'S LIFE.

1778.	Born, April 10th, at Maidstone, Kent.
1783.—(Aged 5.)	Taken to the United States of America by his parents.
1786.—(Aged 8.)	Returns to England.
1793.—(Aged 15.)	A scholar in the Unitarian College, Hackney.[1]
1802.—(Aged 24.)	An art student in Paris.
1805.—(Aged 27.)	Publishes " Essay on the Principles of Human Action."
1806.—(Aged 28.)	Publishes " Free Thoughts on Public Affairs."
1808.—(Aged 30.)	Marries Miss Sarah Stoddart.
1812.—(Aged 34.)	Lectures upon philosophy, before the Russell Institute, London.

[1] Hazlitt was, for the most part, educated at home, by his father, an Unitarian minister.

1814.—(Ag ed 36.) Contributes to the *Edinburgh Review*. Theatrical critic of the *Morning Chronicle*.

1817.—(Aged 39.) "The Round Table" published, the joint work of Leigh Hunt and himself. Publishes "Characters of Shakespeare's Plays."

1818.—(Aged 40.) Lectures upon the English poets, before the Surrey Institute, London. Publishes "A View of the English Stage."

1819.—(Aged 41.) Lectures upon the English comic writers, before the Surrey Institute, London.

1820.—(Aged 42.) Lectures upon the dramatic literature of the age of Elizabeth, before the Surrey Institute, London.

1822.—(Aged 44.) Divorced from his wife. Writes for *The Liberal*.

1823.—(Aged 45.) Publishes "Liber Amoris."

1824.—(Aged 46.) Marries Mrs. Bridgewater, a widow, and goes abroad with her.

1825.—(Aged 47.) Separated from his wife. Returns to England. Publishes "The Spirit of the Age."

1828.—(Aged 50.) Publishes the "Life of Napoleon," vols. 1 and 2.

1830.—(Aged 52 years and 5 months.) Publishes the "Life of Napoleon," vols. 3 and 4, and "Conversations of James Northcote." Dies, September 18th.

WILLIAM HAZLITT.

Precocity.

T HE accounts of Hazlitt's childhood show that
he was an abnormally precocious boy. When
he was twelve years old he went to Liverpool, upon
a visit to some family friends, and wrote letters to
his father containing curiously mature moral and
religious reflections, and considerations of political
issues. All of these boyish letters are remarkable.
They are to be found in W. C. Hazlitt's "Memoirs of
W. Hazlitt." The following extract will give an idea
of their general character: "Saturday afternoon
I . . . went to a Mrs. Bartton's, who appeared
to be an inhospitable English prim 'lady,' if such
she may be called. She asked us, as if she were
afraid we would accept it, if we would stay to tea.
And at the other English person's, for I am sure she
belongs to no other country than to England, I got
such a surfeit of their ceremonial unsociality, that
I could not help wishing myself in America. I had
rather people would tell one to go out of the house
than ask one to stay, and, at the same time, be trembling all over, for fear one should take a slice of
meat, or a dish of tea, with them. Such as these require an Horace or a Shakespeare to describe them."

A year later, when he was thirteen years old, he
wrote a letter upon the proceedings against Dr.

Priestley, which was published in the *Shrewsbury Chronicle.* The style of this composition is so phenomenal, considering the age of its writer, that it may be worth while to give a specimen of it : " Religious persecution is the bane of all religion ; and the friends of persecution are the worst enemies religion has ; and of all persecutions, that of calumny is the most intolerable. Any other kind of persecution can affect our outward circumstances only, our properties, our lives ; but this may affect our characters for ever.

"And here I shall conclude, staying only to remind your anti-Priestlian correspondents, that when they presume to attack the character of Dr. Priestley, they do not so much resemble the wren pecking at the eagle, as the owl, attempting by the flap of her wings to hurl Mount Etna into the ocean ; and that while Dr. Priestley's name 'shall flourish in immortal youth,' and his memory be respected and revered by posterity, prejudice no longer blinding the understandings of men, theirs will be forgotten in obscurity, or only remembered as the friends of bigotry and persecution, the most odious of all characters."

After this, it is not surprising to learn that when he was fourteen he wrote an " Essay upon Laws," which formed the germ of one of his later works, " A Project for a New Theory of Civil and Criminal Legislation." Truly, this must have been a decidedly formidable boy!

For depth, force, and variety of intellectual expression, a finer head and face than Hazlitt's was never seen. I speak of them when his countenance was not dimmed and obscured by illness, or clouded and deformed by those fearful indications of internal passion which he never even attempted to conceal. The expression of Hazlitt's face when anything was said in his presence that seriously offended him, or when any peculiarly painful recollection passed across his mind, was truly awful—more so than can be conceived as within the capacity of the human countenance ; except, perhaps, by those who have witnessed Edmund Kean's last scene of " Sir Giles Overreach " from the front row of the pit. But when he was in good health, and in a tolerable humor with himself and the world, his face was more truly and entirely answerable to the intellect that spoke through it, than any other I ever saw, either in life or on canvas ; and its crowning portion, the brow and forehead, was, to my thinking, quite unequaled, for mingled capacity and beauty.

Personal appearance.

For those who desire a more particular description, I will add that Hazlitt's features though not cast in any received classical mould, were regular in their formation, perfectly consonant with each other, and so finely " chiseled " (as the phrase is), that they produced a much more prominent and striking effect than their scale of size might have led one to expect. The forehead, as I have hinted, was magnificent; the nose precisely that (combining strength with lightness and elegance) which physiognomists have assigned as evidence of a fine and highly cultivated taste ; though there was a peculiar character about the nostrils, like that observable in those of a fiery and unruly horse. The mouth, from its ever-changing form and character, could scarcely be described, except as to its astonishingly varied power of expression, which was equal to, and greatly resembled, that of Edmund Kean. His eyes, I should say, were not good. They were never brilliant, and there was a furtive and at times a sinister look about them, as they glanced suspiciously from under their overhanging brows, that conveyed a very unpleasant impression to those who did not know him. And they were seldom directed frankly and fairly towards you ; as if he were afraid that you might read in them what was passing in his mind concerning you. His head was nobly formed and placed ; with (until the last few years of his life) a profusion of coal-black hair, richly curled ; and his person was of the middle height, rather slight, but well-formed and put together.

Yet all these advantages were worse than thrown away, by the strange and ungainly manner that at times accompanied them. Hazlitt entered a room as if he had been brought back to it in custody ; he shuffled sidelong to the nearest chair, sat himself down upon one corner of it, dropped his hat and his eyes upon the floor, and, after having exhausted his stock of conventional small talk in the words, " It's a fine day " (whether it was so or not), seemed to resign himself moodily to his fate. And if the talk did not take a turn that roused or pleased him, thus he would sit, silent and half-absorbed, for half an hour, or half a minute, as the case might be, and then get up suddenly, with a " Well, good morning," shuffle back to the door, and blunder his way out, audibly muttering curses on his folly, for wittingly

putting himself in the way of becoming the laugh-
ing-stock of — the servants! — PETER G. PATMORE
("My Friends and Acquaintance").

In person Mr. Hazlitt was of the middle size, with
a handsome and eager countenance, worn by sickness and thought; and dark hair, which had curled
stiffly over the temples, and was of late years
sprinkled with gray. His gait was slouching and
awkward, and his dress neglected; but when he began to talk, he could not be mistaken for a common
man.—THOMAS N. TALFOURD ("Thoughts upon W.
Hazlitt").[1]

Hazlitt was of the middle size, with eager, expressive eyes; near which his black hair, sprinkled
sparely with gray, curled round in a wiry, resolute
manner. His gray eyes, not remarkable in color,
expanded into great expression when occasion de-
manded it. Being very shy, however, they often
evaded your steadfast look. They never (as has
been asserted by some one) had a sinister expression; but they sometimes flamed with indignant
glances, when their owner was moved to anger;
like the eyes of other angry men. . . . His
mode of walking was loose, weak, and unsteady;
although his arms displayed strength, which he used
to put forth when he played at rackets with Martin
Burney and others.—BRYAN W. PROCTER ("Recollections of Men of Letters").

---

[1] Hazlitt (William). Literary Remains. 2 vols., 8vo. London,
1836.

*Personal
appearance.*
My first meeting with Mr. Hazlitt took place at
the house of Leigh Hunt, where I met him at supper. I expected to see a severe, defiant-looking
being. I met a grave man, diffident, almost awkward in manner, whose appearance did not impress
me with much respect. He had a quick, restless eye,
however, which opened eagerly when any good or
bright observation was made.—BRYAN W. PROCTER
("Recollections of Men of Letters ").

Dress.
He was untidy in his dress as a rule, and with
this untidiness went, as is mostly the case, a prodi-
gality. . . . He appeared to best advantage
when he was attired for some special occasion. A
gentleman (since dead) who knew him well during
the last thirteen years of his life, said that he was
never more astonished than when he saw Mr. Hazlitt
accoutred in readiness to go to dinner at Mr. Curran's.
He wore a blue coat and gilt buttons, black smalls,
silk stockings, and a white cravat, and he looked
the gentleman. But he did not often do himself
this justice ; the processes of the toilet proved irksome.—WILLIAM C. HAZLITT (" Memoir of W. Hazlitt ").

*Conversa-
tion.*
It has been supposed that Hazlitt was dogmatical
and fond of controversy, and that he resented any
opposition to his opinions. This is an error. He
liked discussion—fair, free talk, upon subjects that
interested him ; but few men ever yielded more
readily to argument, for few ever sought truth more
sincerely. He had no overweening sense of his own

superiority ; indeed, as far as I could perceive, he was
utterly without vanity. . . . In his conversation
he was plain, amusing, convincing. There was nothing of the ambitious or florid style, which is sometimes perceptible in his writings. He was rarely eloquent. Once or twice, when stung by some pertina-
cious controversialist, I have known him exhibit eloquent and impetuous declamation, but in general he
used the most familiar phrases, and made truth, rather
than triumph, the object of discussion. He enjoyed
anecdotes illustrative of character, spoke pithily
upon occasion, and, when in good spirits and good
humor, was the most delightful gossip in the world !
—ANON. (*New Monthly Magazine*, 1830).[1]

*Conversa-
tion.*

In the company of persons with whom he was
not familiar, his bashfulness was painful ; but when
he became entirely at ease, and entered on a favorite topic, no one's conversation was ever more delightful. He did not talk for effect—to dazzle, or
surprise, or annoy—but with the most simple and
honest desire to make his view of the subject entirely apprehended by his hearer. There was sometimes an obvious struggle to do this to his own
satisfaction : he seemed laboring to drag his thought
to light from its deep lurking place ; and, with
modest distrust of that power of expression which
he had found so late in life, he often betrayed a
fear that he had failed to make himself understood,
and recurred to the subject again and again, that
he might be assured he had succeeded.

---

[1] The article from which the foregoing extract is made, is attributed to Barry Cornwall.

In argument he was candid and liberal : there was nothing about him pragmatical or exclusive. . . . He loved "to hear the chimes at midnight," without considering them as a summons to rise. At these seasons, when in his happiest mood, he used to dwell on the conversational powers of his friends, and live over again the delightful hours he had passed with them ; repeat the pregnant puns that one had made ; tell over again a story with which another had convulsed the room ; or expand in the eloquence of a third ; always best pleased when he could detect some talent which was unregarded by the world, and giving alike, to the celebrated and the unknown, due honor.—THOMAS N. TALFOURD ("Thoughts upon W. Hazlitt ").

I found at the conclusion of the evening that when any question arose, the most sensible reply always came from him. Although the process was not too obvious, he always seemed to have reasoned with himself before he uttered a sentence.—BYRAN W. PROCTER (" Recollections of Men of Letters ").

He was accustomed to speak low, . . . with his chin bent in and his eyes widely expanded ; and his voice and manner, as a rule, were apt to communicate an impression of querulousness. His was the tone of a person who related to you a succession of grievances. But when he entered on a theme which pleased or animated him, or when he was in the presence of those whom he knew well, and *trusted*, he cast off a good deal of this air, and his demeanor was easy, yet impassioned.—WILLIAM C. HAZLITT (" Memoir of W. Hazlitt ").

1799.—Another interesting acquaintance L made at this period was with William Hazlitt—a man who has left a deservedly high reputation as a critic ; but at the time I first knew him he was struggling against a great difficulty of expression, which rendered him by no means a general favorite in society. His bashfulness, want of words, slovenliness of dress, etc., made him sometimes the object of ridicule. It will be better, perhaps, if I confine myself at present to describing him as he was at this early period of our acquaintance. He was the younger brother of John Hazlitt, the miniature painter. His first design was to be a dissenting minister ; and for that purpose he went to the Unitarian New College, Hackney. He afterwards thought of becoming a painter, and lived with his brother. At our first interview I saw that he was an extraordinary man. He had few friends, and was flattered by my attentions. . . . At this time he was excessively shy, especially in the company of young ladies, who on their part were very apt to make fun of him. The prettiest girl of our parties was a Miss Kitchener, and she used to drive him mad by teasing him.— HENRY CRABB ROBINSON (" Diary ").

Young, awkward, and unknown.

My acquaintance with William Hazlitt commenced before his name emerged from the " illustrious obscurity " of that private and local fame which had gathered round it, in the small coterie to which he had till then addicted himself. . . . My first interview with him took place in the committee-room of a literary institution, of which I was at that time one of the managers, and had been de-

Awaiting sentence.

puted-by my colleagues to arrange with Hazlitt respecting the details of a course of lectures. . . .

Having been previously cautioned not to be surprised or repelled by any "strangeness" that I
might observe in Hazlitt's manner and personal
appearance, I was shown into the room where he
was, by the librarian, who merely named each to
the other, and then left us together.

On entering, I saw a pale anatomy of a man, sitting uneasily, half on half off a chair, with his legs
tucked awkwardly underneath the rail, his hands
folded listlessly on his knees, his head drooping on
one side, and one of his elbows leaning (not resting)
on the edge of the table by which he sat, as if in
fear of its having no right to be there. His hat had
taken an odd position on the floor beside him, as if
that, too, felt itself as much out of its element as
the owner.

He half rose at my entrance, and, without speaking a word, or looking at me, except with a momentary and furtive glance, he sat down again in a more
uneasy position than before, and seemed to wait
the result of what I might have to say to him, with
the same sort of desperate indifference with which
a culprit may be supposed to wait the sentence of
his judge, after conviction.[1] . . . The picture
which Hazlitt presented when I first saw him in the
little dark, dungeon-like committee-room, . . .
was not unlike that of Sir Joshua's "Ugolino."
There he sat, his anxious and highly intellectual

---

[1] W. C. Hazlitt says, "Leigh Hunt used to describe my grandfather's shake of the hand as something like a fish tendering you
his fin."

face looking upon vacancy ; pale and silent as a ghost ; emaciated as an anatomy ; loose, unstrung, inanimate, as a being whose life is leaving it from sheer emptiness and inanition.—PETER G. PATMORE (" My Friends and Acquaintance ").

Awaiting sentence.

I found Hazlitt living in Milton's house (1819), the very one where he dictated his " Paradise Lost," and occupying the room where, tradition says, he kept the organ on which he loved to play. I should rather say Hazlitt sat in it, for, excepting his table, three chairs, and an old picture, this enormous room was empty and *un*occupied. It was white-washed, and all over the walls he had written in pencil short scraps of brilliant thoughts and phrases, half-lines of poetry, references, etc., in the nature of a commonplace book. His conversation was much of the same kind, generally in short sentences, quick and pointed, dealing much in allusions, and relying a good deal on them for success ; as, when he said, with apparent satisfaction, that Curran was the Homer of blackguards, and afterwards, when the political state of the world came up, said of the Emperor Alexander, that " he is the Sir Charles Grandison of Europe." On the whole, he was more amusing than interesting, and his nervous manner shows that this must be his character.— GEORGE TICKNOR (" Life, Letters, and Journals ").[1]

In his workshop.

Hazlitt always wrote with the breakfast things on the table ; for, as I have said before, they usually

---

[1] Ticknor (George). Life, Letters, and Journals. Edited by G. S. Hillard and Others. 2 vols., 8vo. Boston, 1876.

Methods of work,

remained there till he went out at four or five o'clock to dinner.　He wrote rapidly, in a large hand, as clear as print, made very few corrections, and almost invariably wrote on an entire quire of foolscap, contriving to put into a page of his manuscript exactly the amount (upon an average) of an octavo page of print ; so that he always knew exactly what progress he had made, at any given time, towards the desired goal to which he was travelling—namely, the end of his task.　Unless what he was employed on was a review, he never had a book or paper of any kind about him while he wrote.　In this respect I imagine he stood alone among professional authors.

With respect to Hazlitt's actual method of composition, he never, I believe, thought for half an hour beforehand, as to what he should say on any given subject ; or even as to the general manner in which he should treat it ; but merely, whether it was a subject on which he *had* thought intently at any previous period of his life, and whether it was susceptible of a development that was consistent with the immediate object he might have in view, in sitting down to write on it.　Having determined on these points, and chiefly on the latter, his pen was not merely the mechanical, but (so to speak) the intellectual instrument by which he called up and worked out his thoughts, opinions, sentiments, and even the style and language in which he clothed them : it was the magician's wand with which he compelled and marshaled to his service the powers of his extraordinary mind, and the stores of illustrative material which his early life had been spent in accumulating and laying by for use or pleasure.

He never considered for more than a few moments beforehand the plan or conduct of any composition that he had undertaken, or determined to write, . . . he merely thought for a brief space more or less, till he had hit upon an opening sentence that pleased or satisfied him ; and when that was achieved, he looked upon the thing as done ; for everything else seemed to follow as a natural consequence. . . . When Hazlitt was regularly engaged on any work or article, he wrote at the rate of from ten to fifteen octavo pages at a sitting ; and never, or very rarely, renewed the sitting on the same day. . . . Hazlitt hated writing, and would never have penned a line, and indeed never did, till his necessities compelled him to do so. To think was, and ever had been, the business and the pleasure of his intellectual life—though latterly it had become, on many topics, a fatality and a curse. But to promulgate his thoughts to perverse, or incapable, or unattending ears . . . seemed to him at best but a work of supererogation. . . .

Methods of work.

The three or four hours a day employed . . . in composition enabled him to produce an essay for a magazine, one of his most profound and masterly Table Talks, in two or three sittings ; or a long and brilliant article of thirty or forty pages for the " Edinburgh Review," in about a week. But when he had an entire volume of work in hand he invariably went into the country to execute it, and almost always to the same spot—a little way-side public-house, called " The Hut," standing alone, and some miles distant from any other house, on Winterslow Heath, a barren tract of country on the road to and

III.—13

Methods of work.

a few miles from Salisbury. There, ensconced in a little wainscoted parlor, looking out over the bare heath to the distant groves of Norman Court, some of his finest essays were written; there, in utter solitude and silence, many of his least unhappy days were spent; there, wandering for hours over the bare heath, or through the dark woods of the above-named domain, his shattered frame always gained temporary strength and renovation.—PETER G. PATMORE ("My Friends and Acquaintance").

Facility in composition.

His facility in composition was extreme. We have seen him continue writing (when we went to see him while he was pressed for time to finish an article) with wonderful ease and rapidity of pen, going on as if writing a mere ordinary letter. His usual manuscript was clear and unblotted, indicating great rapidity and sureness in writing, as though requiring no erasures or interlining.—C. and M. C. CLARKE ("Recollections of Writers").

As a lecturer.

January 14, 1812.—Heard Hazlitt's first lecture on the "History of English Philosophy." He seems to have no conception of the difference between a lecture and a book. What he said was sensible and excellent, but he delivered himself in a low, monotonous voice, with his eyes fixed on his MS., not once daring to look at his audience; and he read so rapidly that no one could possibly give to the matter the attention it required. . . . The cause of his reading so rapidly was, that he was told to limit himself to an hour, and what he had prepared would have taken three hours, if it had been read slowly. —HENRY CRABB ROBINSON ("Diary").

Hazlitt's way of life was as little adapted to the ordinary course of things in a " regular " family, as can well be conceived. He always lived (during the period of my intimacy with him) in furnished lodgings, and those of a very secondary class. . . . *Irregular habits.* Hazlitt usually rose at from one to two o'clock in the day—scarcely ever before twelve ; and if he had no work in hand, he would sit over his breakfast (of excessively strong black tea, and a toasted French roll) till four or five in the afternoon—silent, motionless, and self-absorbed, as a Turk over his opium pouch ; for tea served him precisely in this capacity. It was the only stimulant he ever took, and at the same time the only luxury ; the delicate state of his digestive organs prevented him from tasting any fermented liquors or touching any food but beef and mutton, or poultry and game, dressed with perfect plainness. He never touched any but *black* tea, and was very particular about the quality of that, always using the most expensive that could be got : and he used, when living alone, to consume nearly a pound in a week. A cup of Hazlitt's tea (if you happened to come in for the first brewage of it) was a peculiar thing ; I have never tasted anything like it. He always made it himself, half filling the teapot with tea, pouring the boiling water on it and then almost immediately pouring it out, using with it a great quantity of sugar and cream.

To judge from its occasional effect upon myself, I should say that the quantity Hazlitt drank of this tea produced, ultimately, a most injurious effect upon him ; and in all probability hastened his death —which took place from disease of the digestive organs. But its *immediate* effect was agreeable, even to a degree of fascination ; and not feeling any subsequent reaction from it, he persevered in its use to the last, notwithstanding two or three attacks, similar to that which terminated his life.— PETER G. PATMORE (" My Friends and Acquaintance ").

Irregular habits.

When Hazlitt dined at all—which was often not more than two or three times a week—this meal seemed only a sort of preliminary to his everlasting tea, for which he returned home as soon as he had dined, and usually sat over it for a couple of hours. Afterwards he almost inevitably passed two or three hours at one or other of the large theatres, placing himself as invariably in a back corner seat of the second tier of boxes, and, if possible, shrouding himself from view, as if he felt himself " a weed that had no business there," in such a scene of light, gayety, and artificial seeming.—PETER G. PATMORE (" My Friends and Acquaintance ").

Tea and the theatre.

From the time of my first acquaintance with him, Hazlitt had been a determined water-drinker. No temptation ever induced him to transgress his rule of life in this respect ; the only rule he ever prescribed to himself, or could have been likely to keep if he had. But this rule had been imposed upon him by the moral certainty that his life would be the cost of neglecting it ; for, in the early part of his literary career in London, he had been led into an intemperate use of stimulants, which had at length wholly destroyed the healthful tone of his

The trials of abstinence.

digestive organs, and made the utmost caution necessary to prevent those attacks, under one of which he died.

The trials of abstinence.

Of course, in our evening meetings at the Southampton and elsewhere, a glass of grog, or something of the kind, was not wanting to give that *social* flavor to our table-talk which was one of its most pleasant qualities. Indeed, Hazlitt himself could never bear to see the table wholly empty of some emblem of that "taking one's ease at one's inn," which was a favorite feeling and phrase with him ; and immediately his supper-cloth was removed (for *his* corporeal enjoyment on these occasions was confined to the somewhat solid but brief one of a pound or so of rump-steak or cold roast beef), he used to be impatient to know what we were each of us going to take ; and, as each in turn determined the important point, he would *taste* it with us in imagination. It was his frequent and almost habitual practice, the moment the first glass was placed upon the table after supper, to take it up as if to carry it to his lips, then to stop a few moments before it reached them, and then to smell the liquor and draw in the fumes, as if they were "a rich distilled perfume." He would then put the glass down slowly, without uttering a word ; and you might sometimes see the tears start into his eyes, while he drew in his breath to the uttermost, and then sent it forth in a half sigh, half yawn, that seemed to come from the very depths of his heart. At other times he would put the glass down with a less dejected feeling, and exclaim in a tone of gusto that would have done honor to the most earnest of *gas-*

Partaking in fancy.

tronomes over the last mouthful of his *actual* ortolan, "That's fine, by ——!" literally exhilarating, and almost intoxicating himself with the bare imagination of it. He used almost invariably to finish this movement by falling back into a brief fit of dejection, as if stricken with remorse at the irreparable injury he had committed against himself, in having, by an intemperate abuse of a manifest good, forever interdicted himself from the use of it ; for no man ever needed more the judicious use of stimulants, or would, if he could have borne them, have found more unmingled benefit from them.—PETER G. PAT-MORE ("My Friends and Acquaintance").

Hazlitt's judgment and tact as to what would suit the public taste was such, that what he wrote was sure of certain sale, in various quarters, and at a liberal price. So that the labor of a couple of mornings in the week, upon the average, would have amply supplied all his wants, had he chosen to employ himself regularly with that view. Yet nothing could ever persuade him to set to work until his last sovereign was gone, and his credit exhausted with his landlady and his tavern-keeper ; and I have repeatedly known him to leave himself without a half crown to buy him a dinner, or what was still more a necessary of life with him, a quarter of a pound of tea ; and this at a moment, perhaps, when he had just committed some escapade, in the way of revenge for some supposed injury or slight, which had left him without a friend to whom he could persuade himself to apply for the loan of one.—PETER G. PATMORE ("My Friends and Acquaintance").

Partaking in fancy.

Improvidence.

Hazlitt at present gives me great pain by the folly with which he is conducting himself. He has fallen in love to a pitch of insanity, with a lodging-house hussy, who will be his death. He has been to Scotland and divorced his wife, although he has a fine little boy by her; and after doing this, to marry this girl, he comes back and finds she has been making a fool of him in order to get presents, and in reality has been admitting a lover more favored. Hazlitt's torture is beyond expression; you may imagine it. The girl really excited in him a pure, devoted, and intense love. His imagination clothed her with that virtue which her affected modesty induced him to believe in, and he is really downright in love with an ideal perfection, which has no existence but in his own head! He talks of nothing else day and night. He has written down all the conversations without color, literal as they happened; he has preserved all the love-letters, many of which are equal to anything of the sort, and really affecting; and I believe, in order to ease his soul of this burden, means, with certain arrangements, to publish it as a tale of character. He will sink into idiotcy if he does not get rid of it.

Poor Hazlitt! He who makes so free with the follies of his friends, is of all mortals the most open to ridicule. To hear him repeat in a solemn tone and with agitated mouth the things of love he said to her (to convince you that he made love in the true gallant way), to feel the beauty of the sentiment, and then look up and see his old, hard, weather-beaten, saturnine, metaphysical face—the very antidote of the sentiment—twitching all sorts

An affair of the heart.

Lovelorn.

Lovelorn.

of ways, is really enough to provoke a saint to laughter. He has a notion that women have never liked him. Since this affair he has dressed in the fashion, and keeps insinuating his improved appearance. He springs up to show you his pantaloons! What a being it is! His conversation is now a mixture of disappointed revenge, passionate remembrances, fiendish hopes, and melting lamentations.—BENJAMIN R. HAYDON (from a Letter to Miss Mitford, 1822, published in H.'s "Correspondence").

The " Liber Amoris."

There is no doubt that his strong passions and determined likings often interfered with his better reason. His admiration of Napoleon would not allow of any qualification. And in the case of the heroine of the Liber Amoris (Sarah Walker), his intellect was completely subdued by an insane passion. He was, for a time, unable to think or talk of anything else. He abandoned criticism and books as idle matters ; and fatigued every person whom he met by expressions of his love, of her deceit, and of his own vehement disappointment. . . . Upon one occasion I knew that he told the story of his attachment to five different persons in the same day, and at each time entered into minute details of his love story. " I am a cursed fool," said he to me. " I saw J—— going into Will's Coffee-house yesterday morning ; he spoke to me. I followed him into the house ; and whilst he lunched I told him the whole story. Then " (said he) " I wandered into the Regent's Park, where I met one of M——'s sons. I walked with him some time, and on his using some civil expression, by G——!

sir, I told him the whole story." (Here he mentioned another instance, which I forget.) "Well sir," (he went on), "I then went and called on Haydon ; but he was out.   There was only his man, Salmon, there ; but, by G——! I could not help myself.   It all came out ; the whole cursed story ! Afterwards I went to look at some lodgings at Pimlico.   The landlady at one place, after some explanations as to rent, etc., said to me very kindly, 'I am afraid you are not well, sir?'—'No, ma'am,' said I, 'I am not well ;' and on inquiring further, the devil take me if I did not let out the whole story, from beginning to end !"   For a time, I think, that on this point he was substantially insane ; certainly beyond self-control.—Bryan W. Procter ("Recollections of Men of Letters ").

The "Liber Amoris."

During the first week or fortnight after the appearance of (let us suppose) one of "Blackwood's " articles about him, if he entered a coffee-house where he was known, to get his dinner, it was impossible (he thought) that the waiters could be doing anything else all the time he was there, but pointing him out to other guests, as "the gentleman who was so abused last month in ' Blackwood's Magazine.' "   If he knocked at the door of a friend, the look and reply of the servant (whatever they might be) made it evident to him that he or she had been reading " Blackwood's Magazine" before the family were up in the morning !   If he had occasion to call at any of the publishers for whom he might be writing at the time, the case was still worse,—inasmuch that there his bread was at stake, as well as

Sensitiveness to criticism.

that personal civility, which he valued no less. Mr. Colburn would be "not within," as a matter of course ; for his clerks to even ascertain his pleasure on that point beforehand would be wholly superfluous ; had they not all chuckled over the article at their tea the evening before ? Even the instinct of the shopboys would catch the cue from the significant looks of those above them, and refuse to take his name to Mr. Ollier. They would "believe he was gone to dinner." He could not, they thought, want to have anything to say to a person who, as it were, went about with a sheet of "Blackwood's" pinned to his coat-tail like a dish-clout !

Then at home at his lodgings, if the servant who waited upon him did not answer his bell the first time—ah ! 'twas clear—she had read "Blackwood's," or heard talk of it at the bar of the public-house when she went for the beer ! Did the landlady send up his bill a day earlier than usual, or ask for payment of it less civilly than was her custom —how could he wonder at it ? It was "Blackwood's" doing. But if she gave him notice to quit (on the score, perhaps, of his inordinately late hours) he was a lost man ! for would anybody take him in after having read "Blackwood's ?" Even the strangers that he met in the street seemed to look at him askance, "with jealous leer malign," as if they knew him by intuition for a man on whom was set the double seal of public and private infamy ; the doomed and denounced of "Blackwood's Magazine."

This may seem like exaggeration. . . . But . . . . it falls as far short of the truth as it may seem to go beyond it ; . . . not one of the cases to which I have alluded above, but has been in substance detailed to me by Hazlitt himself, as (according to *his* interpretation) a simple matter of fact result of the attacks in question!—P. G. PATMORE ("My Friends and Acquaintance").

Fancies himself ostracized.

In resolving to tell what I know, or have been led to feel, of William Hazlitt, I have determined to "nothing extenuate." I at once, then, confess that the plague-spot of his personal character was an ingrained selfishness, which more or less influenced and modified all the other points of his nature. . . . Let me still further guard against being mistaken by Hazlitt's friends and misinterpreted by his enemies. The defect which I have noticed in his character was little in amount. I never knew him do a base or mean action; and I have known him do many that might fairly claim to be deemed magnanimous in the ordinary acceptation of the term. It would be the basest of libels upon Hazlitt to describe him as a mean-souled man. But the tendency, the taint was there ; though it seldom showed itself in overt acts, and never without a sort of half-struggle to overcome it ; or in default of that, a half-ostentatious exposure of the weakness, as one of which he was not merely conscious, but took to himself more shame for it than his worst enemies would have cast upon him.— PETER G. PATMORE ("My Friends and Acquaintance ").

Selfishness.

With one class of persons—the professed literati of the day—he tried to shine ; with another class—

the opposite of the above—he tried *not* to shine, but, on the contrary, to be and to seem not a whit superior to those about him. In the company of females, whoever they might be, or of whatever class—even with those few who were uniformly kind and cordial in their reception and treatment of him, and of whose respect and good-will he could not reasonably doubt—there was always apparent a dash of melancholy and despondency; and also a resentful feeling, which showed itself from time to time, not in anything he said, but in the fearful expression which used to pass across his face, and which he never even attempted to suppress or conceal—an expression that can only be described by saying that it gave the look of an incarnate demon's to a face that, in the absence of that look, indicated the highest and noblest attributes of the human intellect and character. In speaking of this look, I may remark that, though no *obvious* cause was ever apparent for it, I never remember to have once observed it without being able immediately to assign the cause, even though I may inadvertently have given it myself—for it was always something touching more or less remotely or nearly the *personal* condition and circumstances of the man ; and I might add, it was almost always connected with one of three topics—the downfall of Napoleon—the abuse of some deserving writer from party motives—and (in the case where females were present) in reference to the passion of love. On each of these topics there existed a morbid part in Hazlitt's mind, which no one—friend, foe, or perfect stranger—could touch, or even approach, without exciting a feeling of mingled agony and resentment, that showed itself as I have just described. These topics were strings in the noble instrument of his mind which had been so early and violently overstrained, that nothing could ever restore them to their healthful temperament, or cause them to give out tones capable of making anything but " harsh discords," or music the pathos of which was lost in the pain.—PETER G. PATMORE (" My Friends and Acquaintance ").

The " demon" look.

In no case whatever could Hazlitt's estimates of *persons* be taken implicitly ; because it was impossible for him to prevent—and he never for a moment tried to prevent—his own intense personal feelings from blending with and giving a color to such estimates. And of *living* persons—of those who came, as it were, into hourly intellectual contact with him, by breathing the same air and treading on the same earth—he could not even form, much less set forth, a fair and unbiased opinion.—PETER G. PATMORE (" My Friends and Acquaintance ").

A faulty judge of personal character.

I have seen him more than once, at the Fives Court in St. Martin's Street, on making a bad stroke or missing his ball at some critical point of the game, fling his racket to the other end of the court, walk deliberately to the centre, with uplifted hands imprecate the most fearful curses on his head for his stupidity, and then rush to the side wall and literally dash his head against it !—PETER G. PATMORE (" My Friends and Acquaintance ").

Violence.

*Contradic-
tions of
character.*

It is no less true than it may seem paradoxical, that, with the most *social* disposition of any man I ever met with, and an active and ever present sympathy with the claims, the wants, and the feelings of every human being he approached, Hazlitt was, even by nature, but by circumstances still more so, *a lone man*, living, moving, and having his being, for and to himself exclusively ; as utterly cut off from fulfilling and exercising the ordinary pursuits and affections of his kind, and of his nature, as if he had been bound hand and foot in a dungeon, or banished to a desert. And so, indeed, he was— bound in the gloomiest of all dungeons—that built for us by our own unbridled passions—banished to that dreariest of all deserts, spread out for us by seared hopes and blighted affections.—PETER G. PATMORE ("My Friends and Acquaintance").

*Peculiari-
ties of tem-
per.*

The axiom which bids us "never speak ill of a man behind his back" (as if one might do it with propriety before his face !), was not one of those ranked by Hazlitt among the "wisdom of nations." On the contrary, he spoke what he thought of people, everywhere but in their hearing ; trusting (rather too implicitly, I am afraid) to that tacit compact which recognizes the sacredness of social intercourse. And he cared not what you said of him in return, nor if he heard your injurious estimate of him repeated by half the town ; or if he sought to make reprisals, it was on the hawker, not the originator of the affront. But a *personal* slight or incivility he held to be the most unpardonable of offences, and to be punished and avenged as such.

You might think and call him a rascal or a repro-
bate as much as you pleased ; you might "prove"
him to be a bad writer and a worse man, with perfect impunity ; but if you looked askance upon him
in company, or "cut" him in the street, or even
gave him reason to fancy you had done so, there
was . . . no limit to the revenge he would take
on you, and no rest for him till he had taken it.—
PETER G. PATMORE ("My Friends and Acquaintance ").

*Peculiari-
ties of tem-
per.*

Politics offered the one point which acted on his
temper like monomania. It was capable of chang-
ing him from a reasonable being into a wild beast.
It stirred up the bitter and rancorous feelings that,
to the very last, lay festering in his heart, and eating
into its core like some "poisonous mineral"—de-
posited there by the events that had terminated the
French Revolution; and those feelings were still
more deeply rooted by the subsequent downfall of his
idol, Napoleon, and the restoration of the Bourbons.
I have heard those who knew him in his early youth
say, that it was the great events of the French Revolution, and the new era of thought and of things
that they seemed to create throughout Europe,
which first called forth Hazlitt's intellectual faculties from that dreamy torpor in which they might
otherwise have lain for years longer, perhaps forever. . . . Had his faculties and sensibilities
opened and developed themselves at any other period, or under any other political aspect, than that
of the first French Revolution, he might have been
the very model of a wise and happy man. But as

*Influence of
the French
Revolution.*

it was, his whole intellectual being—his temper, affections, passions, meditations, and pursuits—took

a sinister turn from those events, which never afterwards left it, or at least which was never afterwards
absent when its first exciting cause was recalled
into action. On all matters but political ones Hazlitt's perceptions were almost superhumanly clear
and acute, and his judgment was infallible. But
about the political prospects, tendencies and events
of the day, he was like a child or a woman—either
utterly indifferent to them, or, when not so, regarding them in a light directly opposed to the true one.
—PETER G. PATMORE.—("My Friends and Acquaintance").

A friend of his it was, a friend wishing to love
him, and admiring him almost to extravagance, who

told me, in illustration of the dark sinister gloom
which sat forever upon Hazlitt's countenance and
gestures, that involuntarily when Hazlitt put his
hand within his waistcoat (as a mere unconscious
trick of habit), he himself felt a sudden recoil of
fear, as from one who was searching for a hidden
dagger. Like "a Moor of Malabar," as described
in the Faery Queen, at intervals Hazlitt threw up
his angry eyes, and dark locks, as if wishing to affront the sun, or to search the air for hostility. And
the same friend, on another occasion, described the
sort of feudal fidelity to his belligerent duties, which
in company seemed to animate Hazlitt, as though
he were mounting guard on all the citadels of ma-
lignity under some *sacramentum militaire*, by the
following trait,—that, if it had happened to Hazlitt

to be called out of the room, or to be withdrawn for a moment from the current of the general conversation, by a fit of abstraction, or by a private whisper to himself from some person sitting at his elbow, always on resuming his place as a party to what might be called the public business of the company, he looked round him with a mixed air of suspicion and defiance, such as seemed to challenge everybody by some stern adjuration into revealing whether, during his own absence or inattention, anything had been said demanding condign punishment at his hands. "Has any man uttered or presumed to insinuate," he seemed to insist upon knowing, "during this *interregnum*, things that I ought to proceed against as treasonable to the interests which I defend?" — THOMAS DE QUINCEY ("Essays on the Poets").[1] *Irascibility.*

His manners are to ninety-nine in one hundred singularly repulsive; brow-hanging; shoe-contemplating—strange. . . . He is, I verily believe, kindly natured; is very fond of, attentive to, and patient with children; but he is jealous, gloomy, and of an irritable pride. With all this there is much good in him. He is disinterested; an enthusiastic lover of the great men who have been before us. He says things that are his own, in a way of his own.—SAMUEL T. COLERIDGE (Extract from a Letter quoted in Cottle's "Reminiscences"). *A general estimate.*

While at Fonthill we walked over to Salisbury (a distance of twelve miles) in a broiling sunshine; and

[1] De Quincey (Thomas). Essays on the Poets and other Writers. 16mo. Boston, 1853.

III.—14

I remember, on this occasion in particular, remarking the extraordinary physical as well as moral effect produced on Hazlitt by the sight and feel of "the country." In London the most inobservant person could scarcely pass him in the street without remarking the extreme apparent debility, almost amounting to helplessness, of his air and manner. He used to go drooping and faltering along, like a man just risen from a bed of sickness, seeming scarcely able to support himself without holding by the railings or leaning against the walls ; and invariably looking prone upon the ground, to which he seemed ready to fall at every step. But in the country, especially upon a vast plain or heath, like that over which our path on the present occasion chiefly lay, he was like a being of another species ; his step firm, vigorous, and rapid ; his look eager and onward, as if devouring the way before it, and his whole air and manner buoyant and triumphant, as if a new sense of existence, and new bodily powers had been breathed into him by the objects around.

He spoke on this occasion of having repeatedly walked from forty to fifty miles a day in that fashion formerly, and said that he could do so now with perfect ease and pleasure. Yet in London . . . he would sit as if nailed to his chair, from morning till late at night, day after day, for weeks together— merely creeping out to the theatre, or the Southampton, at ten or eleven o'clock at night, and there taking his seat silently again, and sitting till he was fairly warned away by the extinguished lights and the closing doors.—PETER G. PATMORE ("My Friends and Acquaintance").

His . . . gastric weakness . . . was a constant torment to him ; and his love of all good things in the eatable way . . . tended to aggravate the constitutional tendency to his class of disorder. But it was a way of his to complain of indisposition sometimes, when he called anywhere, and the people of the house were not as pleasant as usual, or something was said which put him out of temper with them and himself. It did not signify very much which side was in fault, so long as matters went amiss, and he did not happen to be in the best cue. A great deal depended on the humor he was in. . . . On such occasions as I have alluded to, he would get up, say he was very ill, with his chin in and his eyes wide open, and make the move to go, with a "Well, good-morning."—WILLIAM C. HAZLITT ("Memoir of W. Hazlitt").

A way of escape.

Like Dr. Johnson, Mr. Hazlitt addressed everybody as *Sir*. The youngest and most intimate of his friends was not exempt from this rule, unless Mr. Hazlitt happened to be in an unusually happy and cordial humor. Mr. C. H. Reynell's sons, whom he knew as well as his own child, were almost invariably saluted in what would now appear a ludicrously formal manner.—WILLIAM C. HAZLITT ("Memoir of W. Hazlitt").

Formality.

Kenny told me that John Lamb (the brother of Charles) once knocked down Hazlitt, who was impertinent to him, and on those who were present interfering, and begging of Hazlitt to shake hands and forgive him, H. said, "Well, I don't care if I do. I am

Indifference to a blow.

a metaphysician, and do not mind a blow ; nothing
but an *idea* hurts *me*."—THOMAS MOORE ("Diary").

A trying peculiarity.

A visit to the theatre in Mr. Hazlitt's company
was not always the most comfortable thing in the
world.   He had a slow way of moving on such occasions, which, to less habitual play-goers, was
highly trying.   He took my mother to the play one
evening . . .;   there was a great crowd, but he
was totally unmoved by that circumstance.   At the
head of the staircase he had to sign the Free Admission Book, and perfectly unconscious that he was
creating a blockade, he looked up at the attendant
in the middle of the operation—a rather lengthy
one with him—and said, "What sort of a house is
there to-night, sir?"   It was a vast relief to his two
companions, my mother and her elder sister, when
they had run the gauntlet of all this, and were safe
in their places.—W. C. HAZLITT ("Memoir of W.
Hazlitt").

Friendly estimates.

I meet, at present, with few persons who recollect
much of Hazlitt.   Some profess to have heard nothing of him except his prejudices and violence ; but
his prejudices were few, and his violence (if violence
he had) was of very rare occurrence.   He was extremely patient, indeed, although earnest when dis-
cussing points in politics, respecting which he held
very strong and decided opinions.   But he circulated
his thoughts on many other subjects, whereon he
ought not to have excited offence or opposition.
. . .   Besides being an original thinker, Hazlitt
excelled in conversation.   He was, moreover, a very

temperate liver : yet his enemies proclaimed to the world that he was wanting even in sobriety. During the thirteen years that I knew him intimately, and (at certain seasons) saw him almost every day, I know that he drank nothing stronger than water ; except tea, indeed, in which he indulged in the morning. Had he been as temperate in his political views as in his cups, he would have escaped the slander that pursued him through life.—BRYAN W. PROCTER (" Charles Lamb : a Memoir ").

Friendly estimates.

Under that straightforward, hard-hitting, direct-telling manner of his, both in writing and speaking, Hazlitt had a depth of gentleness—even tenderness —of feeling on certain subjects ; manly friendship, womanly sympathy, touched him to the core ; and any token of either would bring a sudden expression into his eyes very beautiful as well as very heart-stirring to look upon. We have seen this expression more than once, and can recal its appealing charm, its wonderful irradiation of the strong features and squarely-cut, rugged under portion of the face.—C. and M. C. CLARKE (" Recollections of Writers ").

He was a simple, unselfish man, void of all deception and pretence ; and he had a clear, acute intellect, when not traversed by some temporary passion or confused by a strong prejudice. . . . He hated pretensions supported merely by rank or wealth or repute, or by the clamor of factions. And he felt love and hatred in an intense degree. But he was never dishonest. He never struck down the weak, nor trod on the prostrate. He was never

treacherous, never tyrannical, never cruel.—BRYAN
W. PROCTER ("Recollections of Men of Letters").

*Friendly
estimates.*

I should belie my own conscience, if I said less,
than that I think W. H. to be, in his natural and
healthy state, one of the wisest and finest spirits
breathing. So far from being ashamed of that intimacy, which was betwixt us, it is my boast that I
was able for so many years to have preserved it entire ; and I think I shall go to my grave without
finding, or expecting to find such a companion.—
CHARLES LAMB (Letter to Southey, 1823).

JAMES HENRY LEIGH HUNT.

1784–1859.

INTRODUCTORY NOTE.

IT is hard to conceive of Leigh Hunt as an actual man, a flesh-and-blood reality. He rather seems the creation of a brightly sportive imagination ; a pleasant myth ; a child of Cervantes's brain, born in some mood of airy fantasy.

His nature presents some very curious contradictions. He dearly loved ease and luxury ; one can fancy him spending a long lifetime in the tranquil · enjoyment of the beauties of nature and art. The delicacy of his refinement was almost effeminate. And yet this dainty, fastidious lover of pleasure, this gentle, luxurious, whimsical dreamer performed an amount of work which bore witness to a life of ceaseless industry, and chose to suffer the hardships of a prison rather than to abandon his political principles. Haydon said to him, " You would have been burnt at the stake for a principle, and you would have feared to put your foot in the mud."

What evil genius impelled him, of all men, to meddle with affairs of state ? No man could be more unfit for such employment. His utter inability to cope with the simplest practical details of every-day life, must have insured his failure as a politician. It is fortunate that he soon quitted a field in which it was impossible for him to succeed.

A strange product of English soil! Neither his virtues nor his failings were those of an Englishman. England was the last nation of Europe which might reasonably have been expected to produce such a man. He had many of the engaging traits of French and Italian national character, and he was a living protest against the most obnoxious features of John Bullism—insularity, rapacity, and stolid materialism.

Leigh Hunt's "Autobiography" is one of the most agreeable books of its kind. This, and his correspondence, have been carefully edited, with many personal reminiscences, by his son, Thornton Hunt. There are articles by Thornton Hunt, containing recollections of his father, in the *Cornhill Magazine*, January, 1860, and in the *Atlantic Monthly*, February, 1863. See also A. Ireland's "List of the Writings of W. Hazlitt and Leigh Hunt;" Charles Knight's "Passages from a Working Life;" Hazlitt's "Spirit of the Age;" Carlyle's "Reminiscences;" and F. H. Grundy's "Pictures of the Past."

By far the most satisfying portraiture of Leigh Hunt is (as might be expected) the carefully elaborated sketch by Hawthorne, in "Our Old Home." This work is thoroughly pervaded by the rare and subtle quality of its author's genius ; and in this, and in the note-books of foreign travel, there are comments of great value and suggestiveness upon many distinguished characters. Hawthorne's description of his visit to the aged poet is here reprinted, through the courtesy of Messrs. Houghton, Mifflin & Co.

LEADING EVENTS OF LEIGH HUNT'S LIFE.

1784.   Born, October 19th, at Southgate, Middlesex.

1792.—(Aged 8.) A scholar at Christ's Hospital School.

1799.—(Aged 15.) Leaves Christ's Hospital School.

1801.—(Aged 17.) Publishes "Juvenilia," a volume of poems.

1805.—(Aged 21.) Theatrical critic of *The News*.

1807.—(Aged 23.) Publishes "Critical Essays on the Performers of the London Theatres."

1808.—(Aged 24.) A Clerk in the War Office. Establishes the *Examiner*, with his brother, John Hunt.

1809.—(Aged 25.) Marries Miss Marianne Kent.

1813.—(Aged 29.) Imprisoned for the publication of an article ridiculing the Prince Regent.

1814.—(Aged 30.) Publishes "The Feast of the Poets."

1815.—(Aged 31.) Liberated from prison. Publishes "The Descent of Liberty ; a Mask."

1816.—(Aged 32.) Publishes "The Story of Rimini."

1817.—(Aged 33.) Publishes "The Round Table," the joint work of himself and William Hazlitt.

1818.—(Aged 34.) Publishes "Foliage."

1819.—(Aged 35.) Publishes "Hero and Leander," and "Bacchus and Ariadne."

1822.—(Aged 38.) Arrives in Italy. Co-operates with Byron and Shelley in the publication of *The Liberal*.

1825.—(Aged 41.) Returns to England.

1828.—(Aged 44.) Publishes "Lord Byron and some of his Contemporaries."

1832.—(Aged 48.) Prints "Christianism," for private circulation. His poems are published by subscription.

1834.—(Aged 50.) Edits the *London Journal*.

1835.—(Aged 51.) Publishes "Captain Sword and Captain Pen."

1840.—(Aged 56.) "A Legend of Florence" performed at Covent Garden Theatre. Publishes "The Seer."

1847.—(Aged 63.) Receives a pension of two hundred pounds per annum.

1848.—(Aged 64.) Publishes " The Town."
1850.—(Aged 66.) Publishes his "Autobiography."
1853.—(Aged 69.) Publishes " The Religion of the Heart."
1857.—(Aged 73.) His wife dies.
1859.—(Aged 74 years and 10 months.) Dies, August 28th.

NOTE.—For a better view of Hunt's industry, the reader is referred to Mr. Alexander Ireland's excellent " List of the Writings
of William Hazlitt and Leigh Hunt." 8vo. London, 1868. I am
indebted to Mr. Ireland's careful and authoritative work for the
bibliographic part of the foregoing table.   I have made no record
of a very large part of Hunt's writings.

JAMES HENRY LEIGH HUNT.

L IKE Coleridge and Lamb, he was educated at
Christ's Hospital, . . . and, like Lamb,
he was prevented from going to the University *School life.*
. . . by an impediment in his speech, which,
however, he had the better luck to outgrow. At
school, as afterwards, he was remarkable for exuberance of animal spirits, and for passionate attachment to his friends, but did not evince any great
regard for his studies, except when the exercises
were in verse. His prose themes were so bad that
the master used to crumple them up in his hand,
and throw them to the boys for their amusement.—
Samuel C. Hall ("Book of Memories").

He was tall rather than otherwise,—five feet ten
inches and a half when measured for the St. James'
Volunteers; though in common with men whose *Personal appearance.*
length is in the body rather than the legs, his height
diminished as he advanced in life. He was remarkably straight and upright in his carriage, with a
short, firm step, and a cheerful, almost dashing approach,—smiling, breathing, and making his voice
heard in little inarticulate ejaculations as he met a
friend, in an irrepressible satisfaction at the en-

counter that not unfrequently conveyed high gratification to the arriver who was thus greeted. He
had straight black hair, which he wore parted in
the centre ; a dark but not pale complexion ; features compounded between length and a certain
irregularity of outline, characteristic of the American mould ; black eyebrows, firmly marking the
edge of a brow over which was a singularly upright,
flat, white forehead, and under which beamed a pair
of eyes dark, brilliant, reflecting, gay, and kind, with
a certain look of observant humor, that suggested
an idea of what is called slyness when it is applied
to children or girls. . . . He had a head massive and tall, and larger than most men's—Byron,
Shelley, and Keats wore hats which he could not
put on ; but it was not out of proportion to the
figure, its outlines being peculiarly smooth, and devoid of "bumps." His upper lip was long, his
mouth large and hard in the flesh ; his chin retreating and gentle like a woman's. His sloping shoulders, not very wide, almost concealed the ample
proportions of his chest ; though that was of a compass which not every pair of arms could span.—
THORNTON HUNT (*Cornhill Magazine*, January, 1860).

He was rather tall, as straight as an arrow, and
looked slenderer than he really was. His hair was
black and shining, and slightly inclined to wave ;
his head was high, his forehead straight and white,
his eyes black and sparkling, his general complexion
dark. There was in his whole carriage and manner
an extraordinary degree of life.—THORNTON HUNT
(Introduction to L. H.'s "Autobiography," 1860).

Hunt was a little above the middle size, thin and lithe. His countenance was very genial and pleasant. His hair was black ; his eyes were very dark, but he was short-sighted, and therefore perhaps it was that they had nothing of that fierce glance which black eyes so frequently possess. His mouth was expressive but protruding.—BRYAN W. PROCTER ("Recollections of Men of Letters ").

Personal appearance.

He was tall, but slightly formed, quiet and contemplative in gait and manner, yet apparently affected by momentary impulse ; his countenance brisk and animated, receiving its expression chiefly from dark and brilliant eyes, but supplying unequivocal evidence of that mixed blood which he derived from the parent stock, to which his friend Hazlitt alluded in reference to his flow of animal spirits as well as to his descent, "he had tropical blood in his veins." [1]—SAMUEL C. HALL (" Book of Memories ").

Slim, and perfectly upright ; his handsome, pale, oval face almost without a wrinkle ; his long white locks falling to his shoulders, over those immense shirt collars, which, had they been but starched, would have ended his days long before by cutting his throat. He was a perfect picture of sensitive refinement. I see him striding backwards and forwards up and down his "old Court suburb " study, his dressing-gown, although 'tis evening, flying out behind him, dictating his flowing periods (it was *Beaumont and Fletcher* then) to his too willing facto-

---

[1] Several of his ancestors were from the West Indies.

tum, amanuensis, friend, son, and servant Vincent.
—FRANCIS H. GRUNDY (" Pictures of the Past ").[1]

Personal appearance.

When I saw him last he was yielding to the universal conqueror. His loose and straggling white hair·thinly scattered over a brow. of manly intelligence ; his eyes dimmed somewhat, but retaining that peculiar gentleness yet brilliancy which in his youth was likened to those of a gazelle ; his earnest heart and vigorous mind out-speaking yet, in sentences eloquent and impressive.—SAMUEL C. HALL (" Book of Memories ").

I well remember the last time I saw him at Hammersmith, not long before his death in 1859, when, with his delicate, worn, but keenly intellectual face, his large luminous eyes, his thick shock of wiry grey hair, and a little cape of faded black silk over his shoulders, he looked like an old French abbé.— JOHN FORSTER (" Life of Dickens ").[2]

I found Leigh Hunt living in a pleasant little cottage at Hammersmith (1859). . . . On entering the little parlor, used as a " study," a tall figure, dressed in a morning gown, with a large cape, came forward and grasped my hand with a sort of feminine tenderness and enthusiasm. . . . Leigh Hunt is now nearly eighty years of age ; and yet his complexion has the fairness and freshness of youth. His hair is as white as the

[1] Grundy (Francis H.). Pictures of the Past. London, 1879.
[2] Forster (John). Life of Charles Dickens. 3 vols., 8vo. London, 1872-74.

bloom of the almond tree, and as full and glossy as the head of a child. His brow is broad and beautiful, and his eye as gentle and as clear as that of a woman who has never seen a cloudy day. His heart iş as merry as a bird's, and his look and manner alternately playful and pensive, but without a shadow of sadness.[1]—HIRAM FULLER (" Sparks from a Locomotive ").[2]

Personal appearance.

In his boyhood he had an impediment in his speech, which was assumed to be incurable ; though it seems to have rapidly diminished in his intercourse with the world, and to have left none but the very slightest traces.—THORNTON HUNT ("Correspondence of L. H.").[3]

Stammering.

Unfailing spirits made the great charm of his conversation. The stream flowed gently on, always clear, often sparkling. His vivacity frequently approached to wit, and if there were the slightest touch of satire in his opinions of books or men, it was so subtle and delicate that it was more like the fencing with foils of Congreve's fine gentlemen, than the sword thrusts of one who in his time was foremost in the lists of bold public writers.—CHARLES KNIGHT (" Passages of a Working Life ").[4]

Conversation.

---

[1] For a further account of Leigh Hunt's appearance, see Hawthorne's description, p. 252.

[2] Fuller (Hiram). Sparks from a Locomotive ; or, Life and Liberty in Europe. 12mo. New York, 1859.

[3] Hunt (James Henry Leigh). Correspondence. Edited by his eldest Son. 2 vols., 12mo. London, 1862.

[4] Knight (Charles). Passages of a Working Life during Half a Century. 3 vols., 8vo. London, 1864–65.

III.—15

During an intimacy of many (forty) years, I never heard him utter an oath, although they were then very common ; and I never heard from him an indelicate hint or allusion.—BRYAN W. PROCTER (" Recollections of Men of Letters ").

In a letter to Southey Lamb says of Hunt, " He is one of the most cordial-minded men I ever knew, and matchless as a fireside companion." He also speaks of his having an "air of mild dogmatism," a "condescending to a boyish sportiveness," in his conversation.

. Few men were more attractive "in society," whether in a large company or over the fireside. His manners were peculiarly animated ; his conversation, varied, ranging over a great field of subjects, was moved and called forth by the response of his companion, be that companion philosopher or student, sage or boy, man or woman ; and he was equally ready for the most lively topics or for the gravest reflections—his expression easily adapting itself to the tone of his companion's mind. With much freedom of manners, he combined a spontaneous courtesy that never failed, and a considerateness derived from a ceaseless kindness of heart that invariably fascinated even strangers.—THORNTON HUNT (Introduction to L. H.'s " Autobiography ").

In private intercourse Leigh Hunt was at first timid and reserved, almost to shyness—not from any mental awkwardness, but because of later years he never had robust health. Meeting strangers was always a kind of trial to him, though always ready to receive any with any claim on his attention. His conversation, at first broken and tentative, required but the full consciousness of sympathetic auditors and interlocutors. . . . Not that Leigh Hunt was witty nor in any absolute sense humorous, but that when animated he said everything happily, and could give a quaint, curious turn to the most commonplace conversation. There was never a man who more needed loving hands and voices around him ; and it is a happiness to think that he never wanted them. It was joyous to see how, when silent and depressed—for physical delicacy affected his spirits,—he would brighten up at the pressure of a friendly hand, would answer readily to a cheery voice, and would share in any talk—the chit chat of the day, the nonsense of the hour—with a zest which showed that his heart beat strongest in response to human love.—ANON. (*Athenæum*, September 3, 1859).

Conversation.

Leigh Hunt's conversation was simply perfection. If he were in argument—however warm it might be —he would wait patiently to hear "the other side." Unlike most eager conversers, he never interrupted. Even to the youngest among his colloquists he always gave full attention, and listened with an air of genuine respect to whatever they might have to adduce in support of their view of a question. He was peculiarly encouraging to young aspirants, whether fledgling authors or callow casuists ; and treated them with nothing of condescension, or affable accommodation of his intellect to theirs, or amicable tolerance for their comparative incapacity, but, as it were, placed them at once on a handsome footing

*Conversa-
tion.*

of equality and complete level with himself. When, as was frequently the case, he found himself left master of the field of talk by his delighted hearers, only too glad to have him recount in his own felicitous way one of his " good stories," or utter some of his "good things," he would go on in a strain of sparkle, brilliancy, and freshness like a sun-lit stream in a spring meadow. Melodious in tone, alluring in accent, eloquent in choice of words, Leigh Hunt's talk was as delicious to listen to as rarest music. . . . He used more effusion of utterance, more mutation of voice, and more energy of gesture, than is common to most Englishmen when under the excitement of recounting a comic story ; and this produced corresponding excitement in his hearers, so that the "success" of his good stories was unfailing, and the laughter that followed him throughout was worked to a climax at the close.— Mary Cowden Clarke (" Recollections of Writers ").

*Reading
aloud.*

Leigh Hunt's reading was pre-eminently good. Varied in tone and inflection of voice, unstudied, natural, characteristic, full of a keen sense of the humor of the scenes and the wit of the dialogue, his dramatic reading was almost unequalled : and we can remember his perusal of the Sir Anthony Absolute scenes in Sheridan's " Rivals," and Foote's farce of " The Liar," as pieces of uproarious merriment. Even Dowton himself—and his acted impersonation of Sir Anthony was a piece of wonderful truth for towering wrath and irrational fury—hardly surpassed Leigh Hunt's reading of the part, so masterly a rendering was it of old-gentlemanly wilful-

ness, and comedy-father whirlwind of raging tyranny.
—C. and M. C. CLARKE (" Recollections of Writers ").

He improves upon acquaintance. The author
translates admirably into the man. Indeed the very
faults of his style are virtues in the individual. *Social traits.*
His natural gayety and sprightliness of manner, his
high animal spirits, and the *vinous* quality of his
mind, produce an immediate fascination and intoxication in those who come in contact with him, and
carry off in society whatever in his writings may
to some seem flat and impertinent. From great
sanguineness of temper, from great quickness and
unsuspecting simplicity, he runs on to the public as
he does at his own fireside, and talks about himself,
forgetting that he is not always among friends.
His look, his tone are required to point many things
that he says : his frank cordial manner reconciles you
instantly to a little over-bearing, over-weening self-
complacency. " To be admired he needs but to
be seen :" but perhaps he ought to be seen to be
fully appreciated. . . .
We have said that Lord Byron is a sublime cox-
comb : why should we not say that Mr. Hunt is a
delightful one? There is certainly an exuberance
of satisfaction in his manner which is more than
the strict logical premises warrant, and which dull
and phlegmatic constitutions know nothing of, and
cannot understand till they see it. . . . He sits
at the head of a party with great gayety and grace ;
has an elegant manner and turn of features ; has
continual sportive sallies of wit or fancy ; tells a
story capitally ; mimics an actor or an acquaintance

*Social
traits.*

to admiration ; laughs with great glee and good humor at his own and other people's jokes ; understands the point of an *équivoque* or an observation immediately ; has a taste for, and a knowledge of books,
of music, of medals ; manages an argument adroitly ;
is genteel and gallant ; and has a set of by-phrases
and quiet allusions always at hand to produce a
laugh.'—WILLIAM HAZLITT ("Spirit of the Age").

*Musical
faculty.*

Nature had gifted him with an intense dramatic
perception, an exquisite ear for music, and a voice
of extraordinary compass, power, flexibility, and
beauty.   It extended from the C below the line to
the F sharp above : there were no "passages" that
he could not execute ; the quality was sweet, clear,
and ringing : he would equally have sung the music of *Don Giovanni* or *Sarastro*, or *Oroveso* or *Mao-
metto Secondo*.   Yet nature had not endowed him
with some of the qualities needed for the practical
musician,—he had no aptitude for mechanical con-
trivance, but faint enjoyment of power for its own
sake.   He dabbled on the pianoforte ; delighted to
repeat airs pleasing or plaintive ; and if he would
occasionally fling himself into the audacious revels
of *Don Giovanni*, he preferred to be *Lindoro* or *Don
Ottavio ;* and still more, by the help of his falsetto, to
dally with the tender treble of the *Countess* in *Figaro*
or *Polly* in *Beggar's Opera*.   This waiving of the
potential, this preference for the lightsome and
tender, ran through all his character,—save when
duty bade him draw upon his sterner resources ;
and then out came the inflexibility of the Shewell

---

¹ See Hawthorne's account of Hunt's conversation, p. 256 *et seq.*

and the unyielding determination of the Hunts.
But as soon as the occasion passed, the manner
passed with it; and the man whose solemn, clear-
voiced indignation had made the very floor and
walls vibrate was seen tenderly and blandly exten-
uating the error of his persecutor and gayly confess-
ing to a community of mistake.—THORNTON HUNT
(*Cornhill Magazine*, January, 1860).

Firmness.

I was first introduced to Leigh Hunt at a party,
when I remember he sang a cheery sea-song with
much spirit in that sweet, small baritone voice
which he possessed.   His manner—fascinating, animated, full of cordial amenity, and winning to a
degree of which I have never seen the parallel—
drew me to him at once, and I fell as pronely in
love with him as any girl in her teens falls in love
with her first-seen Romeo.—MARY COWDEN CLARKE
("Recollections of Writers ").

*A girl's en-
thusiasm.*

His comparative estimates of authors were perhaps sometimes at fault.   He liked Milton more,
and Spenser far more, than Shakespeare.   I never
saw a volume of that greatest of dramatists and
poets in his house; but the beloved Spenser was always there, close at hand, for quotation or reference.—BRYAN W. PROCTER (" Recollections of Men
of Letters ").

*Literary
taste.*

His memory was marvellous; and to try him in
history, biography, bibliography, or topography,
was to draw forth an oral "article " on the topic in
question.   Ask him where was the Ouse, and he
would tell you of all the rivers so called; what were

Memory.

the books on a given subject, and you had the list.
. . . His conversation was an exhaustless *Curios-*
Memory. *ities of Literature.* The delighted visitor *read* his
host,—but it was from a talking book, with cordial
voice naturally pitched to every change of subject,
animated gesture, sparkling eyes, and overflowing
sympathy.—THORNTON HUNT (*Cornhill Magazine*,
January, 1860).

One characteristic of Leigh Hunt, for which few
gave him credit, was his great capacity for work.
Industry. His writings were the result of immense labor and
painstaking, of the most conscientious investigation
of facts, where facts were needed ; and of a complete
devotion of his faculties towards the object to be accomplished. Notwithstanding his great experience,
he was never a very rapid writer. He corrected,
excised, reconsidered, and elaborated his productions
(unless when pressed for time), with the most minute attention to details.—E. O. [Edmund Ollier ?]
(*Spectator*, September 3, 1859).

His whole existence and his habit of mind, were
essentially literary. If it were possible to form any
Absorbed in computation of the hours which he expended
literature. severally in literary labor and in recreation, after
the manner of statistical comparisons, it would be
found that the largest portion of his hours was devoted to hard work in the seclusion of the study, and
that by far the larger portion of the allotted " recreation " was devoted to reading, either in the study
or in the society of his family.—THORNTON HUNT
(Introduction to L. H.'s " Autobiography ").

Those who knew him best will picture him to themselves clothed in a dressing gown, and bending his head over a book or over the desk. At some periods of his life he rose early, in order that he might get to work early, . . . for the most part, however, he habitually came down "too late" for breakfast, and was no sooner seated sideways at the table than he began to read. After breakfast he repaired to his study, where he remained until he went out to take his walk. He sometimes read at dinner, though not always. At some periods of his life he would sleep after dinner; but usually he retired from the table to read. He read at tea-time, and all the evening read or wrote.—THORNTON HUNT (Introduction to L. H.'s "Autobiography").

Absorbed in literature.

There was surely never a man of so sunny a nature, who could draw so much pleasure from common things, or to whom books were a world so real, so exhaustless, so delightful. I was only seventeen when I derived from him the tastes which have been the solace of all subsequent years.—JOHN FORSTER ("Life of Dickens").

Sunny nature—Free from envy.

He was very good-tempered; thoroughly easy tempered. He saw hosts of writers, of less ability than himself, outstripping him on the road to future success, yet I never heard from him a word that could be construed into jealousy or envy; not even a murmur.—BYRAN W. PROCTER ("Recollections of Men of Letters").

Leigh Hunt's whole teaching of himself as well as others, inculcated a perception of cheerfulness as a

A teacher of cheerfulness. duty, not for the selfish gain of the one man himself, but for the sake of making the happier atmosphere for others, and of rendering the more perfect homage to the Author of all good and happiness. . . . The sense of existence was to him a ceaseless perception of the beauty unfolded in the universe.— THORNTON HUNT ("Correspondence of L. H.")

Love of truth. In one of his letters to me he writes :—" I would rather be considered a hearty loving nature than anything else in the world, and if I love truth, as I do, it is because I love an apple to be thought an apple, and a hand a hand, and the whole beauty and hopefulness of God's creation a truth instead of a lie." He was justified in saying of himself that he had "two good qualities to set off against many defects—that he was not vindictive and spoke the truth."—SAMUEL C. HALL ("Book of Memories").

Kindly judgment of his contemporaries. All his "notes" concerning his contemporaries (I have some of them still) were genial, cordial, and laudatory, affording no evidence of envy, no taint of depreciation. . . . This generosity of thought and heart is conspicuous in all his writings. . . . He who might have said so many bitter things, utters scarcely one ; he who might have galled his enemies to the quick, does not stab even in thought.[1] —SAMUEL C. HALL ("Book of Memories").

---

[1] One exception must be noted—his book upon Lord Byron and some of his Contemporaries. This was manifestly written in a very bitter spirit, and, in his old age, Hunt expressed regret for having published it.

He was held up to shame as an enemy of religion, whereas he was a man from whose heart there came a flowing piety spreading itself over all nature and in every channel in which it was possible to run. I remember a passage in one of his writings in which he says he never passed a church, of however unreformed a faith, without an instinctive wish to go in and worship for the good of mankind. And all this obloquy, all this injustice, all this social cruelty never for one' moment soured the disposition or excited a revengeful feeling in the breast of this good man.

"A superstition of good."

He had as it were—I have no other phrase for it —a superstition of good. He did not believe in the existence of evil, and when it pressed against him, in the bitterest form against himself, he shut his eyes to it. . . . We know that through all the difficulties of a more than usually hard life he kept to the end a cheerfulness of temper which the most successful might have envied.—LORD HOUGHTON (from an Address delivered in 1869).

Whenever and wherever I met this charming person, I learned a lesson of gentleness and patience ; for, steeped to the lips in poverty as he was, he was ever the most cheerful, the most genial companion and friend. He never left his good-nature outside the family circle, as a Mussulman leaves his slippers outside a mosque, but he always brought a smiling face into the house with him. T—— A——, whose fine floating wit has never yet quite condensed itself into a star, said one day of a Boston man, that he was " east-wind made flesh."

Genial, despite poverty.

Leigh Hunt was exactly the opposite of this; he was compact of all the spicy breezes that blow. In his bare cottage at Hammersmith the temperament of his fine spirit heaped up such riches of fancy that kings, if wise ones, might envy his magic power.— JAMES T. FIELDS (" Old Acquaintance ").[1]

Genial, despite poverty.

Religious views.

His religion (which he styles, in a letter to me, . . . "a sort of luxurious natural piety") was cheerful, hopeful, sympathising, universal in its benevolence. and entirely comprehensive in charity, but it was not the religion of the Christian. . . . He recognized Christ, indeed, but classes him only among those—not even foremost of *them*—who were lights in dark ages ; . . . Confucius, Socrates, Epictetus, Antoninus. Jesus was their "martyred brother," nothing more.—SAMUEL C. HALL (" Book of Memories").

Enjoyment of nature.

He was fond of writing and talking about the country, but knew little of its *flora* and *fauna* beyond some dozen of flowers and half a dozen birds. A few flowers in a glass of water on his writing-table was to him a garden, and a "look-out" upon a distant green field was his country life. The rest was an imaginary Italy. I once heard him discourse while standing in front of a bed of winter cabbages covered with a sparkling hoar-frost, as though it was Nature's jewelry of emeralds and diamonds set in frosted silver ; and assuredly I have read something of a similar kind in one of his es-

---

[1] Fields (James T.). Old Acquaintance : Barry Cornwall and some of his Friends. 32mo. Boston : J. R. Osgood & Co. 1876.

says. But I have been recently reminded by Lord
Houghton of a far more striking instance of a de-
gree of simplicity that could not perceive there was   *Enjoyment
of nature.*
anything ludicrous in its grave counsels, when earnestly exhorting a poor man, if he could not afford
to buy flowers, to take home a handful of grass to
his wife, so that they might contemplate Nature by
that means.—RICHARD H. HORNE ("Mrs. Browning's
Letters ").[1]

Though Leigh Hunt is not deep in knowledge,
moral, metaphysical, or classical, yet he is intense
in feeling, and has an intellect forever on the alert.   *Mental
alertness—
He is like one of those instruments on three legs,   Supersensitiveness.*
which, throw it how you will, always pitches on
two, and has a spike sticking forever up and ever
ready for you. He "sets" at a subject with a scent
like a pointer. He is a remarkable man, and created
a sensation by his independence, his courage, his
disinterestedness in public matters. . . . As a
man, I know none with such an affectionate heart,
if never opposed in his opinions. He has defects,
of course ; one of his great defects is getting inferior
people about him to listen, too fond of shining
at any expense in society, and a love of approbation from the darling sex, bordering upon weakness. . . .
He is a man of sensibility tinged with morbidity,
and of such sensitive organization of body, that the

---

[1] Browning (Elizabeth Barrett). Letters addressed to R. H.
Horne. Edited by S. R. T. Mayer. 2 vols., 8vo. London,
1877. (*This volume also contains reminiscences of contemporaries,
by R. H. Horne.*) .

plant is not more alive to touch than he. I remember once, walking in a field, we came to a muddy
Mental alertness— Supersensitiveness. place concealed by the grass. The moment Hunt
touched it, he shrank back, saying, " It's muddy ! "
as if he meant that it was full of adders.—BENJAMIN
R. HAYDON (Extract from a Letter to Wilkie, published in Haydon's Correspondence).

A favorite luxury. He liked . . . to sit in a large and very easy
chair he had, wrapped in his dressing-gown, surrounded by attentive young ladies who adored him ;
one or more of them—I have seen two—gently
smoothing his long locks in most irritating fashion
to others sometimes, whilst all hung upon his flowing periods, sparkling with that graceful wit and
airiness for which he was so famous.'—FRANCIS H.
GRUNDY (" Pictures of the Past ").

His estimate of praise. He accepted praise less as a mark of respect from
others, than as a delight of which all are entitled to
partake, such as spring weather, the scent of flowers,' or the flavor of wine.— BRYAN W. PROCTER
(" Recollections of Men of Letters ").

Eccentricities as to food. His most remarkable piece of oddity was in his
eating, especially his suppers. He " would take a
fancy," and indulge freely night after night in a
thoroughly indigestible supper of anything which
accident or circumstance might have suggested,

---

¹ Mr. Grundy writes of Leigh Hunt's old age.
² An anonymous writer in the Dublin University Magazine, November, 1861, says, in an article entitled "Leigh Hunt's last
Evening at Home," that Hunt had no sense of smell, and quotes
Hunt's own statement that such was the fact.

from corned beef to Welsh rarebit or Scotch porridge, recommending it eagerly as the most wholesome of eatable things ; then after a week or so of
indulgence, he would have brought on a fit of in-
digestion, upon which he would abuse the innocent,
if indigestible, cause of his illness, "up hill and
down dale." When better he would adopt something else, with similar "praise, blame, and result."

*Eccentrici-
ties as to
food.*

The following interviews are given as nearly ver-
batim as I can remember them after this lapse of
time. Call the time Wednesday evening at nine
P.M. Scene, the drawing-room at Kensington ;
Leigh Hunt seated by himself at table ; on table,
white cloth and tray ; on the tray, three eggs boiled
hard, salt, butter, pepper, and bread. Leigh Hunt
loq. : "Ha, how are you ? I am eating my supper,
you see. Do you eat supper ? If you do, take my
advice, and have regularly every night, at half-past
nine precisely, three eggs boiled hard, with bread
and butter. I have had them now every evening
for five nights, and there is not, I assure you, anything more wholesome for supper. One sleeps so
soundly, too," etc.

Next scene, Friday, time and circumstances as
before, save that the condiment under present consideration is a Welsh rarebit, with mustard, etc. I
enter. Hunt to me : "Ha, how are you ? Have
you seen Vincent ? I am just getting supper, you
see. Do you ever eat supper ? If you do, I pray
you, *never* take boiled eggs ; they are, without any
exception, the most indigestible, nightmare-produc-
ing, etc. They have nearly killed me. No ; the
lightest and most palatable supper I have ever taken

*Eccentrici-
ties as to
food.*

is a Welsh rarebit with Scotch ale. This is the second day I have taken it, and I do assure you," etc. On Monday next it would be liver and bacon. His longest love in my time was his old love, dried fruit, bread, and water—his Italian memory.—FRANCIS H. GRUNDY (" Pictures of the Past ").

*Whims
about exer-
cises.*

He was curiously eccentric even when in his best moods. He would take his exact number of constitutional strides backwards and forwards at exactly the same hour daily : so many made a mile, and not one more or less would he take or give ;.another turn would have been destruction.—FRANCIS H. GRUNDY (" Pictures of the Past ").

*Lack of
business
ability.*

I had never attended, not only to the business part of the *Examiner*, but to the simplest money matter that stared at me on the face of it. I could never tell any body who asked me, what was the price of its stamp ! Do I boast of this ignorance ? Alas ! I have no such respect for the pedantry of absurdity as that. I blush for it ; and I only record it out of a sheer painful movement of conscience, as a warning to those young authors who might be led to look upon such folly as a fine thing ; which at all events is what I never thought it myself. I did not think about it at all, except to avoid the thought : and I only wish that the strangest accidents of education, and the most inconsiderate habit of taking books for the only ends of life, had not conspired to make me so ridiculous.—LEIGH HUNT (" Autobiography ").

It was no affectation when he declared himself entirely incompetent to deal with the simplest ques-

tion of arithmetic. The very commonest sum was a
bewilderment to him. . . . It was a born inca-
pacity, similar to that of people who cannot distin- *Arithmetic.*
guish the notes of music or the colors of the prism.
. . . He regarded himself as a sort of idiot in the
handling of figures; and he was consequently inca-
pacitated for many subjects which he could handle
very well when they were explained to him in another
form.—THORNTON HUNT ("Correspondence of L.
H.").

One afternoon Leigh Hunt drove up to the door
in a hansom. I met him at the door, where he was
beaming benevolently at the cabman, who was beam- *Adventure*
ing too. Says Leigh Hunt after the usual salutations, *with a*
"Fine fellow that!" I ask how, for neither man, *cabman.*
cab, horse, nor harness seemed particularly "fine."
"Well," says Leigh Hunt "I found him returning
from Hammersmith, and he said as an empty he
would take me for half fare" (the whole fare was
about three shillings), "so I told him to drive on.
He drove nicely and steadily, and now when I asked
him his fare, he left it to my honor. You know
nothing could be fairer than that, so I said I was
sorry to say that I had only two half sovereigns in
my pocket, would one of them do? I could give
him that, and, if not enough, he could call at so-and-
so, or I could borrow it from you. 'Oh, that would
do,' he said ; he would not trouble you. He took it,
thanked me, and was getting on to his cab when I
stopped him to say that I was pleased with him, and
that I should be returning about nine to-night, when,
if he liked, he might come for me, and receive the
III.—16

same fare back. He said he would, but now he has driven away so suddenly as you opened the door that I hardly know what to think."—FRANCIS H. GRUNDY ("Pictures of the Past").

Self-por-traiture.

I felt age coming on me, and difficulties not lessened by failing projects : nor was I able, had I been ever so inclined, to render my faculties profitable "in the market." . . . A man can only do what he can do, or as others will let him. Suppose he has a conscience that will not suffer him to reproduce the works of other people, or even to speak what he thinks commonplace enough to have become public property. Suppose this conscience will not allow him to accommodate himself to the opinion of editors and reviewers. Suppose the editors and reviewers themselves will not encourage him to write on the subjects he understands best, perhaps do not understand the subjects themselves ; or, at least, play with him, and delay him, and keep him only as a resource when their own circle fails them. Suppose he has had to work his way up through animosities, political and religious, and through such clouds of adversity as, even when they have passed away, leave a chill of misfortune round his repute, and make "prosperity" slow to encourage him. Suppose, in addition to all this, he is in bad health, and of fluctuating as well as peculiar powers ; of a temperament easily solaced in mind, and as easily drowsed in body ; quick to enjoy every object in creation, every thing in nature and in art, every sight, every sound, every book, picture, and flower, and at the same time really qualified to do nothing, but either to preach the enjoyment of those objects in modes derived from his own particular nature and breeding, or to suffer with mingled cheerfulness and poverty the consequences of advocating some theory on the side of human progress. Great may sometimes be the misery of that man under the necessity of requesting forbearance or undergoing obligation ; and terrible will be his doubts, whether some of his friends may not think he had better have had a conscience less nice, or an activity less at the mercy of his physique.—LEIGH HUNT ("Autobiography"). *Self-por-traiture.*

In his presentation of his father's moral nature and intellectual qualities, Mr. Hunt is . . . faithful and touching.[1] Those who knew Leigh Hunt will see the bright face, and hear the musical voice again, when he is recalled to them in this passage : " Few men were more attractive in society, whether in a large company or over the fireside. His manners were peculiarly animated ; his conversation, varied, ranging over a great field of subjects, was moved and called forth by the response of his companion. . . . With much freedom of manners, he combined a spontaneous courtesy that never failed, and a considerateness derived from a ceaseless kindness of heart, that invariably fascinated even strangers. . . . His animation, his sympathy with what was gay and pleasurable ; his avowed doctrine of cultivating cheerfulness, were manifest on the surface, and could be appreciated *Dickens's explanation concerning " Harold Skimpole."*

---

[1] The reference is to Thornton Hunt's Introduction to the revised edition of his father's autobiography.

by those who knew him in society, most probably even exaggerated as salient traits, on which he himself insisted *with a sort of gay and ostentatious wilfulness."*

Dickens's explanation concerning "Harold Skimpole."

The last words describe one of the most captivating peculiarities of a most original and engaging man, better than any other words could. The reader is besought to observe them, for a reason that shall presently be given. . . . Four or five years ago, the writer of these lines was much pained by accidentally encountering a printed statement, "that Mr. Leigh Hunt was the original of Harold Skimpole in Bleak House." . . . The fact is this :—

Exactly those graces and charms of manner which are remembered in the words we have quoted, were remembered by the author of the work of fiction in question, when he drew the character in question. Above all other things, that "sort of gay and ostentatious wilfulness" in the humoring of a subject, which had many a time delighted him, and impressed him as being unspeakably whimsical and attractive, was the airy quality he wanted for the man he invented. Partly for this reason, and partly (he has since often grieved to think) for the pleasure it afforded him to find that delightful manner reproducing itself under his hand, he yielded to the temptation of too often making the character *speak* like his old friend. He no more thought—God forgive him !—that the admired original would ever be charged with the imaginary vices of the fictitious character, than he has himself ever thought of charging the blood of Desdemona and Othello on the innocent academy model who sat for Iago's leg in the picture.—CHARLES DICKENS (*All the Year Round*, December 24, 1859).

I have seen him in many situations calculated to try the nerves, and never saw him moved by personal fear. He has been in a carriage of which the horses ran away, and seemed only to enjoy the rapidity of the motion ; in fact, I believe he could scarcely present to his mind the chances of personal mischief that were before us. I have seen him threatened, more than once, by brutal and brawny rustics, whom he instantly approached with an animated and convincing remonstrance. I have seen him in a carriage nearly carried away by a flooded river, his whole anxiety being centred in one of his children, whom he thought to be more exposed than himself. I have seen him for weeks together, each hour of the day, in imminent danger of shipwreck, and never observed the slightest solicitude, except for those about him. . . . But there *was* a species of fear which beset him in every situation of life—it was, lest he might not do quite what was right ; lest some terrible evil should be inflicted upon somebody else ; and this thought, if he reflected, did sometimes paralyse his action and provoke evident emotion.—THORNTON HUNT (" Introduction to L. H.'s Autobiography ").

Courage.

Those who imagine that Leigh Hunt was indifferent to his pecuniary obligations, in the most curious manner invert the true state of the case. He was so incessantly haunted by them, so over-anxious to

Anxiety about debts.

fulfil all that was due from him, that he often para-
lysed his own powers. At a later day, he had the
Anxiety about debts. means of not only keeping pace with the time, but
of recovering these arrears ; . . . he never pre-
termitted the endeavor, and derived immense satisfaction from the progress made.—THORNTON HUNT
(" Correspondence of L. H.").

His friend, Mr. Reynell, tells me . . . that in
his later days Mr. Hunt often said to him his great
wish was, that when he died he should not owe to
any one a half-penny. He had borrowed from the
good Duke of Devonshire a sum of £200, and *returned it to him*. . . . Hunt was indebted to Mr.
Reynell—a debt incurred by Mr. Reynell becoming
surety for him in 1832. . . . Twenty years afterward he repaid that sum—on receiving the first
instalment of Shelley's legacy—as he had promised he
would do.—SAMUEL C. HALL (" Book of Memories ").

Perhaps the mastering trait in his character was
a conscientiousness which was carried even to ex-
Conscien-tiousness. tremes. While he possessed an uncertain grasp of
material facts, . . . and viewed things most
distinctly when they were presented to his mind in
the mirror of some abstraction, he never was able
to rest with a final confidence in his own judgment.
The anxiety to recognise the right of others, the
tendency to " refine," which was noticed by an early
school companion, and the propensity to elaborate
every thought, made him, along with the direct
argument by which he sustained his own conviction,
recognise and almost admit all that might be said
on the opposite side. If, indeed, the facts upon

which he had to rely had become matter of literary record, he would collect them with an unwearied industry of research ; but in the action of life these resources did not always avail him ; and the excessive anxiety to take into account all that might be advanced on every side, with the no less excessive wish to do what was right, to avoid every chance of wrong, and, if possible, to abstain from causing any pain, begot an uncertainty of purpose for which I can find no known prototype except in the character of Hamlet.—THORNTON HUNT (" Introduction to L. H.'s Autobiography "). *Conscientiousness.*

His life was in several respects, a life of trouble, though his cheerfulness was such that he was, upon the whole, happier than some men who have had fewer griefs to wrestle with. . . . Leigh Hunt's was an essentially human nature, rich and inclusive. . . . It has been said occasionally that Leigh Hunt was a weak man. He had, it is true, particular weaknesses, as evinced in his want of business knowledge, and in a certain hesitation of judgment on some points, which his son has aptly likened to the ultra deliberation of Hamlet, and which was the result of an extreme conscientiousness. But a man who had the courage to take his stand against power on behalf of right [1]—who, in the midst of the sorest *Not a weak man.*

---

[1] In 1813 Hunt and his brother were sentenced to two years' imprisonment for a very severe article upon the Prince Regent (afterwards George IV.), which had been published in the *Examiner*. The Government made several offers of compromise, upon condition that no more articles of the same kind should be published in the *Examiner*. These offers were rejected, and the brothers went to prison for two years.

temptations, maintained his honesty unblemished by a single stain—who, in all public and private *Not a weak man.* transactions, was the very soul of truth and honor —who never bartered his opinion or betrayed his friend—could not have been a weak man.—CHARLES DICKENS (*All the Year Round*, December 24, 1859).

Leigh Hunt was here [1] almost nightly, three or four times a week, I should reckon ; he came always *Carlyle's sketches.* neatly dressed, was thoroughly courteous, friendly of spirit, and talked like a singing-bird. Good insight, plenty of a kind of humor too ; I remember little warbles in the tones of his fine voice which were full of fun and charm. We gave him Scotch porridge to supper ("nothing in nature so interesting and delightful") ; she played him Scotch tunes ; a man he to understand and feel them well. His talk was often enough (perhaps at first oftenest), literary, biographical, autobiographical, wandering into criticism, reform of society, progress, etc., etc., on which latter points he gradually found me very shocking (I believe—so fatal to his rose-colored visions on the subject).—THOMAS CARLYLE ("Reminiscences").

Our commonest evening sitter, for a good while, was Leigh Hunt, who lived close by, and delighted to sit talking with us (free, cheery, idly melodious as bird on bough), or listening, with real feeling, to her old Scotch tunes on the piano, and winding up with a frugal morsel of Scotch porridge (endlessly admirable to Hunt). I think I spoke of this

---

[1] At Carlyle's house in London.

above? Hunt was always accurately dressed these evenings, and had a fine, chivalrous, gentlemanly carriage, polite, affectionate, respectful (especially to her), and yet so free and natural. Her brilliancy and faculty he at once recognized, none better, but there rose gradually in it, to his astonished eye, something of positive, of practically steadfast, which scared him off a good deal; the like in my own case too, still more, which he would call "Scotch," "Presbyterian," who knows what; and which gradually repelled him, in sorrow, not in anger, quite away from us, with rare exceptions, which, in his last years, was almost pathetic to us both. Long before this he had gone to live in Kensington, and we scarcely saw him except by accident. His household, while in "4 Upper Cheyne Row," within few steps of us here, almost at once disclosed itself to be huggermugger, unthrift, and sordid collapsed, once for all, and had to be associated with on cautious terms, while he himself emerged out of it in the chivalrous figure I describe. Dark complexion (a trace of the African, I believe), copious, clean, strong black hair, beautifully shaped head, fine beaming serious hazel eyes; seriousness and intellect the main expression of the face (to our surprise at first); he would lean on his elbow against the mantel-piece (fine, clean, elastic figure, too, he had, five feet ten or more), and look round him nearly in silence, before taking leave for the night, "as if I were a Lar," said he once, "or permanent household god here" (such his polite, aerial-like way). Another time, rising from this Lar attitude, he repeated (voice very fine) as if in sport of parody, yet with

Carlyle's sketches.

something of very sad perceptible, "While I to sulphurous and penal fire " . . . as the last thing before vanishing.—THOMAS CARLYLE ("Reminiscences ").

His hair is grizzled, eyes black-hazel, complexion of the clearest dusky-brown ; a thin glimmer of a smile plays over a face of cast-iron gravity. He never laughs—can only titter, which I think indicates his worst deficiency. His house excels all you have ever read of—a *poetical Tinkerdom*, without parallel even in literature. In his family room, where are a sickly large wife and a whole shoal of well-conditioned wild children, you will find half a dozen old rickety chairs gathered from half a dozen different hucksters, and all seemingly engaged, and just pausing, in a violent *hornpipe*. On these and around them, and over the dusty table and ragged carpet, lie all kinds of litter—books, papers, egg-shells, scissors, and last night when I was there the torn heart of a half-quartern loaf. His own room above-stairs, into which alone I strive to enter, he keeps cleaner. It has only two chairs, a bookcase, and a writing-table ; yet the noble Hunt receives you in his Tinkerdom in the spirit of a king, apologizes for nothing, places you in the best seat, takes a window-sill himself if there is no other, and there folding closer his loose-flowing 'muslin-cloud' of a printed nightgown in which he always writes, commences the liveliest dialogue on philosophy and the prospects of man (who is to be beyond measure 'happy' yet) ; which again he will courteously terminate the moment you are bound to go : a most interesting, pitiable, lovable man, to be used kindly but with discretion.—THOMAS CARLYLE (From two letters of 1834, in Froude's "Carlyle").

Mr. Hunt is a man of the most indisputably superior worth ; a *Man of Genius* in a very strict sense of that word, and in all the senses which it bears or implies : of brilliant varied gifts, of graceful fertility, of clearness, lovingness, truthfulness ; of child-like open character ; also of most pure, and even exemplary private deportment ; a man who can be other than *loved* only by those who have not seen him, or seen him from a distance through a false medium. . . . Well seen into, he *has* done much for the world ;—as every man possessed of such qualities, and freely speaking them forth in the abundance of his heart for thirty years long, must needs do ; *how* much they that could judge best would perhaps estimate highest.—THOMAS CARLYLE ("Memoranda concerning Mr. Leigh Hunt").[1]

A great cynic's judgment.

As he advanced in life, from youth to middle age, he was a living refutation of the worldly maxims which attribute generosity to youth, and harder virtues to maturity and old age. In literature, as in daily life, as he grew older he became kindly and considerate to a fault.—ANON. (*Athenæum*, September 3, 1859).

Mellowing with age.

He has been censured for literary affectation and for personal improvidence, but only by those who

---

[1] Printed in Alexander Ireland's List of the Writings of William Hazlitt and Leigh Hunt, etc. 8vo. London, 1868.

*A son's
estimate.*
do not understand the real elements of his character. The leading ideas of his mind were, first,
earnest duty to his country at any cost to himself ;
next, the sacrifice of any ordinary consideration to
personal affection and friendship ; and lastly, the
cultivation of " the ideal," especially as it is developed in imaginative literature. His life was
passed in an absolute devotion to these three principles. A one-sided frankness has blazoned to the
world the sacrifices which he accepted from friends,
but has whispered nothing of the more than com-
mensurate sacrifices made on his side ; and the
simplicity that rendered him the creature of the
library in which he lived entered into the expression of all his thoughts and feelings.—THORNTON
HUNT (*Atlantic Monthly*, February, 1863).

*Haw-
thorne's
visit.*
He was then [1] at Hammersmith, occupying a very
plain and shabby little house, in a contiguous range
of others like it, with no prospect but that of an
ugly village street, and certainly nothing to gratify
his craving for a tasteful environment, inside or
out. A slatternly maid-servant opened the door for
us, and he himself stood in the entry, a beautiful
and venerable old man, buttoned to the chin in a
black dress-coat, tall and slender, with a countenance quietly alive all over, and the gentlest and
most naturally courteous manner. He ushered us
into his little study, or parlor, or both,—a very for-
lorn room, with poor paper-hangings and carpet,
few books, no pictures that I remember, and an
awful lack of upholstery. I touch distinctly upon

[1] About 1855.

these external blemishes and this nudity of adorn-
ment, not that they would be worth mentioning in
a sketch of other remarkable persons, but because
Leigh Hunt was born with such a faculty of enjoy-
ing all beautiful things that it seemed as if Fortune
did him as much wrong in not supplying them as
in withholding a sufficiency of vital breath from ordinary men.   All kinds of mild magnificence, tempered by his taste, would have become him well ;
but he had not the grim dignity that assumes naked-
ness as the better robe.

*Haw-
thorne's
visit.*

I have said that he was a beautiful old man.   In
truth I never saw a finer countenance, either as to
the mould of features or the expression, nor any
that showed the play of feeling so perfectly without
the slightest theatrical emphasis.   It was like a
child's face in this respect.   At my first glimpse of
him, when he met us in the entry, I discerned that
he was old, his long hair being white and his
wrinkles many ; it was an aged visage, in short,
such as I had not at all expected to see, in spite of
dates, because his books talk to the reader with the
tender vivacity of youth.   But when he began to
speak, and as he grew more earnest in conversation,
I ceased to be sensible of his age ; sometimes, indeed, its dusky shadow darkened through the gleam
which his sprightly thoughts diffused about his face,
but then another flash of youth came out of his eyes
and made an illumination again.   I never witnessed
such a wonderfully illusive transformation, before
or since ; and, to this day, trusting only to my recollection, I should find it difficult to decide which
was his genuine and stable predicament,—youth or

age.   I have met no Englishman whose manners seemed to me so agreeable, soft, rather than polished, wholly unconventional, the natural growth of a kindly and sensitive disposition without any reference to rule, or else obedient to some rule so subtile that the nicest observer could not detect the application of it.

His eyes were dark and very fine, and his delightful voice accompanied their visible language like music.   He appeared to be exceedingly appreciative of whatever was passing among those who surrounded him, and especially of the vicissitudes in the consciousness of the person to whom he happened to be addressing himself at the moment.   I felt that no effect upon my mind of what he uttered, no emotion, however transitory, in myself, escaped his notice, though not from any positive vigilance on his part, but because his faculty of observation was so penetrative and delicate ; and to say the truth, it a little confused me to discern always a ripple on his mobile face, responsive to any slightest breeze that passed over the inner reservoir of my sentiments, and seemed thence to extend to a similar reservoir within himself.   On matters of feeling, and within a certain depth, you might spare yourself the trouble of utterance, because he already knew what you wanted to say, and perhaps a little more than you would have spoken. His figure was full of gentle movement, though, somehow, without disturbing its quietude ; and as he talked, he kept folding his hands nervously, and betokened in many ways a fine and immediate sensibility, quick to feel pleasure or pain, though scarcely capable, I should imagine, of a passionate experience in either direction. There was not an English trait in him from head to foot, morally, intellectually, or physically. Beef, ale, or stout, brandy, or port wine, entered not at all into his composition. In his earlier life, he appears to have given evidences of courage and sturdy principle, and of a tendency to fling himself into the rough struggle of humanity on the liberal side. It would be taking too much upon myself to affirm that this was merely a projection of his fancy world into the actual, and that he never could have hit a downright blow, and was altogether an unsuitable person to receive one. I beheld him not in his armor, but in his peacefullest robes. Nevertheless, drawing my conclusion merely from what I saw, it would have occurred to me that his main deficiency was a lack of grit. Though anything but a timid man, the combative and defensive elements were not prominently developed in his character, and could have been made available only when he put an unnatural force upon his instincts. It was on this account, and also because of the fineness of his nature generally, that the English appreciated him no better, and left this sweet and delicate poet poor, and with scanty laurels in his declining age. . . .

Hawthorne's visit.

Leigh Hunt loved dearly to be praised. That is to say, he desired sympathy as a flower seeks sunshine, and perhaps profited by it as much in the richer depth of coloring that it imparted to his ideas. In response to all that we ventured to express about his writings (and, for my part, I went quite to the extent of my conscience, which was a long way, and there left the matter to a lady and a young girl, who happily were with me), his face shone, and he manifested great delight, with a perfect, and yet delicate, frankness for which I loved him. He could not tell us, he said, the happiness that such appreciation gave him ; it always took him by surprise, he remarked, for—perhaps because he cleaned his own boots, and performed other little ordinary offices for himself—he never had been conscious of anything wonderful in his own person. And then he smiled, making all the poor little parlor about him beautiful thereby. It is usually the hardest thing in the world to praise a man to his face ; but Leigh Hunt received the incense with such gracious satisfaction (feeling it to be sympathy, not vulgar praise), that the only difficulty was to keep the enthusiasm of the moment within the limit of permanent opinion. A storm had suddenly come up while we were talking ; the rain poured, the lightning flashed, and the thunder broke ; but I hope, and have great pleasure in believing, that it was a sunny hour for Leigh Hunt. Nevertheless, it was not to my voice that he most favorably inclined his ear, but to those of my companions. Women are the fit ministers at such a shrine.

He must have suffered keenly in his lifetime, and enjoyed keenly, keeping his emotions so much upon the surface as he seemed to do, and convenient for everybody to play upon. Being of a cheerful temperament, happiness had probably the upper hand. His was a light, mildly joyous nature, gentle, graceful, yet seldom attaining to that deepest grace which

results from power ; for beauty, like woman, its
human representative, dallies with the gentle, but
yields its consummate treasure only to the strong.
I imagine that Leigh Hunt may have been more
beautiful when I met him, both in person and character, than in his earlier days.   As a young man I
could conceive of his being finical in certain moods,
but not now, when the gravity of age shed a venerable grace about him.   I rejoiced to hear him say
that he was favored with most confident and cheering anticipations in respect to a future life ; and
there were abundant proofs, throughout our interview, of an unrepining spirit, resignation, quiet
relinquishment of the worldly benefits that were
denied him, thankful enjoyment of whatever he
had to enjoy, and piety, and hope shining onward
into the dusk,—all of which gave a reverential cast
to the feeling with which we parted from him.   I
wish he could have had one full draught of prosperity before he died.   As a matter of artistic propriety, it would have been delightful to see him
inhabiting a beautiful house of his own, in an Italian climate, with all sorts of elaborate upholstery
and minute elegances about him, and a succession
of tender and lovely women to praise his sweet
poetry from morning to night.   I hardly know
whether it is my fault, or the effect of a weakness
in Leigh Hunt's character, that I should be sensible
of a regret of this nature, when, at the same time,
I sincerely believe that he has found an infinity of
better things in the world whither he has gone.

At our leave-taking he grasped me warmly by
both hands, and seemed as much interested in our

*Haw-
thorne's
visit.*

III.—17

whole party as if he had known us for years. All this was genuine feeling, a quick luxuriant growth out of his heart, which was a soil for flower-seeds of rich and rare varieties, not acorns, but a true heart, nevertheless. Several years afterwards I met him for the last time at a London dinner-party, looking sadly broken down by infirmities ; and my final recollection of the beautiful old man presents him arm in arm with, nay, if I mistake not, partly embraced and supported by, another beloved and honored poet, whose minstrel-name, since he has a week-day one for his personal occasions, I will venture to speak. It was Barry Cornwall, whose kind introduction had first made me known to Leigh Hunt.—NATHANIEL HAWTHORNE ("Our Old Home").[1]

---

[1] Hawthorne (Nathaniel). Our Old Home : a Series of English Sketches. 16mo. Boston : Ticknor & Fields, 1863. (The preceding extract from Hawthorne is reprinted in this volume by the courtesy of Messrs. Houghton, Mifflin, & Co.)

BRYAN WALLER PROCTER.

1787–1874.

INTRODUCTORY NOTE.

"BARRY CORNWALL" was the youngest of this little company of friends, and he outlived them all by many years. He saw the dawn of Wordsworth's fame; he saw the full development of the powers of Tennyson and of Browning; and he lived to witness the rise of poets, who have demonstrated the inability of the highest technical skill to conceal or atone for dearth of feeling and poverty of imagination.

His long life was prosperous and happy; unmarked by stirring incidents or strange experiences. The quiet beauty of his character was sullied by no departures from the even course of mental and moral sanity. Men of this kind do not invite remark. Biographers miss in them the sharp contrasts which give the light and shade essential to an effective picture. Still it is surprising how very few accounts we have of Procter. The leading facts of his life, and some pleasant personal reminiscences, are recorded in a volume edited by Coventry Patmore, and entitled "Bryan Waller Procter: an Autobiographical Fragment, and Biographical Notes." This is the only memoir of him, nor is it at all likely that a more formal and extended work will be attempted.

His nature was gentle and retiring ; warmly affectionate, yet not effusive ; calmly and steadily
cheerful, rather than gay ; as far removed from dul-
ness as from boisterous hilarity. " The tradition
of such a character," says Mr. Patmore, " has the
power of lingering in the world, even when the life
has been so uneventful as to leave little scope for biography or even for anecdote." A serenity and harmony, too rarely seen in the lives of literary men,
form the essential charm of Procter's character, and
give a sense of repose and relief to all our thoughts
of this happily constituted man.

LEADING EVENTS OF PROCTER'S LIFE.

1787.   Born, November 21st, in London.
1800, *circa.*—(Aged 13.) A scholar at Harrow.
1815.—(Aged 28.) Contributes poems to the *London Literary Ga-
                zette.*
1816.—(Aged 29.) Comes into possession of property, upon the
                death of his father.
1819.—(Aged 32.) Publishes " Dramatic Scenes."
1820.—(Aged 33.) Publishes " A Sicilian Story," and " Marcian
                Colonna."
1821.—(Aged 34.) His tragedy of " Mirandola," performed at
                Covent Garden Theatre.
1823.—(Aged 36.) Publishes " The Flood of Thessaly," and other
                poems.
1824.—(Aged 37.) Marries Miss Skepper.
1831.—(Aged 44.) Called to the bar.   Publishes   " English
                Songs."
1832.—(Aged 45.) Appointed Commissioner of Lunacy. Publishes
                second edition of " English Songs."
1835.—(Aged 48.) Publishes the " Life of Edmund Kean."
1861.—(Aged 74.) Resigns his office of Commissioner.
1866.—(Aged 79.) Publishes " Charles Lamb, a Biography."
1874.—(Aged 86 years and 10 months.) Dies, October 4th.

BRYAN WALLER PROCTER.

THE poet's figure was short and full, and his voice had a low, veiled tone habitually in it, which made it sometimes difficult to hear distinctly what he was saying. When in conversation he liked to be very near his listener, and thus stand, as it were, on confidential ground with him. His turn of thought was cheerful among his friends, and he proceeded readily into a vein of wit and nimble expression. Verbal felicity seemed natural to him, and his epithets, evidently unprepared, were always perfect. He disliked cant and hard ways of judging character. He praised easily. He had no wish to stand in anybody's shoes but his own, and he said, "There is no literary vice of a darker shade than envy." Talleyrand's recipe for perfect happiness was the opposite to his. He impressed every one who came near him as a born gentleman, chivalrous and generous in a marked degree, and it was the habit of those who knew him to have an affection for him. Altering a line of Pope, this counsel might have been safely tendered to all the authors of his day,—

Sketch of general characteristics.

"Disdain whatever *Procter's mind* disdains."

JAMES T. FIELDS ("Old Acquaintance ").

Carlyle's recollections.

A decidedly rather pretty little fellow, Procter, bodily and spiritually; manners prepossessing, slightly London-elegant, not unpleasant; clear judgment in him, though of narrow field; a sound honorable morality, and airy friendly ways; of slight neat figure, ·vigorous for his size; fine genially rugged little face, fine head; something curiously dreamy in the eyes of him, lids drooping at the *outer* ends into a cordially meditative and droopng expression; would break out suddenly now and then into opera attitude and a *Là ci darem la mano* for a moment; had something of real fun, though in London style. Me he had invited to "his garret," as he called it, and was always good and kind and so continues, though I hardly see him once in a quarter of a century.—THOMAS CARLYLE (" Reminiscences ").

Voice and manner.

A plain, middle-sized, English-looking gentleman, elderly, with white hair, and particularly quiet in his manners. He talks in a somewhat low tone without emphasis, scarcely distinct. . . . His head has a good outline, and would look well in marble. . . . He said that in his younger days he was a scientific pugilist, and once took a journey to have a sparring encounter with the Game-Chicken. Certainly no one would have looked for a pugilist in this subdued old gentleman. . . . He is slightly deaf.—NATHANIEL HAWTHORNE (" English Note-Books ").[1]

[1] Hawthorne (Nathaniel). Passages from English Note-books. 2 vols., 12mo. Boston: Fields, Osgood & Co., 1870.

He had a modest—nay, shy—manner in company ; heightened by a singular nervous affection, a kind of sudden twitch or contraction, that spasmodically flitted athwart his face as he conversed upon any lofty theme, or argued on some high-thoughted topic.—MARY COWDEN CLARKE (" Recollections of Writers ").

Voice and manner.

There are three or four individuals who used to form part of those pleasant *symposii,*[1] to whom the nature of these Recollections calls upon me to refer more particularly. . . . The most distinguished of these was the amiable and gifted poet, so universally known to the reading world under the name of Barry Cornwall. This gentleman used but seldom to grace our simple feasts of " reason " (or of folly, as the case might be) ; but when he did look in by accident, or was induced by Hazlitt's request to come, everything went off the better for his presence ; for, besides the fact of Hazlitt's being fond of his society, and, at the same time, thinking so highly of his talents as always to talk his best when he (Procter) was a partaker of the talk, there is an endearing something in the personal manner of that exquisite writer, an appearance of gentle and genial sympathy with the feelings of those with whom he talks, which has the effect of exciting towards him that *personal* interest from which it seems itself to spring, and in the absence of which the better feelings and mental characteristics incident to social converse are seldom if ever called forth. In Procter Hazlitt always found

A choice companion.

---

[1] Mr. Patmore is here alluding to the evening gatherings at inns and coffee-houses, where Hazlitt was often present.

A choice companion.

a man of fine and delicate intellectual pretensions, who was nevertheless eager and pleased to listen, with attention and interest, to all the little insignificant details of his daily life. . . . There is . . . between the writings of that delightful poet and his personal character a beautiful correspondence and relationship, which, to those who know him, cause them to act and re-act upon each other, till the result is a pervading sense of gentle sweetness of temperament, and genial goodness of heart. —PETER G. PATMORE ("My Friends and Acquaintance ").

Methods of work.

Miss Martineau, in her short sketch of Mr. Procter, first published in the *Daily News*, tells us that "his favorite method was to compose when he was alone in a crowd, and he declared that he did his best when walking London streets." He had "an odd habit of running into a shop to secure his verses, often carrying them away on scraps of crumpled paper in which cheese or sugar had been wrapped." —COVENTRY PATMORE (in Procter's "Autobiographical Recollections," etc.)

A dinner at Lady Blessington's.

The blaze of lamps on the dinner table was very favorable to my curiosity, and as Procter and D'Israeli sat directly opposite me, I studied their faces to advantage. Barry Cornwall's forehead and eye are all that would strike you in his features. His brows are heavy ; and his eye, deeply sunk, has a quick, restless fire, that would have arrested my attention, I think, had I not known he was a poet. His voice has the huskiness and elevation of a man more accustomed to think than converse, and it was never heard except to give a brief and very condensed opinion, or an illustration, admirably to the point, of the subject under discussion.—NATHANIEL P. WILLIS ("Pencillings by the Way"). *A dinner at Lady Blessington's*

Most of Mr. Procter's intimate friends must have heard him refer, with more pride perhaps than he ever expressed in his other achievements, to the fact that, upon just occasion, he could and did hold his own at Harrow by his pugilistic abilities ; a circumstance to which he, no doubt, looked back with the greater satisfaction of conscience, inasmuch as he was somewhat under-sized (though well-made), and highly sensitive in nerves.—COVENTRY PATMORE (in Procter's "Autobiographical Recollections," etc.) *One of his few boasts.*

Who that ever came habitually into his presence can forget the tones of his voice, the tenderness of his gray retrospective eyes, or the touch of his sympathetic hand laid on the shoulder of a friend ! The elements were indeed so kindly mixed in him that no bitterness, or rancor or jealousy had part or lot in his composition. No distinguished person was ever more ready to help forward the rising and as yet nameless literary man or woman who asked his counsel and warm-hearted suffrage. His mere presence was sunshine to a new-comer into the world of letters and criticism, for he was always quick to encourage, and slow to disparage anybody. Indeed to be *human* only entitled any one who came near him to receive the gracious bounty of his good-ness and courtesy. He made it the happiness of his *Kindliness.*

Kindliness. life never to miss, whenever opportunity occurred, the chance of conferring pleasure and gladness on those who needed kind words and substantial aid.— JAMES T. FIELDS ("Old Acquaintance)."

A general estimate of his character. No one who has passed an hour in the company of Charles Lamb's "dear boy" can ever lose the impression made upon him by that simple, sincere, shy, and delicate soul. His small figure, his head, not remarkable for much besides its expression of intelligent and warm good-will, and its singular likeness to that of Sir Walter Scott ; his conversation, which had little decision or "point" in the ordinary sense, and often dwelt on truths which a novelty-loving society banishes from its repertory as truisms, never disturbed the effect, in any assemblage, of his real distinction. His silence seemed wiser, his simplicity subtler, his shyness more courageous than the wit, philosophy, and assurance of others.—COVENTRY PATMORE (in Procter's "Autobiographical Recollections," etc.).

EVENINGS WITH THE LAMBS.

Sketches by Procter and Talfourd.

EVENINGS WITH THE LAMBS.

THE descriptions of Lamb's "Wednesday evenings," by Procter and Talfourd, may fitly conclude this volume. The first extract is from Procter's biography of Lamb :

"When you went to Lamb's rooms on the Wednesday evenings (his 'At Home'), you generally found the card table spread out, Lamb himself one of the players. On the corner of the table was a snuff-box ; and the game was enlivened by sundry brief ejaculations and pungent questions, which kept alive the wits of the party present It was not 'silent whist'! I do not remember whether, in common with Sarah Battle, Lamb had a weakness in favor of 'Hearts.' I suppose that it was at one of these meetings that he made that shrewd remark which has since escaped into notoriety: 'Martin' (observed he), 'if dirt were trumps, what a hand you would hold!' It is not known what influence Martin's trumps had on the rubber then in progress.—When the conversation became general, Lamb's part in it was very effective. His short, clear sentences always produced effect. He never joined in talk unless he understood the subject ; then, if the matter in question interested him, he was not slow in showing his earnestness ; but I never heard him

argue or talk for argument's sake.   If he was indifferent to the question, he was silent.

" The supper of cold meat, on these occasions,
was always on the side-table ; not very formal, as
may be imagined ; and every one might rise, when
it suited him, and cut a slice or take a glass of porter,
without reflecting on the abstinence of the rest of
the company.   Lamb would, perhaps, call out and
bid the hungry guest help himself without ceremony.   After the game was won (and lost) the ring
of the cheerful glasses announced that punch or
brandy and water had become the order of the
night.   . . .

" Politics were rarely discussed amongst them.
Anecdotes, characteristic, showing the strong and
weak points of human nature, were frequent enough.
But politics (especially party politics) were seldom
admitted.   Lamb disliked them as a theme for evening talk ; he perhaps did not understand the subject scientifically.   And when Hazlitt's impetuosity
drove him, as it sometimes did, into fierce expressions upon public affairs, these were usually received in silence ; and the matter thus raised up
for assent or controversy was allowed to drop.

" Lamb's old associates are now dead. ' They that
lived so long,' as he says, 'and flourished so steadily,
are all crumbled away.'   The beauty of these evenings was, that every one was placed upon an easy
level.   No one out-topped the others.   No one—
not even Coleridge—was permitted to out-talk the
rest.   No one was allowed to hector another, or to
bring his own grievances too prominently forward,
so as to disturb the harmony of the night.   Every

one had a right to speak, and to be heard ; and no one was ever trodden or clamored down (as in some large assemblies) until he had proved that he was not entitled to a hearing, or until he had abused his privilege. I never, in all my life, heard so much unpretending good sense talked, as at Charles Lamb's social parties. Often a piece of sparkling humor was shot out that illuminated the whole evening. Sometimes there was a flight of high and earnest talk, that took one half way towards the stars."

The same scenes are thus described by Talfourd, in his " Final Memorials of Charles Lamb :"

" Now turn to No. 4 Inner Temple Lane, at ten o'clock, when the sedater part of the company are assembled, and the happier stragglers are dropping in from the play. Let it be any autumn or winter month, when the fire is blazing steadily, and the clean-swept hearth and whist-tables speak of the spirit of Mrs. Battle, and serious looks require 'the rigor of the game.' The furniture is old-fashioned and worn ; the ceiling low, and not wholly unstained by traces of 'the great plant,' though now virtuously forborne : but the Hogarths, in narrow black frames, abounding in infinite thought, humor, and pathos, enrich the walls ; and all things wear an air of comfort and hearty English welcome. Lamb himself, yet unrelaxed by the glass, is sitting with a sort of Quaker primness at the whist-table, the gentleness of his melancholy smile half lost in his intentness on the game ; his partner, the author of 'Political Justice' (the majestic expression of his large head not disturbed by disproportion of

III.—18

his comparatively diminutive stature), is regarding
his hand with a philosophic but not a careless eye ;
Captain Burney, only not venerable because so
young in spirit, sits between them ; and H. C. R.,
who alone now and then breaks the proper silence,
to welcome some incoming guest, is his happy partner—true winner in the game of life, whose leisure
achieved early, is devoted to his friends! At another table, just beyond the circle which extends
from the fire, sit another four. The broad, burly,
jovial bulk of John Lamb, the Ajax Telamon of the
slender clerks of the old South Sea House, whom
he sometimes introduces to the rooms of his younger
brother, surprised to learn from them that he is
growing famous, confronts the stately but courteous Alsager ; while P., 'his few hairs bristling' at
gentle objurgation, watches his partner M. B.,
dealing with 'soul more white' than the hands of
which Lamb once said, 'M., if dirt were trumps,
what hands you would hold!' In one corner of the
room, you may see the pale, earnest countenance
of Charles Lloyd, who is discoursing 'of fate, free-
will, fore-knowledge absolute,' with Leigh Hunt ;
and, if you choose to listen, you will scarcely know
which most to admire—the severe logic of the melancholy reasoner, or its graceful evasion by the
tricksome fantasy of the joyous poet. Basil Montague, gentle enthusiast in the cause of humanity,
which he has lived to see triumphant, is pouring
into the outstretched ear of George Dyer some
tale of legalized injustice, which the recipient is
vainly endeavoring to comprehend. Soon the room
fills ; in *slouches* Hazlitt from the theatre, where his

stubborn anger for Napoleon's defeat at Waterloo
has been softened by Miss Stephens's angelic notes,
which might chase anger, and grief, and fear, and
sorrow, and pain from mortal or immortal minds ;
Kenney, with a tremulous pleasure, announces that
there is a crowded house to the ninth representa-
tion of his new comedy, of which Lamb lays down
his cards to inquire ; or Ayrton, mildly radiant,
whispers the continual triumph of ' Don Giovanni,'
for which Lamb, incapable of opera, is happy to
take his word.   Now and then an actor glances on
us from 'the rich Cathay' of the world behind the
scenes, with news of its brighter human-kind, and
with looks reflecting the public favor—Liston, grave
beneath the weight of the town's regards—or Miss
Kelly, unexhausted in spirit by alternating the
drolleries of high farce with the terrible pathos of
melodrama—or Charles Kemble mirrors the chivalry
of thought, and ennobles the party by bending on
them looks beaming with the aristocracy of nature.
Meanwhile Becky lays the cloth on the side-table,
under the direction of the most quiet, sensible, and
kind of women—who soon compels the younger
and more hungry of the guests to partake largely
of the cold roast lamb or boiled beef, the heaps of
smoking roasted potatoes, and the vast jug of porter, often replenished from the foaming pots, which
the best tap of Fleet Street supplies.   Perfect freedom prevails, save when the hospitable pressure of
the mistress excuses excess ; and perhaps, the physical enjoyment of the play-goer exhausted with
pleasure, or of the author jaded with the labor of
the brain, is not less than that of the guests at the

most charming of aristocratic banquets.   As the hot water and its accompaniments appear, and the severities of whist relax, the light of conversation thickens : Hazlitt, catching the influence of the spirit from which he has lately begun to abstain, utters some fine criticism with struggling emphasis ; Lamb stammers out puns suggestive of wisdom, for happy Barron Field to admire and echo ; the various driblets of talk combine into a stream, while Miss Lamb moves gently about to see that each modest stranger is duly served ; turning, now and then, an anxious loving eye on Charles, which is softened into a half-humorous expression of resignation to inevitable fate, as he mixes his second tumbler ! "

LIST OF WORKS QUOTED.

LIST OF WORKS QUOTED.

ALLIBONE (SAMUEL AUSTIN). Critical Dictionary of English Literature, and British and American Authors. 3 vols., 8vo. Philadelphia, 1859–71.

ATHENÆUM, September 3, 1859. Anonymous article upon Leigh Hunt.

BABSON (J. E.). Eliana : Being the hitherto Uncollected Writings of Charles Lamb. 8vo. New York and Boston, 1864.

BALMANNO (MARY). Pen and Pencil. 8vo. New York : D. Appleton & Co., 1858.

BROWN (JOHN, M. D.). Horæ Subsecivæ. 2 vols., 12mo. Edinburgh, 1858–61. (Reprinted in Boston as "Spare Hours," 1866.)

BROWNING (ELIZABETH BARRETT). Letters Addressed to R. H. Horne, Edited by S. R. T. Mayer. 2 vols., 8vo. London, 1877. (This volume also contains reminiscences of contemporaries, by R. H. Horne.)

CARLYLE (THOMAS). Life of John Sterling. London, 1851.
——— Reminiscences. Edited by J. A. Froude. 8vo. London, 1881.

CARLYON (CLEMENT, M.D.). Early Years and Late Reflections. 3 vols., 12mo. London, 1856.

CLARKE (CHARLES COWDEN). Reminiscences. *Gentleman's Magazine*, February, 1874.
——— (CHARLES COWDEN and MARY COWDEN). Recollections of Writers. 12mo. London, 1878.
——— (MARY COWDEN). Article upon Lamb. *Gentleman's Magazine*, December, 1873.

COLERIDGE (HENRY N., editor). Specimens of the Table-talk of S. T. Coleridge. 2 vols., 16mo. New York, 1835.

COLERIDGE (SAMUEL T.). Biographia Literaria. Edited with Biographical Supplement, by H. N. and Sara Coleridge. 2 vols., 12mo. London, 1847.

CONWAY (MONCURE D.). The English Lakes and their Genii. *Harper's Magazine*, December, 1880.

COTTLE (JOSEPH). Reminiscences of S. T. Coleridge and R. Southey. Crown 8vo. London, 1847.

CRANBROOK (LORD). Christopher North. *National Review*, April, 1884.

DE QUINCEY (THOMAS). Biographical Essays. 16mo. Boston, 1851.

—— Essays on the Poets and other Writers. 16mo. Boston, 1853.

—— Literary Reminiscences. 2 vols., 16mo. Boston : Ticknor & Fields, 1851.

—— Narrative and Miscellaneous Papers. 2 vols., 16mo. Boston, 1853.

DIBDIN (THOMAS FROGNALL). Reminiscences of a Literary Life. 8vo. London, 1836.

DICKENS (CHARLES). Article upon Leigh Hunt. *All the Year Round*, December 24, 1859.

DUBLIN UNIVERSITY MAGAZINE, November, 1861. Anonymous article upon "Leigh Hunt's Last Evening at Home."

EDINBURGH REVIEW, July, 1856. Anonymous article upon Rogers.

EMERSON (RALPH WALDO). English Fruits. 12mo. Boston, 1856.

FIELDS (JAMES T.). Old Acquaintance : Barry Cornwall and Some of his Friends. 32mo. Boston : J. R. Osgood & Co., 1876.

FITZGERALD (PERCY). Charles Lamb ; his Friends, his Haunts, and his Books. 12mo. London, 1876.

FORSTER (JOHN). Article upon Lamb. *New Monthly Magazine,* 1835.

—— Life of Charles Dickens. 3 vols., 8vo. London, 1872-74.

FOX (CAROLINE). Memories of Old Friends. Being Extracts from the Journals and Letters of Caroline Fox, from 1835 to 1871. Edited by Horace Pym. 8vo. London, 1882.

FRASER'S MAGAZINE, July, 1878. Letters of Lamb, Southey, and Coleridge to Matilda Betham.

FROUDE (JAMES ANTHONY). Thomas Carlyle. A History of the First Forty Years of his Life. 2 vols., 8vo. London and New York, 1882.

—— Thomas Carlyle. A History of his Life in London. 2 vols., 8vo. London, 1884.

FULLER (HIRAM). Sparks from a Locomotive, or Life and Liberty in Europe. 12mo. New York, 1859.

GILLIES (ROBERT PEARCE). Memoirs of a Literary Veteran. 3 vols., 12mo. London, 1854.

GILLMAN (JAMES). Life of S. T. Coleridge. Vol. I. 8vo. London, 1838. (Only one volume was published.)

GRAVES (ROBERT PERCIVAL). Recollections of Wordsworth. Afternoon Lectures on Literature and Art. Vol. V. 12mo. London, 1869.

GREVILLE (CHARLES C. F.). A Journal of the Reigns of King George IV. and King William IV. Edited by Henry Reeve. 3 vols., 8vo. London, 1874.

GRUNDY (FRANCIS H.). Pictures of the Past. London, 1879.

HALL (SAMUEL C.). A Book of Memories of Great Men and Women of the Age. 4to. London, 1876.

—— Retrospect of a Long Life. 8vo. London and New York, 1883.

HAWTHORNE (NATHANIEL). Our Old Home : A Series of English Sketches. 16mo. Boston : Ticknor & Fields, 1863.

HAWTHORNE (NATHANIEL). Passages from English Note-books. 2 vols., 12mo. Boston : Fields, Osgood & Co., 1870.

HAYDON (FREDERICK W.). Benjamin Robert Haydon ; Correspondence and Table Talk, with a Memoir. 2 vols., 8vo. London, 1876.

HAZLITT (WILLIAM). Literary Remains. 2 vols., 8vo. London, 1836.

———— The Plain Speaker : Opinions on Books, Men, and Things. 2 vols., 8vo. London, 1826.

———— The Spirit of the Age. 8vo. London, 1825.

HAZLITT (WILLIAM CAREW). Memoirs of William Hazlitt. 2 vols., 12mo. London, 1867.

HEMANS (FELICIA D.). Poetical Works. With a Memoir by her Sister, Mrs. Hughes. 7 vols., 12mo. London, 1839.

HOGG (JAMES). Poetical Works. With Autobiography. 5 vols., 16mo. Glasgow, 1838–1840.

HOOD (THOMAS). Works. 4 vols., 12mo. New York, 1852–53.

HORNE (RICHARD HENGIST). A New Spirit of the Age. 2 vols., 8vo. London, 1844.

HUGHES (THOMAS). Memoir of Daniel Macmillan. 12mo. London, 1882.

HUNT (JAMES HENRY LEIGH). Autobiography and Reminiscences. 3 vols., 16mo. London, 1850.

———— Correspondence. Edited by his Eldest Son. 2 vols., 12mo. London, 1862.

HUNT (THORNTON). Article upon Leigh Hunt. *Cornhill Magazine,* January, 1860.

———— Article upon Leigh Hunt. *Atlantic Monthly,* February, 1863.

———— (*editor*). Autobiography of L. Hunt. 12mo. London, 1860.

IRELAND (ALEXANDER). List of the Writings of William Hazlitt and Leigh Hunt, etc. 8vo. London, 1868.

JERDAN (WM.). Men I have Known. 8vo. London, 1866.

KNIGHT (CHARLES). Passages of a Working Life during Half a Century. 3 vols., 8vo. London, 1864-65.

LAMB (CHARLES). Elia. Essays which have appeared under that signature in the *London Magazine.* 12mo. London, 1823.

LESLIE (CHAS. ROBERT). Autobiographical Recollections. Edited by Tom Taylor. 2 vols., 12mo. London, 1860.

L'ESTRANGE (REV. A. G.). The Literary Life of the Rev. Wm. Harness. London, 1870.

LOCKHART (JOHN GIBSON). Peter's Letters to his Kinsfolk. 3 vols., 8vo. Edinburgh, 1819.

MACKAY (CHARLES). Forty Years' Recollections, from 1830 to 1870. 2 vols., 8vo. London, 1877.

MACKENZIE (ROBERT SHELTON). Life of Charles Dickens. 12mo. Philadelphia, 1870.

MARTINEAU (HARRIET). Autobiography. Edited by M. W. Chapman. 2 vols., 8vo. Boston : Houghton, Mifflin & Co., 1877.

MILNES (RICHARD MONCKTON, LORD HOUGHTON). Address Delivered in 1869.

MOORE (THOMAS). Memoirs, Journal, and Correspondence. Edited by Lord John Russell. 8 vols., 8vo. London, 1853-56.

MYERS (FREDERICK W. H.). Wordsworth. 12mo. London and New York, 1881. (English Men of Letters. Edited by John Morley.)

NEW MONTHLY MAGAZINE, 1830. Anonymous article (attributed to Barry Cornwall) upon Hazlitt.

PATMORE (PETER GEORGE). My Friends and Acquaintance. 3 vols., 8vo. London, 1854.

PAUL (REV. CHAS. KEGAN). William Godwin: His Friends and Contemporaries. 2 vols., 8vo. London, 1876.

PROCTER (BRYAN WALLER). Article upon Charles Lamb. *Athenæum,* January, 1835.

—— Autobiographical Fragment, and Biographical

Notes, with Sketches of Contemporaries, &c.   Edited
by C.[oventry] P.[atmore] 12mo. London, 1877.

PROCTER (BRYAN WALLER.)   Charles Lamb ; a Memoir.
8vo. London, 1866.

QUARTERLY REVIEW, August, 1834. Anonymous article
upon Coleridge.

ROBINSON (HENRY CRABB). Diary, Reminiscences, and
Correspondence. Edited by T. Sadler. 3 vols., 8vo.
London, 1869.

SOUTHEY (ROBERT) and CAROLINE BOWLES. Correspondence. Edited by Edward Dowden. 8vo. Dublin and
London, 1881.

SPECTATOR, September 3, 1859. Article upon Leigh Hunt.
By E. O. (Edmund Ollier ?)

TALFOURD (THOMAS NOON). Final Memorials of Charles
Lamb. 2 vols., 12mo. London, 1848.

——Letters of Charles Lamb.   With a Sketch of His
Life. 2 vols., 12mo. London, 1837.

TICKNOR (GEORGE). Life, Letters, and Journals. Edited by
G. S. Hillard and Others. 2 vols., 8vo. Boston, 1876.

TWICHELL (REV. JOSEPH H.). Article upon Lamb. *Scribner's Magazine*, March, 1876.

WATTS (ALARIC ALFRED). Alaric Watts. A Narrative
of His Life. 2 vols., 8vo. London, 1884.

WESTWOOD (THOMAS). Article upon Lamb. *Notes and
Queries*, September, 1866.

WILLIS (NATHANIEL PARKER). Famous Persons and
Places. 12mo. New York : Charles Scribner, 1854.

—— Pencillings by the Way. 12mo. New York : Charles
Scribner, 1853.

WORDSWORTH (REV. CHRISTOPHER). Memoirs of William Wordsworth. Edited by Henry Reed.   2 vols.,
16mo. Boston : Ticknor & Fields, 1851.

YOUNG (REV. JULIAN CHARLES). A Memoir of Charles
M. Young, Tragedian, with Extracts from his Son's
Journal. 12mo. London and New York, 1871.

INDEX.

www.ingramcontent.com/pod-product-compliance
Lightning Source LLC
Chambersburg PA
CBHW060549030726

47498CB00005B/1329